MONUMENTAL COINS

COINS

Buildings & Structures on Ancient Coinage

Marvin Tameanko

Published by

 krause publications

700 E. State Street • Iola, WI 54990-0001

Please call or write for our free catalog. Our toll-free number to place an order or obtain a free catalog is 800-258-0929 or please use our regular business telephone 715-445-2214 for editorial comment and further information.

ISBN: 0-87341-713-5
Library of Congress Catalog Card Number: 98-87366

Printed in the United States of America

Main cover photo: Chris Pritchard
Cover coin photos: Courtesy Ben Damsky

DEDICATION

I dedicate this work to my wife Bette Ann and, through her, to the spouses of all ancient coin collectors.

Our partners in life may never understand our fascination with "little bits of old metal," but they still accompany us to coin shows and conventions, and wait patiently in hotel lobbies or in nearby shopping malls while we hunt through dealers' trays looking for that one coin that will make our dreams come true.

CONTENTS

PART I

OVERVIEW

Foreword

Readers of The Celator are well acquainted with the work of Marvin Tameanko, which has frequently graced the journal's pages over the past decade. It is seldom that one author can appeal to the diverse interests represented in a field as broad as ancient numismatics, but Marvin has earned the respect of collectors and professional numismatists in many specialties. This is partly because the focus of his research—architectural and historical themes in coinage—has relativity to almost every numismatic series and culture.

Equally, this respect is a reflection of the caliber of his works. Marvin's encyclopedic grasp of images and meaning serves him well in synthesizing and organizing material from the vast corpus of numismatic and archaeological literature. The development of this book has been a labor of love, as all who know Marvin will attest. The author's passion for his subject is immediately evident and his style of presentation is reminiscent of the great storytellers of the past. Reading these chapters is as much a joy as it is an enlightenment. That comfortable style is further enhanced by the nostalgic use of line drawings which Marvin himself has drawn. The use of line art was common in the pre-photography era, and with its special charm is a perfect mode of portraying architecture on ancient coins. This again is a personal reflection of the author, who is obviously a romantic, and often treats us to a special kind of 19th century connoisseurship.

The pages that follow are entertaining to read, but they are also a wonderful resource and reference for any collector interested in the images on ancient coinage. Not only is there much to be enjoyed, there is much to learn from them. Indeed, we have never read an article by Marvin Tameanko that did not provide new insights and facts which spark the imagination and give cause to ponder the mysteries of the ancient world. Having so many of those articles at hand in one convenient volume will be a most welcome addition to every numismatic library. Finally, we should say that a modern study of architectural motifs on ancient coins has been badly needed. There have been very few works on this subject in the past century, and the few which have made it to press have been rather limited in scope. We are therefore grateful for this book and heartily commend it to anyone who finds ancient history, coinage or architecture appealing.

Wayne G. Sayles
Gainesville, Missouri

Preface

Buildings and monuments are the most remarkable subjects illustrated on ancient coinage. They take second place only to the magnificent, photo-like portrait busts that have transformed ancient coins into classical works of art. The engravings of these structures are important because they often describe monuments that have disappeared from history without a trace. In fact, the coins may be the only surviving physical records that such edifices ever existed. While the technology of ancient coin making remained relatively constant over 1,000 years, the architecture of that same time period changed to reflect the development of society, and the buildings shown on these coins are often mirrors of the science, art, and culture of the civilizations that produced them.

There have been many excellent books written about the architecture on ancient coins, beginning with *Architectura Numismatica* by T. L. Donaldson, first published in 1859. Donaldson was a famous British architect, and his book is a romantic study of 92 classical coins more suitable for Victorian age antiquarians than for the numismatists of today. However, there are many up-to-date, scholarly books and articles about architecture on ancient coins available to the coin collecting community.[1] These studies utilize the most recent research, but they are essentially catalogs of the coins with the addition of historical and archaeological notes. The descriptions of the buildings are severely limited, and little information about the plans, construction, details, and original appearance of the architecture is given. Also, the context and historical background of these ancient monuments is frequently disregarded, and the structures are rarely "brought to life" for the reader. The buildings shown on coins are sometimes treated as remote and intangible artifacts that were engraved as abstract or symbolic designs. This book takes the approach that the architectural subject was of equal importance to the coin itself and deserves equal attention. The buildings were truly "benchmarks" of the culture in which they existed, and they often formed a vital part of the physical environment that shaped the foundations of Western civilization.

In this book I classify the coins by building types, such as temples, harbors, or public spaces, and not by geographical area, historical age, or emperor's reign. I have also tried to add an element of "wonder" and "joy" to the descriptions of the architecture because ancient buildings instilled these emotions in the people who used them, and do so even today. Anyone who has stood before the remains of the Parthenon in Athens, especially on a moonlit night, will understand my reasons for treating these monuments with some passion.

The contents of this book are illustrated by line drawings of the coins, computer-generated plans of the structures, and freehand sketches of the reconstructions of the buildings. Line drawings of the coins are used instead of photographs for several reasons. First, obtaining and reproducing photographs of unworn ancient coins is difficult, and line drawings can reveal the fine details which are often obscured by wear, corrosion, or a weak strike of the dies. However, photographs of more than one half of the coins in the text are illustrated in the plates at the end of the book. Second, using line drawings is an old tradition in reference books on ancient coins, and because the subject of this book deals with ancient art and architecture as well as numismatics, it seemed appropriate to

---

[1] The most notable and useful books are *Coins and Their Cities* by Martin Jessop Price and Bluma L. Trell, published in 1977, and *The Monuments of Ancient Rome as Coin Types* by Philip V. Hill, published in 1989. These three authors have also written numerous articles on the subject which appeared in several periodicals such as *Numismatich E Antichita Classiche*, the *Numismatic Chronicle*, and *Archaeology* magazine.

use a venerable art form for the illustrations. Third, in collecting the information for the book, I found it necessary to draw and redraw all of the coins in my notes in order to better understand the artistic composition and the techniques used by the artists to render the buildings. These line drawings are records of my research and I believe that they deserve to be displayed alongside the text. Fourth, all architects and engineers make drawings and use them as technical communication and for the documentation of concepts. As this book pays homage to the ancient architects and engineers who created the buildings, I felt that it would be suitable to use the same graphic techniques they used, and still use today. Also, I am convinced that the ancient coin artists made sketches of their designs on papyrus or parchment, and then executed the work from these drawings. Line drawings were the genesis of the coins as well as of the buildings, and it is proper that this book uses the same illu-strative medium as was used by the original artists and designers.

I wish to thank the following for providing the photographs used in the plates of the book: Classical Numismatic Group, Inc. (P.O. Box 479, Lancaster, PA 17608 USA); Leu Numismatics Ltd. (In Gassen 20, CH-8001 Zurich, Switzerland); Superior Stamp and Coin (9478 West Olympic Blvd., Beverly Hills, CA 90212 USA); Andrew Daneman (formerly with Numismatic Fine Arts International, Inc.); and Steve Rubinger of Antiqua Inc. (20969 Ventura Blvd., Suite 11, Woodland Hills, CA 91364 USA). Additionally, I'd like to thank Ben Damsky for providing the color photographs used on the dust jacket of this book.

Some of the information in this book appeared in different forms or as articles in the *Society for Ancient Numismatics (SAN) Journal,* or in *The Celator* and *Coin News* magazines over the past fifteen years. I am grateful to Walker Carlton, editor emeritus of the *SAN Journal*, Wayne G. Sayles, publisher/editor of *The Celator,* and to John W. Mussell, managing editor of *Coin News,* for their constant encouragement over the years. I give special thanks to the editor of this book, Steven A. Sayles, for his resourceful, tireless service and his knowledgeable contribution to the honing and polishing of a raw and rough manuscript. As I am responsible for everything in this book, I accept the blame for any errors and misinterpretations but, by the same token, I claim the credit for anything written here that enlightens, informs, and delights the reader.

Abbreviations, References, and Bibliography

The following abbreviations are used for the references cited throughout this book:

Primary or Classical Sources

Ammianus: *Roman History* by Ammianus Marcellinus, translated by J.C. Rolfe, Loeb Classical Library, Harvard University Press, Cambridge, 1937.

Appian: *Roman History* by Appian, translated by H.E. White, Loeb Classical Library, Harvard University Press, Cambridge, 1912.

Augustan History: *Lives of the Later Caesars* or the *Augustan History*, translated by Anthony Birley, Penguin Classics, London, 1976.

Dio Cassius: *Roman History* by Dio Cassius, translated by E.W. Cary, Loeb Classical Library, Harvard University Press, Cambridge, 1924.

Frontinus: *Strategems, Aqueducts* by Frontinus, translated by T. Ashby, Loeb Classical Library, Harvard University Press, Cambridge, 1925.

Herodian: *History of the Period after Marcus Aurelius* translated by C.R. Whittaker, Loeb Classical Library, Harvard University Press, Cambridge, 1961.

Herodotus: *The History of Herodotus* translated by G. Rawlinson, E.P. Dutton and Co., New York, 1926.

Hesiod: *Works and Days* by Hesiod, translated by H.G. Evelyn-White, Loeb Classical Library, Harvard University Press, Cambridge, 1936.

Josephus: *The Works of Josephus* translated by W. Whiston, Hendrickson Publishers, Massachusetts, 1992.

Livy: *Roman History* by Livy, translated by B.O. Forster et al, Loeb Classical Library, Harvard University Press, Cambridge, 1959.

Lucan: *Civil War* by Lucan, translated by J.D. Duff, Loeb Classical Library, Harvard University Press, Cambridge, 1928.

Pausanias: *Guide to Greece* by Pausanias, translated by Peter Levi, Penguin Classics, London, 1979.

Pliny: *Letters of Pliny the Younger* translated by Betty Radice, Penguin Classics, London, 1969.

Pliny the Elder: *Natural History* by Pliny the Elder, translated by H. Rackhman et al, Loeb Classical Library, Harvard University Press, Cambridge, 1938.

Plutarch: *Parallel Lives* by Plutarch, translated by B. Perrin, Loeb Classical Library, Harvard University Press, Cambridge, 1926.

Res Gestae: *Res Gestae Divi Augusti* edited by P.A. Brunt and J.M. Moore, Oxford University Press, Oxford, 1967.

Strabo: *The Geography of Strabo* translated by H.L. Jones, Loeb Classical Library, Harvard University Press, Cambridge, 1933.

Suetonius: *The Twelve Caesars* by Suetonius, translated by Robert Graves, Allan Lane, London, 1979.

Tacitus: *The Complete Works of Tacitus* translated by Moses Hadas, The Modern Library, New York, 1942.

Vitruvius: *De Architectura*, also called *The Ten Books on Architecture*, by Vitruvius, translated by M.H. Morgan, Dover Publications, New York, 1960.

Virgil: *The Aeneid* by Virgil, translated by W.F. Jackson, Penguin Classics, London, 1956.

Secondary Sources

Avi Yonah: *Illustrated Encyclopedia of the Classical World* by Michael Avi Yonah and Israel Shatzman, Harper and Row, New York, 1975.

Banister Fletcher: *A History of Architecture on the Comparative Method* by Banister Fletcher, The Athlone Press, London, 1961.

Boatwright: *Hadrian and the City of Rome* by Mary Taliaferro Boatwright, Princeton University Press, New Jersey, 1987.

Dal Maso: *Rome of the Caesars* by L.B. Dal Maso, Bonechi-Edizioni, Florence, undated.

Donaldson: *Architectura Numismatica* by T.L. Donaldson, Argonaut Library, Chicago, 1965.

Grant: *Roman Anniversary Issues* by Michael Grant, Attic Books, New York, 1977.

Hill: *The Monuments of Ancient Rome as Coin Types* by Philip V. Hill, Seabys, London, 1989.

JRA: *Journal of Roman Archaeology*, University of Michigan, Ann Arbor.

Lanciani: *The Ruins and Excavations of Ancient Rome* by Rodolfo Lanciani, Bell Publishing, New York, 1967.

Lempriere: *Lempriere's Classical Dictionary* by J. Lempriere, Bracken Books, London, 1984.

Nash: *Pictorial History of Ancient Rome* by E. Nash, A. Zwemmer, London, 1961.

NC: *Numismatic Chronicle,* Royal Numismatic Society, London, various years.

Ogilvie: *The Romans and their Gods* by R.M. Ogilvie, Ancient Culture and Society, Chatto and Windus, London, 1979.

Platner and Ashby: *A Topographical Dictionary of Ancient Rome,* by S. Platner and T. Ashby, Oxford, 1929.

Price and Trell: *Coins and Their Cities* by Martin Jessop Price and Bluma L. Trell, V.C. Vecchi and Sons, London, 1977.

RN: *Revue Numismatique*, Paris, various years.

Richter: *A Handbook of Greek Art* by Gisela Richter, E.P. Dutton, New York, 1980.

Rivoira: *Roman Architecture* by G.T. Rivoira, Hacker Art Books, New York, 1972.

Robertson: *Greek and Roman Architecture*, second edition, by D.S. Robertson, Cambridge University Press, London, 1974.

Stevenson: *A Dictionary of Roman Coins* by S.W. Stevenson, Seabys, London, 1964.

Ward-Perkins: *Roman Architecture* by John B. Ward-Perkins, in the *History of World Architecture* series, Harry N. Abrams, New York, 1977.

Zanker: *The Power of Images in the Age of Augustus* by Paul Zanker, University of Michigan Press, Ann Arbor, 1988.

Numismatic References

Alfoldi: *Die Kontorniate Medallions* by A. and E. Alfoldi, Berlin, 1976.

BMC Greek: *A Catalogue of Greek Coins in the British Museum* in 29 volumes, Arnaldo Forni reprint, Bologna, 1965.

BMC Roman: *Coins of the Roman Empire in the British Museum* by H. Mattingly et al, British Museum Publications, London, 1983.

Cayon: *Los Sestercios del Imperio Romano* by Juan R. Cayon, Madrid, 1984.

Cohen: *Description Historiques des Monnaies Frappees Sous L'empire Romain* by Henry Cohen, Forni, Bologna reprint, undated.

Curtis: *The Tetradrachms of Roman Egypt* by James W. Curtis, Argonaut Publishers, Chicago, 1969, reprinted 1990.

Dattari: *Monete Imperiale Greche, Numi Avgg. Alexandrini: Catalogo Della Collezione G. Dattari* by Giovanni Dattari, Bologna reprint, 1974.

Gnecchi: *I Medaglioni Romani* by F. Gnecchi, Bologna reprint, 1977.

Head: *Historia Numismatica, A Manual of Greek Numismatics* by Barclay V. Head, Oxford University Press, 1911.

Hendin: *Guide to Biblical Coins* by David Hendin, Amphora Books, New York, 1987.

Hill: *The Monuments of Ancient Rome as Coin Types*, as above.

Mildenberg: *Typos VI, The Coinage of the Bar Kokhba War* by Leo Mildenberg, Verlag Sauerlander, Frankfurt am Main, 1984.

Milne: *Catalogue of Alexandrian Coins* by J.G. Milne, Ashmolean Museum, Oxford, 1971.

Price and Trell: *Coins and Their Cities,* as above.

RIC: *The Roman Imperial Coinage* by C.H.V. Sutherland, R.A.G. Carson, H. Mattingly, E.A. Sydenham et al, Spink and Son, London, 1926-84.

RPC: *Roman Provincial Coinage*, Vol. 1, by Burnett, Amandry, Ripolles, British Museum Press and Bibliotheque Nationale, 1992.

Sear GIC: *Greek Imperial Coins and Their Values* by David R. Sear, Seabys, London, 1982.

Sear Greek: *Greek Coins and Their Values*, in 2 volumes, by David R. Sear, Seabys, London, 1978.

Sear Roman: *Roman Coins and Their Values* by David R. Sear, Seabys, London, 1988.

Toynbee: *Roman Medallions* by J.M.C. Toynbee, The American Numismatic Society No. 5, New York, 1944.

Von Aulock: *Sylloge Nummorum Graecorum, Deutschland, Sammlung Von Aulock*, Verlag Gebr Mann, Berlin, 1967.

Chapter 1

Introduction

In ancient days architects and engineers formed a single profession or guild of designers and master-builders. The title of "engineer" did not exist, and the Greeks referred to a construction or design expert as an *Architekton.* The Romans later borrowed this Greek term to make up their own Latin title of *Architectus.* Greek architects were reputed to have specialized in design, proportion, and beauty in their buildings, while the Romans experimented with materials and new methods of construction, and then applied them to the Greek designs which they slavishly copied. Architects were held in high esteem by the ancients because they were an elite of military officers in charge of constructing the vital fortifications, weapons, and machines of war. The architects who designed and built civilian structures were usually slaves, indentured to the state or to aristocratic house-holds. This was not unusual in the ancient world; slaves also dominated the other noble professions of medicine, business management, and teaching. Pliny the Younger, A.D. 61-112, a Roman senator and author who was appointed as a provincial governor by the emperor Trajan, A.D. 98-117, recorded the details of daily life in the Roman provinces. In one of his letters to the emperor, Pliny mentioned the fact that many of the architects he met were former slaves or Greeks *(Letters of Pliny,* 10.40). In Roman imperial times, beginning in the 1st century A.D., architecture became a more important profession to the growing nation, and Roman citizens began to practice as civil architects.

The ancient architect was an all-round person who designed buildings, dabbled in art, served as a military officer, and performed the duties of a civil or municipal engineer. A Roman architect and author named Marcus Vitruvius Pollio, writing around 29 B.C., is well known to historians because he wrote the only surviving ancient treatise on architecture. His ten books on the subject, called *De Architectura,* were later studied by medieval and Renaissance architects such as Leonardo da Vinci, Bramante, and Michelangelo. Vitruvius' *Ten Books on Architecture* were so popular as a source of information that they were re-published in 1485 and have been reprinted constantly since then. His influence is still felt by modern architects, who were probably educated in a school where the educational philosophy was based on the principles Vitruvius wrote down in the first century B.C. According to Vitruvius, the knowledge of an architect should be a combination of the theoretical and the practical. He said that an architect should "be educated, skillful with the pencil, instructed in geometry, know much history, have followed the philosophers with attention, have an understanding of music, have some knowledge of medicine, know the opinions of the jurists, and be acquainted with astronomy".[1]

From historical records we know quite a bit about the lives of the architects/engineers of the ancient world. In some cases we know more about them than we know about the famous architects of today. Going back to the beginnings of recorded history, an inscription carved on a wall in an Egyptian tomb reported that the architect of the first stone, stepped pyramid for the pharaoh Zoser, in the 30th century B.C., was a priest named Imhotep. The Bible mentions Hiram of Tyre, a half-Jewish artisan with the same name as the king of Tyre, who was probably the principal architect of

---

[1] *Vitruvius, The Ten Books on Architecture,* translated by M.H. Morgan, Dover Publications, London, 1960, Book I, Chapter I, 3, page 5.

the Solomonic temple in Jerusalem.[2] In ancient mythology we find the tale of the architect/artist Daedalus of Athens, who worked for King Minos of Crete sometime in the 14th century B.C. Daedalus supposedly constructed the Labyrinth for the Minotaur, a half-bull, half-man monster. Held captive on Crete, Daedalus ingeniously constructed wings made of feathers and wax so that he and his son, Icarus, could fly to freedom. However, Icarus, intoxicated by the exuberance of flight, soared too close to the sun, his wings melted, and he fell to his death in the sea.

More reliable than myths, historical literature reveals the names and accomplishments of numerous architects. Herodotus, the Greek "Father of History," reported how the architect Mandrocoles the Samian constructed the boat bridge used by the Persian king Darius I, in 512 B.C., to cross over the Bosphorus strait during his invasion of Greece. Inscriptions on temple walls record that in 447-446 B.C. the architects of the famous Parthenon, on the Acropolis in Athens, were Iktinos and Kallikrates. Vitruvius related the story of Dinocrates, the famous court architect of Alexander the Great, 356-323 B.C. This artisan caught Alexander's attention by appearing at an audience dressed as Hercules, Alexander's patron deity. Dinocrates had oiled his skin to a high shine, wore only a lion skin draped over his shoulder, and carried a large club. This self-promoting architect endeared himself to Alexander by proposing the grandiose scheme of sculpting Mount Athos, the highest mountain in Greece, into a colossal statue of a man. In his left hand the statue would hold an entire city, and in his right an enormous bowl to receive the waters of the rivers that descended from the mountain.[3] Dinocrates became Alexander's personal architect, and in 331 B.C. designed the new city of Alexandria in Egypt. In this same city, an inscription recorded that one of the "Seven Wonders of the World," the Pharos lighthouse, was designed by the architect Sostratos of Knidos for King Ptolemy II, 285-247 B.C. Historical documents also report that a Roman architect named Cossutius was employed by Antiochus IV, 175-164 B.C., to design the great Temple of the Olympian Zeus in Athens. Cossutius may have been responsible for introducing the best Greek styles of architecture into early Rome. The architects who served the emperor Nero, A.D. 54-68, and the designers of his magnificent Domus Aureus—or the "Golden House" palace— were two Romans named Severus and Celer.[4] They also supposedly designed the Claudian aqueduct, the macellum (market) of Nero, and the Neronian baths in Rome. In Roman imperial times, the names of several architects were registered as favorites of the emperors. Rabirius served as architect to the emperor Domitian, A.D. 81-96, and constructed his finest buildings. Apollodorus of Damascus was the principal architect of the emperor Trajan, A.D. 98-117. He was responsible for the bridge over the Danube, which can be seen in the sculpture on Trajan's Column, the Forum of Trajan, the harbors at Ostia and Centumcellae, and the many temples built during the emperor's reign. The emperor Hadrian, A.D. 117-138, was a talented self-taught architect, but he employed the services of Apollodorus until this architect foolishly criticized the emperor's design for the Temple of Venus and Roma. Hadrian also commissioned the services of an architect named Decrianus to move a gigantic bronze statue of Nero that was over 110 feet high. Decrianus used twenty-four elephants to do the job, moving the statue in its upright position.[5] This catalog of famous ancient architects and their accomplishments could continue with many more names, but the point has been made, and the listing can end in the 2nd century A.D. with an architect named Amandus. He probably designed the Roman frontier fortress of Birrens, Scotland, near Hadrian's Wall, around A.D. 158. Amandus erected a stele in the fort dedicated to Brigantia, the tutelary

---

[2] *I Kings*, VII, 13, 40.

[3] *Vitruvius*, as above, Book II, Introduction, 3, page 35.

[4] *Roman Architecture,* by G.T. Riviora, Hacker Art Books, New York, 1972, page 71, quoting the data from Tacitus, *The Annals of Rome*, XV, 42.

[5] *Lives of the Later Caesars*, also called the *Augustan History*, Hadrian 19.12, translated by A. Birley, Penguin Classics, London, 1976, page 65.

10

A stele erected by the architect Amandus, found in 1895 in Birrens fortress in Scotland.

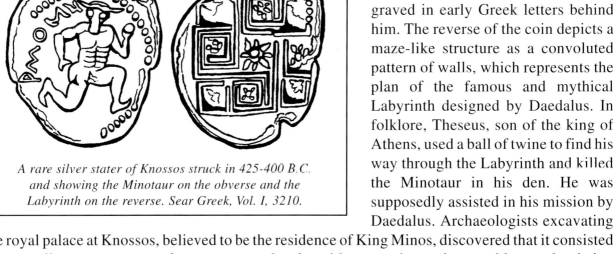

A rare silver stater of Knossos struck in 425-400 B.C. and showing the Minotaur on the obverse and the Labyrinth on the reverse. Sear Greek, Vol. I, 3210.

goddess of the native Brigantes tribe. In the inscription on this monument, Amandus labels himself proudly as an *"ARCITECTVS."*[6]

The ancient architects and engineers were honored by the exhibition of their great works on the coinage of the times. Buildings were a commonly used subject, and there were thousands of Greek and Roman architectural coins struck from 100 B.C. to A.D. 400. These coins were significant to the state because they were the main advertising or propaganda vehicles used to show the devotions, deeds, and accomplishments of the ruler. Also, whenever a temple was shown on a coin, the religion, cult practice, deified ruler, or the deity represented by the structure was being initiated or promoted.

Perhaps the first and earliest ancient coins to include a building as part of their designs were the silver staters struck at the city of Knossos on the island of Crete. These crude coins were manufactured in 425 to 400 B.C. This date-line places these coins in the earliest stages of the development of struck coinage. The coins show the figure of the legendary Minotaur, running to the right and holding a round stone in his left hand. The legend KNOMI, referring to Knossos, is crudely engraved in early Greek letters behind him. The reverse of the coin depicts a maze-like structure as a convoluted pattern of walls, which represents the plan of the famous and mythical Labyrinth designed by Daedalus. In folklore, Theseus, son of the king of Athens, used a ball of twine to find his way through the Labyrinth and killed the Minotaur in his den. He was supposedly assisted in his mission by Daedalus. Archaeologists excavating the royal palace at Knossos, believed to be the residence of King Minos, discovered that it consisted of a puzzling arrangement of rooms on two levels, with many zigzagging corridors and twisting stairways, some leading to dead ends. This complex palace plan may have been the source of the myth that the Labyrinth was a tangled maze.

This labyrinthine structure was used on the coins of Knossos for many centuries, well into the Roman imperial era. A later coin, struck in 300-270 B.C., shows a classical plan of the legendary maze on the reverse. This plan is so well engraved that, if a labyrinth did exist as some kind of a

6 *Scotland's Roman Remains,* by Lawrence Keppie, John Donald Publishing Ltd., Edinburgh, 1986, page 76.

religious precinct or as a tourist attraction in ancient Knossos, the coin could have been used as a guide map to show visitors how to enter and exit the maze. The obverse shows a beautiful bust of the goddess Hera facing left.

See plates, coin 1.

A silver stater of Knossos struck in 300-270 B.C. The reverse shows the plan of the classical Labyrinth. Sear Greek, Vol. I, 3217.

Legendary buildings make up only a small part of the architecture represented on coinage. Most coins show real buildings located on actual sites in historical cities, and the details displayed on these coins reveal much information about the structures. Architectural historians claim that to understand the culture, science, and aesthetic aspirations of a nation, we need only examine their architecture. Numismatists suggest that to comprehend the art, technology, economics, and wealth of a society, we need only observe its coinage. Perhaps by combining these two thoughts into one, in a study of the architecture shown on coinage, we can obtain a broader and deeper understanding of our founding civilizations.

Chapter 2

Ancient Architecture

Ancient people assigned religious and mystical qualities to their buildings. This tradition probably arose in primitive times when protection from the natural elements, enemies, and predators was so important to sustaining life that people came to regard their shelters as sacred. This concept continued into classical times, and can be seen in the ritual practice of priests laying out new cities by plowing a sanctified furrow around the perimeter of the community.

A cuneiform inscription from Persepolis in ancient Persia, 485-465 B.C.

This ceremonial custom is depicted on ancient coins by a priest or ruler guiding a plow pulled by a team of oxen. The construction of temples and important civic buildings was never started without first depositing statues of deities, animal sacrifices, or coins in the foundations, and most buildings contained some religious image as a protective icon. Also, ancient civilizations revered their great buildings and attributed them directly to their gods. The cuneiform inscription shown here was found at Persepolis, carved in four prominent locations on the gateway pylons of the great palace of the Persian king Xerxes I, the biblical Ahasuerus, 485-465 B.C. It translates into English as *"Whatever seems beautiful we made by the grace of god."*

Most of the large buildings constructed in the ancient world evolved directly from earlier, primitive wooden prototypes. When these structures were translated into stone or masonry, the wooden forms were retained and became decorative and symbolic. This recollection and reuse of older shapes can be seen in the construction of circular stone columns as imitations of the round tree trunks used for posts in olden days. The Greeks began this transformation of wood technology into a stone vernacular, enhanced the decorative aspects of the retained forms, and produced some of the most elegant temples ever constructed in history.

The Greek love of philosophy and geometry, combined with their search for perfection and beauty, led to the creation of mathematical proportioning systems which were applied to buildings as dogmatic rules of construction. All decoration was formalized or prescribed, and used on Greek buildings as symbolic elements. The Romans, more practical in their approach to buildings, fully adopted the Greek designs but developed better construction methods using concrete materials, arches, and domes. However, the Roman architects, entranced by the beauty of Greek architecture, copied the rules of proportion and decoration set out by Grecian artists and applied them to most of their buildings. This adaptive process can be illustrated by the "Orders of Columns" created by the ancient architects for use in the design of buildings. The Orders were prototype designs of columns that dictated the function, spacing, size, height, decoration, and appearance of the various members, and thereby guaranteed beautiful proportions. For example, the Doric column, invented in the 7th century B.C., was a squat, tapered, heavily fluted column with an unadorned capital. Its height was, by the rules applied to this Order, six times the diameter of the shaft. This column had no separate base, and simply sat on the floor of the temple. The Doric column was later recommended by the Romans to support heavy loads, or it was used on the lower floors of multi-storey structures. The Ionic column, invented just a little later than the Doric, was tall, usually nine times its diameter, and slender, with an ornate capital made up of spiral volutes at the four corners. The shaft of this column was more delicately fluted than the Doric Order, and the base was a round, cushion-like shape, sometimes set on a square pad. Vitruvius saw the Doric column as *male* because it was strong, powerful, and solid. He considered the Ionic column to be *female,* elegant and beautiful, because he related the flowing volutes of the Ionic capital to the curly hair of a woman and the fancy fluting of the shaft to the folds of a dress.

The Corinthian column, developed in the 5th century, was taller than the Ionic Order. The capital of this column was very ornate and fashioned to look like a basket of acanthus leaves with their tendrils curling around the top at the corners. The shaft was fluted and the base was a cushion form similar to that of the Ionic Order. The Romans became very fond of the exquisite Corinthian column and created a similar new type by combining the spiral volutes of the Ionic with the capital of the Corinthian Order. This new column was called the Composite Order, and it first appeared on the triumphal arch of Titus, constructed in Rome in A.D. 81. Also, the Romans often used an Etruscan adaption of the Greek Doric Order, and modified it to make a new style called the Tuscan. These columns usually had a smooth shaft and a high rectangular base. However, the Roman architects were inventive and often tampered with the rigid rules of the Orders by adding high, rectangular plinths as bases at the bottoms of all the columns, or by using fluted or smooth column shafts indiscriminately.

These various Orders of columns were clearly shown on coins by the distinctive shape of the capitals. It appears that the mint engravers tried to show building details on coins, such as the column capitals, as consistently and accurately as possible.

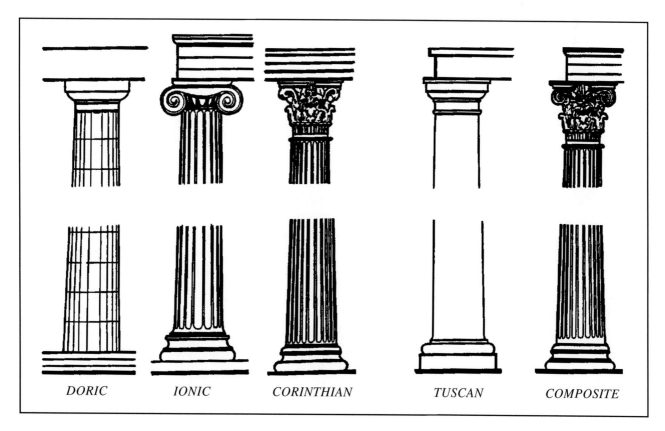

DORIC *IONIC* *CORINTHIAN* *TUSCAN* *COMPOSITE*

14

A bronze coin, 29 millimeters in diameter (AE29) struck in the time of Hadrian, A.D. 117-138, at the city of Corinth, showing the Doric column and the statues commemorating the tomb of Lais. BMC Greek 12, 691.

A bronze diobol of Alexandria struck under Hadrian, A.D. 117-138, showing an Ionic column surmounted by a basket of grain and poppy heads and flanked by two serpents. Dattari, 1928.

An AE29 struck in Sagalassus, Pisidia by Macrinus, A.D. 217-218, showing a Corinthian column between two shrines of the Dioskuroi. BMC Greek 19, 27.

The designs of the column Orders and the capitals were so symbolic and significant that they were often used by themselves as the principal feature on a coin. The most remarkable coin using a column as a main theme is one struck in the city of Corinth, to commemorate a famous 4th century B.C. courtesan named Lais. According to the poet Aulus Gellius (*Attic Nights* 1.8), Lais demanded the princely sum of 10,000 drachma for her services from Demosthenes, the renowned Athenian orator. As one drachma was a day's wages for a worker in Greece at that time, the fee was astronomical. This coin actually honors Lais' tomb, which was a popular tourist attraction and is described by the geographer and travel writer Pausanias (*Guide to Greece, Book II, 4*). The tomb's monument was a large Doric column surmounted by the statue of a lioness with a prostrate ram between her forepaws. Presumably, Lais was the lioness and Demosthenes, if he paid her outrageous fee, was the unfortunate ram.

Another coin struck at Alexandria in Egypt displayed an Ionic column on its reverse. In this case, the column had religious associations with the temple of Serapis or to other fertility temples in Egypt. The snakes flanking the column and the basket of grain with poppy heads on top were also common fertility symbols.

The much admired Corinthian column also appeared as a principal feature on some coins. A coin struck at Sagalassus in Pisidia shows this column type flanked by two circular altars dedicated to the Dioskuroi, the mythical heavenly twins known to the Romans as Castor and Pollux.

The Greek or Roman names for the elements and parts of ancient buildings have been incorporated into the English language, and as these terms are commonly used by historians and numismatists in describing architecture shown on coins, they are presented here as an illustrated glossary.

Similarly, the terminology of the elements of the plan of a typical ancient temple is shown as an illustration below.

For the purposes of this study, the building materials and methods of construction used for ancient buildings are of secondary importance to the designs, but as the materials of the structures are often shown on coins by joint lines, it is necessary to provide some explanations.

Ancient Greek buildings were constructed with solid blocks of stone, usually marble. These were laid up without mortar, but the blocks were so heavy and the joints so accurately fitted that only a metal "H" or dovetail clamp was needed to hold the stones together. Later, cheaper construction relied on masonry as a core structure, and this was faced with thin slabs of stone or covered with thick stucco that was made to look like stone by scoring lines in the surface to represent joints.

The Romans introduced concrete as a building material after the discovery of a natural, volcanic cement called pozzuolana. Strong walls were sometimes constructed with brick layers in the front and back of the wall, and concrete poured into the cavity between. Concrete was also used to make arched and dome structures by pouring the wet material into wooden formwork. The ancients had devised heavy cranes which worked by using multiple pulleys, windlasses, and treadwheels. These could move and lift very heavy loads, and slaves provided the manpower needed to operate the machinery.

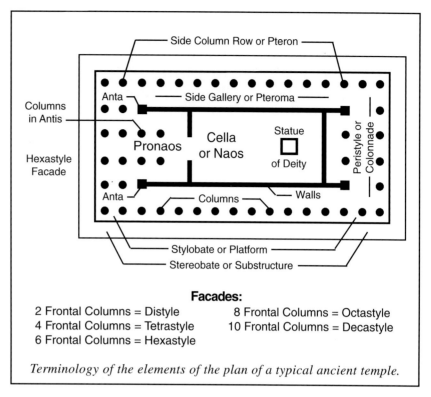

Facades:

2 Frontal Columns = Distyle   8 Frontal Columns = Octastyle
4 Frontal Columns = Tetrastyle   10 Frontal Columns = Decastyle
6 Frontal Columns = Hexastyle

Terminology of the elements of the plan of a typical ancient temple.

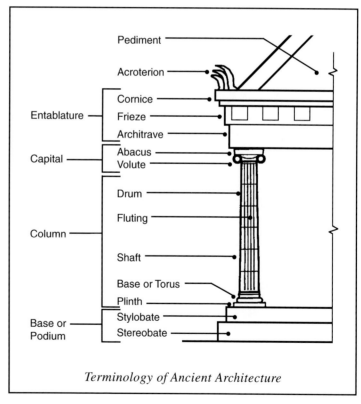

Terminology of Ancient Architecture

According to Pliny the Elder, the Romans had a large variety of local building stones such as travertine, tufa, basalt, limestone, and marble. They also imported granite, porphyry, serpentine, alabaster, and fancy marbles of many patterns and colors from the provinces. The Italian forests provided for structural timbers such as pine and fir, and Gaul or other northern provinces produced strong woods such as oak, elm, alder, and cedar. With all these resources, the ancient architects could create marvellous buildings of enormous sizes. The remains of five-story apartment buildings have been found in Ostia and Rome, and the concrete dome constructed for Hadrian's Pantheon in Rome is 142 feet (43 meters) in diameter. This dome size was exceeded only in the 15th century. The ruins of wonderful ancient buildings still impress visiting tourists, and many of these monuments are fully illustrated on ancient coins—the tiny physical documents that have survived the ages.

Chapter 3

Ancient Coinage

Coinage, as we know it, was supposedly invented in the 7th century B.C. Up to that time, the ancients used barter systems to facilitate trade and commerce. To establish the worth of various unequal commodities, the traders used some precious object as a measure or standard of value. This was usually an item that everyone could recognize as being of a fixed worth. For example, the Chinese and other eastern nations first used the rare cowrie shell as a standard of value, and goods were priced as equal to so many cowries. The cowrie shell was later replaced by other items of a known worth, such as a knife, spade, or a pair of pants. To us, this seems a strange and unwieldy system, but it functioned satisfactorily for many centuries. When the Chinese introduced metal tokens to replace the barter measure of value, they made the metal pieces in the shapes of the original, fixed value commodities, that is cowrie shells, knives, spades, and pairs of pants.

The ancient Greeks used a handful of iron roasting spits as an early standard of value. These common barbeque implements were thin rods of worked iron which could also be used as the raw material to make tools. The term "drachma," *drachme* in Greek, which was applied to coins by later Greeks, actually means "a handful" and refers to the traditional value of a handful of spits. The early Romans used animals as a standard of value, and later the term "pecunia," meaning cattle, *pecus* in Latin, was applied to their money.

When lumps of precious metal became the standard measure of value, the traders had to weigh all of the bits and pieces offered as payment in order to determine their equivalent worth. One enterprising merchant stamped a mark on all the pieces of metal in his possession, so that he would recognize them when they returned to him in trade, and he would not have to weigh them again. This idea developed into the practice of some individuals or civic authorities placing an official mark on the metal tokens that circulated in the city. Such a mark testified to the purity and weight of the metal, and guaranteed its acceptance by merchants. This, briefly, is the origin of stamped or struck currency. The early use of religious symbols or the images of deities on coins provided an element of sacredness to the coinage, and suggested that the gods sanctioned and protected the integrity of the currency.

The first coins were fabricated from a naturally occurring alloy of silver and gold called *electrum*. These lumps of metal, called staters, were first introduced by the Lydians or by the Ionian Greeks. The historian Herodotus, 484-420 B.C., said that "So far as we have any knowledge, the Lydians were the first nation to introduce the use of gold and silver coins and the first who sold goods by retail." (Herodotus, Book I, chapter 94). There are two theories about the reason for making these early coins. One is that the ancients used small bits of precious metal instead of spoils of war to pay off the mercenary soldiers they employed.[1] The second hypothesis, and the one most favoured by historians, is that these coins were made to replace the awkward barter systems then used in trade and commerce. Neither of these theories can be proven conclusively, but the earliest coins were rough, bean shape pieces of metal of a fairly uniform weight. They were stamped on

---

[1] *Ancient History from Coins,* by C. Howgego, Routledge, London, 1995, page 3.

one side with some symbol, and on the other side by a punch mark made with the blunt tool used to force the metal into the die. Later, the punch was also engraved with a symbol so that both sides of the coin contained some device which identified the city, country, ruler, or authority that issued the coinage.

Electrum staters were replaced by gold and silver coinage in Lydia by the king Kroisos (Croesus in Latin), 561-547 B.C. However, some historians argue that a bi-metallic coinage was first introduced by the Persians, who struck the famous silver siglos and the gold darics apparently at about the same time. When the Persians conquered Lydia in 546 B.C., they supposedly replaced the staters of Kroisos with their own currency. In response to this foreign intrusion, the Ionian Greeks, the most prominent traders in the Mediterranean world at that time, developed their own denominations based on a weight standard established at the city of Aigina. This coinage consisted of a silver didrachm, showing the city's badge, a turtle, equal to the older stater and weighing 12 grams. The Greeks promoted their new silver coinage for commercial transactions and were responsible for its widespread use.

Later, the cities in Attica became dominant in the Greek world, and they introduced a lighter silver coinage in the Attic weight standard, with a didrachm that weighed only 8.5 grams. These Greek coin designs and standards became universal when Alexander the Great, 337-323 B.C., completed his conquest of the Persian empire, and they were imitated by other nations ranging from India to Great Britain. The Romans began using Greek style coins from the end of the 4th century B.C., copying the designs of the neighbouring Greek colonial cities in Italy.

The next step in the general development of coins was the introduction of a base metal, token coinage. The Etruscans in Italy had used base metal, mostly bronze pieces measured by weight, as a form of money as early as the 6th century B.C. The Romans adopted this concept, and used it in an altered form up into the Second Punic War, 218-201 B.C., when they introduced new gold and silver denominations to accompany a modified bronze currency.

In the Greek series of coins, silver denominations always predominated. The basic denomination was the drachma, called a drachm and pronounced as "dram" in English, but the tetradrachm, a four-drachm piece, was the prestige silver piece of its time. The size and weight of the drachma varied greatly from locality to locality and changed frequently over the years. The drachma also had several fractions and multiples that produced lower and higher denominations. Architectural subjects usually appeared on the drachm, didrachm, and tetradrachm denominations in the Greek and the later Roman provincial series. The Greeks also used an unpopular bronze token coinage, probably first introduced in Macedon at the end of the 5th century B.C., and this developed into the so-called Greek imperial or Roman provincial series of coins struck under the Roman emperors. These coins often show architecture on their reverses. In most cases we are uncertain as to the names of these bronze denominations, although some of them are mentioned in historical documents. Numismatists usually refer to them by the Latin abbreviation of the bronze metal, "AE," followed by the diameter of the coin in millimeters. For example, a provincial *AE22* is a bronze coin, 22 millimeters in diameter. Gold denominations in the Greek series were very rare and did not display architectural subjects.

The Romans developed their own distinctively Latin series of denominations. The basic early coin was the As (plural—Asses), a large, bronze, heavy ingot weighing one Roman pound, about 327.5 grams. (The word As is capitalized in this book to avoid confusion with the preposition "as.") Because of inflation, the bronze coins were gradually reduced in size and weight. Later, a silver series was introduced in which the principal coin, the denarius (plural—denarii), was equal to 16 reduced size-Asses. This relationship varied over the centuries, and new denominations were introduced whenever inflation affected the economy. The basic gold coin, the aureus (plural—

aurei), was equivalent to 25 denarii. Later, multiples of the As produced a double As, the dupondius (plural—dupondii), and the sestertius (plural—sestertii) equal to eight Asses. Fractions of the As were the half As, called a semis (plural—semisses), and the quarter As, the quadrans (plural—quadrantes). In later years, the denarius was replaced as the basic silver coin by a double denarius called the antoninianus (plural—antoniniani). Because of worsening economic conditions, by the late 3rd century A.D. the antoninianus was reduced to a copper module with only a silver wash on its surface, and then it deteriorated into a small copper coin. A series of larger bronze coins, such as the follis (plural—folles), was later introduced to restore the integrity of the currency. These were accompanied by a silver coin called the siliqua (plural—siliquae) and a gold denomination, the solidus. This is a very rough outline of the history of ancient coinage, but it provides some background information for the coins displaying buildings and monuments that were struck only in a period from the 1st century B.C. to about A.D. 400.

The Greek and Roman coin artists and engravers were exceptionally fine craftsmen. Most historians claim that they were slaves, but some scholars prefer to believe that they were freed slaves called *freedmen* (as compared to *freemen* who were born-free citizens), or at least slaves given special privileges. It is difficult to believe that artists could produce such marvellous work while living under the intimidating conditions of enslavement. Numismatists also believe that the engravers carved the coin dies without optical aids. It is suggested that young slaves with keen eyes or those who suffered from severe myopia would work on the dies until they destroyed their eyesight. However, ancient literature mentions "burning glasses," that is, magnifying lenses to start fires. Pliny the Elder remarks that a glass globe filled with water and facing the sun could be used to "set clothes on fire" (*Natural History,* Book XXXVI, lxvii.199). Also, the emperor Nero is said by Pliny (*Natural History,* Book XXXVII, xvi.64) to have used a magnifying glass made out of an emerald (smaragdus) as an eyepiece to observe distant gladiators in the arena. As the technology for producing all types of glass was highly developed in the ancient world, we can assume that it was possible to make simple convex lenses that could magnify an object by a power of three and be used as an aid to engravers.

Most buildings are engraved on coins to show a two-dimensional view of the front facade, sometimes called the front elevation, of the structure. Ancient temples and many other buildings were designed so that the front facade was the most important element of the composition, and this frontal view was most commonly exhibited on coinage in two dimensions. When views other than the two-dimensional appeared on coinage, early art historians and numismatists lacked the knowledge to identify the graphic technique used. These scholars were unaware that the ancients had not only invented the three-dimensional graphics system called *linear perspective,* but also had introduced some sophisticated techniques which are only being re-discovered by artists today.[2] A brief examination of ancient wall paintings and the designs on coins can prove this conclusively.

Also, ancient literature describes the method for drawing a linear perspective so clearly that the terms used appear to have been taken from a modern dictionary of graphic techniques. Vitruvius gives a definition of perspective drawing in his work (Book VII, Intro. 11) which is technically superior to the one given in today's Webster's dictionary. From the engravings on ancient coins, it is evident that the ancient artists were familiar with all the three-dimensional drawing systems that we today call axonometrics, obliques, linear perspectives, and vanishing axis perspectives. Up to very recent times, art historians claimed that linear perspective was invented by the artists of the Renaissance, sometime in the early 15th century. However, one ancient

2 *Glide Projection, Lateral Architectural Drawing,* by Kevin Forseth, Van Nostrand Reinhold Co., New York, 1984.

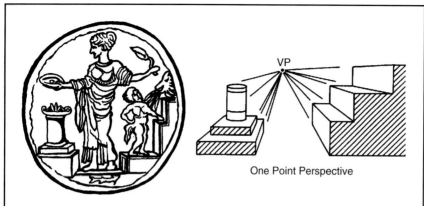

One Point Perspective

A Greek silver tetradrachm of the city of Himera, Sicily, struck in 482-472 B.C. BMC Greek 2.24. The column base at the left and the fountain monument on the right are delineated in perfect one-point, eye-level perspective, in exactly the same technique used by artists today.

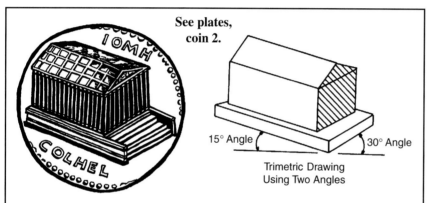

See plates, coin 2.

15° Angle   30° Angle

Trimetric Drawing
Using Two Angles

Left: an AE25 struck at Heliopolis in Syria, modern day Baalbeck in Lebanon, by Septimius Severus, A.D. 193-211, showing the large Temple of Jupiter Heliopolitanus. Sear GIC 2265. Right: a diagramatic analysis of the coin's design showing the axonometric (trimetric in this case) drawing technique.

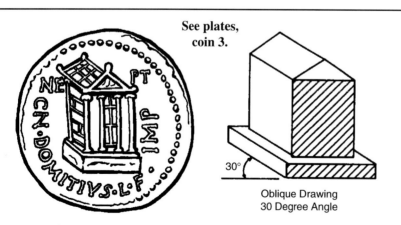

See plates, coin 3.

30°

Oblique Drawing
30 Degree Angle

Left: a Roman Republican aureus struck by Cn. Domitius Ahenobarbus in 40-41 B.C., showing the Temple of Neptune in Rome using an oblique drawing technique. Syd. 1176. Right: an analysis of the coin's composition showing the oblique graphic method used to provide a three-dimensional view.

coin from Sicily, BMC Greek 2.24, shows that the Greeks had mastered the technique as early as 482 B.C., and that the Renaissance artists had merely rediscovered it 1,500 years later.

Axonometric techniques produce a drawing of a building showing two of its sides, both projected at an angle to the horizontal. When this angle is 30 degrees, it is called an *isometric* drawing. When other angles are used, it is called a *dimetric* or *trimetric* drawing. Ancient coins display several types of axonometric renderings of buildings with the two sides drawn at a variety of different angles. See Sear GIC 2265.

Oblique drawings are those that show the front wall or facade of the building as a two-dimensional view, and the side wall, either on the left or right, projected at an angle to the front. See Syd. 1176. Ancient coin artists employed several forms of the oblique drawing technique, including one peculiar and inventive type where the side wall is drawn at a zero degree angle so that it is on a horizontal line with the front wall. This produces a double facade or elevation showing two sides of the building and the corner in two dimensions, an effective method for engravers to create the illusion of a three-dimensional composition. See RIC Nero 510.

Linear perspective is a drawing system in which

receding lines, which give the optical illusion of the third dimension or the depth of the composition, radiate from a vanishing point (VP) on a horizon line. Perspective, in all its forms, was well known to the ancients and was used occasionally to engrave the buildings on the reverses of coins. As well as the common eye-level perspectives, artists could draw aerial and multi vanishing point views. See Sear GIC 3954.

In modern coin catalogs and reference books, numismatists unfamiliar with technical graphics and its terminology often refer to these renderings of buildings as three-quarter views, or as distorted compositions. Sometimes the catalogers confuse axonometrics and obliques with perspective engravings, and label them all incorrectly.

Far in advance of these common techniques, ancient artists experimented with innovative perspective methods using a vanishing axis on which multiple vanishing points could be used to view a building from several positions along a horizontal or vertical line of sight. For example, see RIC Trajan 577.

The ancient coin artists frequently carried their drawing experiments to the extreme, and boldly combined several graphics systems to achieve views of buildings in which a plan or top view, a facade or elevation, and an axonometric or a perspective

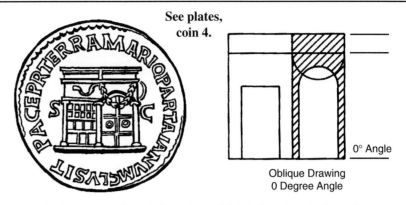

Left: a sestertius of Nero, A.D. 54-68, showing the Temple of Janus in Rome, with the doors closed, using an oblique technique with a zero angle projection for the side. RIC 510. Right: a diagram of the coin's design illustrating the unusual zero angle, oblique method which looks like a two-dimensional rendering.

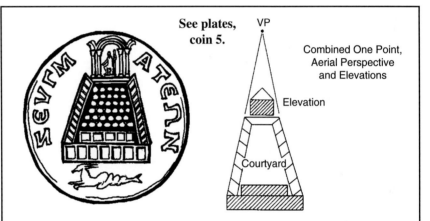

Left: an AE30 of the city of Zeugma in Syria struck by Philip I, A.D. 244-249, showing a one point, aerial view of a temple and sacred precinct. Sear GIC 3954. Right: a diagram analyzing the coin's design to show the aerial perspective, vanishing point, and horizon line used.

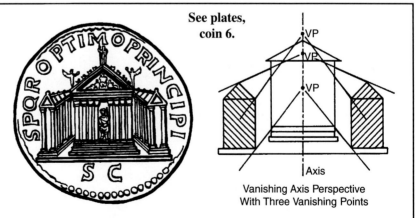

Left: an As of Trajan, A.D. 98-117, showing the complex Temple of Jupiter Victor in Rome by using a vanishing axis type of perspective with three vanishing points. RIC 577. Right: a diagramatic analysis of the coin's design showing the vanishing axis and multiple vanishing point method used in the composition.

22

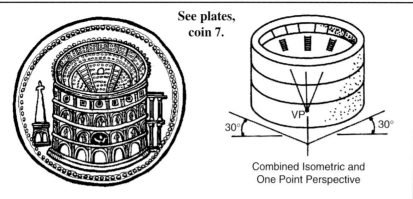

See plates, coin 7.

Combined Isometric and
One Point Perspective

Left: a sestertius of Titus, A.D. 79-81, showing the Colosseum, exterior and interior at the same time, by combining a perspective and an axonometric. RIC 110. Right: a diagram analyzing the coin and illustrating the combination of graphic techniques and an axonometric of 30 degrees (isometric).

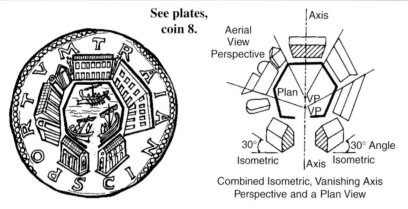

See plates, coin 8.

Aerial View Perspective

Axis

Plan

VP

VP

30° Isometric

30° Angle Isometric

Axis

Combined Isometric, Vanishing Axis
Perspective and a Plan View

Left: a sestertius of Trajan, A.D. 98-117, showing the entire new port at Ostia by combining a harbor plan, axonometric and vanishing axis perspective for the buildings. RIC 632. Right: a diagram analyzing the coin's use of a combined plan, axonometric (isometric) and a vanishing axis with two vanishing points.

See plates, coin 9.

A gigantic AE42 struck in the city of Pergamum, Mysia, by Caracalla, A.D. 198-217, showing two temples in oblique and one in front elevation. A seated statue of the god Aesclepius can be seen in the central temple. In his final years, the emperor was constantly worried about his health and this coin commemorated his visit to the famous Temple of Aesclepius, the god of healing, in Pergamum in 214. Sear GIC 2534.

rendering were combined to give an unusual multi-view composition. See RIC Titus 110 and RIC Trajan 632.

Ancient coin engravers also used "artistic license," or graphic shortcuts, to overcome the small and odd shaped areas provided by the coin's circular surface. This resulted in several standard artistic conventions which many historians mistakenly blame on carelessness, inept workmanship, or the lack of skill of the artist. These well known conventions consisted of omitting the central columns of a temple in order to show the cult statue inside the sanctuary, omitting some of the columns when space was unavailable on the coin, placing statues, which were behind objects and hidden, in positions above these objects so that they could be seen, using simple dots or pellets to represent statues, and adding non-existent, whimsical statuary to the tops of temples to better define the roof edge.

With all these techniques and tricks-of-the-trade at their fingertips, the engravers could produce remarkable compositions. We need only examine some of their architectural coins to see the imaginative talent and genius of these ancient coin artists. For example, see Sear GIC 2534.

Often the most accomplished craftsmen in the country were given the task of producing the designs of the architectural coins. Many of their engravings are outstanding, and some have never been surpassed even in modern times. It is presumed that the best artisans in the mint engraved the bust of the emperors or empresses on the obverse (head's side) of the coin, while the second or third best carved the reverse (tail's side). However, the resulting coinage, both obverses and reverses, were spectacular works of art, and were often truly magnificent. An excellent example of this can be seen on a coin of Nicaea in Bithynia, Sear GIC 510.

An AE30 of the city of Nicaea, Bithynia, struck by Claudius, A.D. 41-54, for his third wife, the infamous Valeria Messalina, showing a wonderful portrait of the empress and a two-story building on the reverse. While the composition of the coin is excellent, it is apparent that the bust on this obverse is rendered in a superior fashion to the architecture on the reverse. Similar to Sear GIC 510.

PART II

EARLY ARCHITECTURE
ON COINS

Chapter 4

The Temple of Artemis at Ephesos

The earliest building that was archaeologically connected to ancient coinage and which also appeared on coins is the famous Temple of Artemis, located in the city of Ephesos (Ephesus in Latin). This temple was named as one of the classical "Seven Wonders of the World." These marvelous works of art and architecture were traditionally listed as the Pyramids at Giza, the Hanging Gardens of Babylon, the Temple of Artemis at Ephesos, the Statue of Zeus at Olympia, the Mausoleum of Halicarnassus, the Colossus of Rhodes, and the Pharos of Alexandria. The Temple of Artemis was always placed third on this list, but it is the "wonder" few people can ever remember. Descriptions of this renowned temple appeared in the works of several ancient authors, such as *Herodotus, Vitruvius, Strabo, Pliny the Elder,* and *Pausanias.* Also, references to this temple and to Ephesos appeared in the New Testament, *Acts 19, 24-28,* when the merchants of the city rioted against St. Paul's preaching of the Christian doctrine. To some of the ancient authors, the Temple of Artemis was the most impressive of all the Seven Wonders, and they ranked it as number one on their personal lists. Pausanias, the Roman geography and travel writer, A.D. 174, said that "Ionia enjoys the finest climate and its sanctuaries are unmatched in the world. The first for size and opulence is the sanctuary of the Ephesian goddess."[1]

According to the geographer Strabo, 64 B.C.-A.D. 21, the Greek colony at Ephesos on the coast of Ionia, modern day Turkey, was established by Argive and Athenian colonists in the 11th century B.C. These Greek settlers intermarried with the native tribes and adopted the local goddess of the area, re-naming her Artemis. Artemis later became Diana in Latin mythology, and the Romans, as well as the apostle St. Paul, knew the temple in Ephesos as the "Temple of Diana of the Ephesians." In the early years of the city only a small shrine and a religious precinct were built for the worship of this deity, but in the 6th century B.C. a grand temple was erected. This first temple was completed and dedicated by King Croesus of Lydia, 560-546 B.C., who ruled over Ionia at that time, and who is credited with introducing the first bi-metallic coinage. The historian Herodotus, 484-420 B.C., says that the golden heifers and many of the columns of the Temple of the Ephesian Artemis were gifts of King Croesus.[2] However, many historians now claim that the first temple was built much earlier, either in the 8th century B.C. or in the mid 7th century B.C.

Archaeologists, excavating Ephesos in 1905, discovered a votive foundation deposit of the 6th century B.C. under the altar area of the temple built by Croesus. This offering consisted of jewellery, statuettes of female divinities made of wood, gold, and ivory, and 93 of the earliest known Greek coins. This find became famous because it was one of the first groups of early Ionian electrum coins found in a dateable archaeological site, and the hoard was used to establish the basic chronology of these early coins.[3] This chronology is presently under dispute, and some numis-

---

[1] *Pausanias, Description of Greece*, Book VII, Chapter V, translated by J.G. Frazer, Macmillan and Co., London, 1898, Vol I, page 333.

[2] *History,* by Herodotus, translated by G. Rawlinson, E.P. Dutton and Co., New York, 1930, Vol. I, Book I, Chapter 92, page 48.

[3] Originally described in *The British Museum Excavations at Ephesus, The Coins,* by B. Head, pages 74-93, but also in *Archaic and Classical Greek Coins,* by Colin M. Kraay, University of California Press, Berkeley, 1976, pages 20-30. Perhaps *Coinage in the Greek World,* by I. Carradice and Martin Price, Seabys, London, 1988, gives the most accurate account on pages 24-27.

matists are proposing an even earlier date for the deposit. However, the hoard contained several electrum and silver lumps of metal, and many archaic coins struck by the city-states in the area around Ephesos. These consisted of seven "dumps" or unmarked lumps of silver, two electrum lumps without any marks, three plain electrum pieces with only an incuse square punch mark, and four electrum coins with striated surfaces and simple punch marks on the other sides. The remaining 80 coins consisted of eight different, later denominations ranging from a half stater to the tiny ninety-sixth stater. They were struck by several local cities, including Miletus, Phocaea, Ephesos, and perhaps Teos. These coins showed designs of animals or parts of animals such as lions, goats, cocks, griffins, beetles, seals, bulls, stags, or horses. Only one coin showed a crude male, human head. The stag is considered to be the civic emblem of Ephesos, the seal is associated with Phocaea, the lion with Miletus, and the griffin with Teos. Because the coins have no inscriptions, more positive identifications were not possible, but the hoard provided a glimpse into the early stages of coinage before 600 B.C. and it traced the development of coin making from crude, unmarked metal lumps to the earliest types of struck coinage.

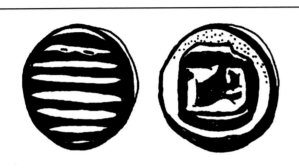

An early electrum coin, probably a one-sixth stater, weighing 2.36 grams, found in the Temple of Artemis in 1905. It has a striated field on the obverse and a square punch mark on the reverse. Sear Greek, 3433. Also Archaic and Classical Greek Coins *by C.M. Kraay, no. 51, plate 3.*

According to legend, on the night of Alexander the Great's birth in 356 B.C., a Greek named Herostratus set fire to the Temple of Artemis. He committed this terrible crime in a frivolous attempt to become famous and to have his name go down in history. The temple was immediately rebuilt with money collected from the citizens of Ephesos and from communities all over Asia. This new building was erected directly on the ruins of the old structure, and the temple the Greeks and Romans knew as one of the Seven Wonders of the World was this second temple. The name of the architect for this edifice was recorded by Strabo as Cherisphron, and Vitruvius confirms this in his book by recording the architects as Cherisphron of Gnossus (Knossos in Crete) and his son, named Metagenes.[4] The temple was later enlarged by a priest of Artemis called Demetrius and a citizen of Ephesos named Paeonius.

Pliny the Elder, in his work *Natural History*, Book XXXVI, 21, described in great detail how the temple was constructed. Because the area around Ephesos was prone to earthquakes, the structure was placed in a marsh, where the water-logged ground was expected to cushion it from tremors and shocks. To stabilize the soil, the builders first put down a thick layer of compacted charcoal, and on top of that, a layer of sheepskins with unshorn fleece. Vitruvius, in his writings about building construction, mentions the use of charcoal to fill in swampy soil, but the reason for the sheepskins is unknown. They may have acted as a waterproof membrane to prevent water seeping under the foundations. The marshland site was also probably chosen for religious reasons; the bogs contained several sacred springs. However, the swampy site did not protect the temple from damage during earthquakes, and over the years, the temple subsided into the mud.

From ancient records, we know that the temple contained a cult statue of Artemis in the cella

---

4 *De Architectura, The Ten Books on Architecture,* by Vitruvius, translated by M.H. Morgan, Dover Publications, New York, 1960, Book VII, 16, page 200. Book III, page 75.

sculptures. Many of the statues were the work of Praxiteles, the leading Athenian sculptor who had made the well known Aphrodite of Cnidos, the prototype for the famous Venus de Milo. Also, many large paintings were placed on the walls of the temple. One was a renowned equestrian portrait of Alexander the Great painted by Apelles, the greatest painter of his day. There is a charming tale told by Pliny the Elder in *Natural History,* Book XXXV, 96, about the great skill of this artist. A competition was held among the leading artists of Greece to see who could paint the best picture of a horse. Apelles learned that the other artists were bribing the judges, so he brought a live horse into the hall and showed it all the paintings being exhibited. The horse was unresponsive to the work of the other artists, but when it saw Apelles' picture, it began to neigh at the painted horse as if it was alive. The panel of judges, now including the horse, unanimously awarded the prize to Apelles.[5]

The cult statue of the Ephesian Artemis was a strange image, very different from the traditional form of the Greek Artemis, who was always portrayed as a youthful, slim, virgin huntress dressed in a short gown and carrying a bow and arrows. Similarly, the Romans worshipped an image of Artemis/Diana that was a young, virgin goddess of the moon, the ethereal twin sister of the sun god, Apollo. However, the Artemis of Ephesos was obviously the image of an eastern, earth-mother deity, personifying the fruitfulness and fertility of women and nature. This divine function perhaps identified the Ephesian Artemis more closely with the mythology of Cybele, the "Magna Mater" or Great Mother of the Roman religion. The statue of the Ephesian deity was a matronly figure dressed in a rigid, sheath-like gown with plaques showing animals and bees attached to the fabric. This gown resembles a column or tree trunk, but some historians see it as an Egyptian mummy case and describe it as such. Similar column-like sculptures are sometimes described in numismatic literature as "terminal" statues. The head, hands, chest, and toes of the goddess project from the sheath. Her head bears a high, cylindrical, turreted head-dress, and her head is backed by a nimbus or halo. Among Artemis' attributes are the stag and the bee. These appear prominently in the plaques on her gown and can be seen accompanying the image of the goddess on many coins. Also, the bee and stag became the official emblem or coat-of-arms of the city of Ephesos, and were used on the coinage struck at the city's mint.

Although this image of the goddess is unusual, it is noted in studies of ancient Greek religion that the Spartans worshipped a fertility version of Artemis, surnamed "Orthia" (meaning "straight"), which was represented by a statue with a post-like body and wings, wearing a rigid sheath skirt and a high turreted crown headdress.[6] The image of the Spartan Artemis Orthia may have been the direct inspiration for the Ephesian Artemis. The unique feature of the statue of Artemis at Ephesos, and that which sets it apart from all other images of this deity, is that her chest is "polymaste" or multi-breasted, probably to suggest fecundity. These breasts make the statue look very eastern, almost Indian in character. The breast forms have been interpreted by various authors as representing ostrich eggs, acorns, bags of amulets, or palm dates, but their shapes and location on the statue make them unmistakably human breasts. The polymaste Artemis was so powerful as a talisman for fertility that her image was made into small silver statues and sold to women in the market places of the city. Details of this form of Artemis can be clearly seen on a Roman copy of the statue presently in the National Archaeological Museum in Naples, Italy, and on Roman

[5] This tale is often dramatically rewritten where the equestrian picture of Alexander the Great in the Temple of Artemis is made the subject of the horse's appraisal, with Alexander himself as the judge. For this version, see 'Apelles' in *Lempriere's Classical Dictionary,* by J. Lempriere, Bracken Books, reprint of the 1865 edition, London, 1984, page 65.
[6] *Epilogmena to the Study of Greek Religion and Themis,* by Jane E. Harrison, University Books, New York, 1966, page 114.

30

See plates, coin 10.

The cult statue of the Ephesian Artemis with stags at her feet, seen on a cistophoric tetradrachm of Hadrian, A.D. 117-138, struck at Ephesos. RIC, Hadrian 525. The same statue appears on a cistophoric tetradrachm struck for Agrippina Junior and Claudius which shows Artemis, but without the stags at her feet. RIC, Claudius 54.

A bronze coin of Ephesos, struck under Antoninus Pius, A.D. 138-161, showing the temple of Artemis with her cultic statue in the center and an image of the goddess, or a priestess dressed as her, appearing in the central window of the pediment. Sear, GIC 1409 or BMC Greek, 14, 78, 234.

See plates, coin 11.

A cistophoric tetradrachm of Ephesos, struck under Claudius, A.D. 41-54, showing the temple with the three windows in the pediment, but only four columns on the facade. RIC, Claudius 53.

cistophoric silver tetradrachms struck for the emperors Claudius and Hadrian. The Artemis of Ephesos was also worshipped in several other nearby cities, and her image can be seen on bronze coins struck in Ionia, Lydia, Phrygia, and even distant Samaria. (See Sear, GIC 1587, 2724, 1801, 2188, 4008, 4034, 4093, 5062, and 5124. Also RIC Hadrian 525.)

In the rituals of the cult of Artemis, the goddess was "epiphanes", that is, a divinity that made a physical appearance during ceremonies. To provide for this spiritual revelation, her temple had three windows in the pediment, the triangular end of the roof, where the statues of the goddess or a priestess dressed as the deity could be revealed to the worshippers gathered below. This act of epiphany is actually represented on several of the coins that depict the facade of the temple of Artemis by showing the windows containing statues. See Sear GIC 1409.

A silver cistophoric tetradrachm of Claudius, A.D. 41-54, shows the windows in the pediment, used for the epiphany, in greater detail. However, only four columns are shown on this temple. This is a good example of the "artistic license" taken by the coin engraver to create an abbreviation of the temple's facade when there was not enough room on the coin's surface to show all of the eight columns, or when the craftsman was not skillful enough to represent the entire facade. See RIC Claudius 53.

Pliny the Elder began his lengthy description of the temple by praising it as a "Graecae magnificae", a Greek magnificence. It supposedly took 120 years to build, and most of the monarchs and nations of Asia Minor contributed to the cost. When he saw the building, still under construction in 334 B.C., Alexander the Great was so impressed he proposed that if the temple was dedicated in his name, he would pay all the remaining costs to

Great was so impressed he proposed that if the temple was dedicated in his name, he would pay all the remaining costs to complete it. The elders at Ephesos, wishing to be independent of Alexander's ambitions and political influence, diplomatically declined the offer by respectfully suggesting that it would be inappropriate for one god to contribute to the temple of another.[7]

Modern archaeological excavations of the temple site began in 1863 with an English team led by J.T. Wood. Many fragments of architecture and sculpture were recovered over the next ten years, including one sculptured column base. These are now on display in galleries of the British Museum. Excavations by Austrian archaeologists continued the work, and they discovered additional fragments and information. Also, the temple is clearly shown in great detail on numerous coins struck at Ephesos and other Asian cities under the Roman emperors from Claudius, A.D. 41, until Trajan Decius, 251. These coins are so accurate that, in the past, the best reconstruction drawings of the structure were made directly from them.

Pliny said that the building was 425 feet (128 m) long, 200 feet (60 m) wide, with 127 columns, 60 feet (18 m) high, donated by the kings of neighbouring nations. He also said that 36 columns had unusual bases made with sculptured panels. Archaeological excavation of the site indicated that the temple was probably only about 342 feet (104 m) long by 163 feet (49 m) wide, but still an impressive size. Vitruvius recorded that the Temple of Diana at Ephesos was made with Ionic columns, "octastyle," that is eight columns wide and "dipteral," meaning that it had two rows of columns forming a colonnade at the sides (*Vitruvius,* Book III, chapter II, 7). The size of the plan mentioned by Pliny does not comply with the classical, mathematical proportions dictated as a rule for the design of Ionic temples. Pliny was obviously quoting secondhand or thirdhand information, and he probably never saw or measured the temple. Vitruvius, on the other hand, as one of the court architects of the emperor Augustus, may be considered a more reliable source for information on ancient buildings. The major discrepancy in Pliny's account is the number of columns in the temple. He said that there were 127, an uneven number. This would not permit a symmetrical plan with an equal number of columns on each end, a format which ancient architects insisted upon, especially for temples.

Some recent reconstruction drawings of the Temple of Artemis have tried to accommodate Pliny's 127 columns by showing eight columns in the front and nine on the rear facade. Such an unbalanced composition would have been avoided by ancient architects, who were strict purists when it came to symmetry in their buildings, and this would be the only ancient temple ever constructed in that way. However, the figure of 127 columns has been cleverly discounted by some scholars, who blame a punctuation error in the copies of Pliny's writing for this uneven number. Pliny records the columns in his Latin text as "- columnae CXXVII a singulis regibus factae -." This is usually translated as "- 127 columns each made by a king -." Some authors say that there should be a comma between the numbers C and XXVII, so that the words would actually read as "- 100 columns, (comma) 27 each made by a king."[8] This is a more logical translation, because 127 independent kings would be difficult, if not impossible, to find in the Asia of those times. It also provides for the even number of columns required for the greatly preferred symmetrical temple plan.

Following Vitruvius' description of the octastyle and dipteral Temple of Artemis, using the details of the coins and the figure of 100 columns, it is possible to draw a more reasonable reconstruction of the temple. The 36 sculpted columns mentioned by Pliny could be the most visible 32

---

[7] Quoted from an original ancient source in "The Temple of Artemis at Ephesus", by B.L. Trell, in *The Seven Wonders of the World,* edited by P. Clayton and Martin Price, Dorset Press, New York, 1988, page 78.

[8] *Pausanias, Description of Greece,* Comments in Vol. 3, by J.G. Frazer, Macmillan and Co., London, 1898, page 434.

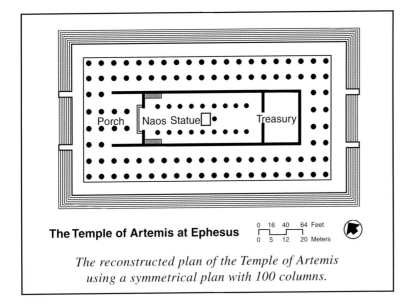

The Temple of Artemis at Ephesus

0 16 40   64 Feet
0   5   12   20 Meters

The reconstructed plan of the Temple of Artemis using a symmetrical plan with 100 columns.

The author's reconstruction of the Artemisium of Ephesus as an octastyle, dipteral temple using the details on the coins and the description given by Vitruvius.

A recently discovered coin of Ephesos struck for Maximus, A.D. 235-238, now in the British Museum collection. It shows an octastyle temple with sculpted columns, the large architrave beam, the cult statue, the three windows, and the statues of Amazons in the pediment. This is the same engraving of the temple used on coins struck at Ephesos for Antoninus Pius, A.D. 138-161. See Sear GIC 1409.

columns that made up the front and back colonnade of the temple, plus the 4 columns located "in antis"—in the porch. Using only 100 columns, the reconstruction still exhibits the impressive "forest of columns" mentioned by many ancient authors in their descriptions of this great temple structure.

Pliny recorded that some of the 36 sculpted columns were carved by the great Greek artist Scopas. He was the famous sculptor who made several of the statues for the Mausoleum of Halicarnassus, another of the Seven Wonders of the World located in a city near Ephesos. These sculptures appeared only on the base drums of the columns, and they are clearly seen on many of the coins depicting the temple. See Sear GIC 1409. In confirmation of this description, a large fragment of a sculpted column base was discovered in the excavations of the site in 1869.

Also, a huge stone formed the lintel beam over the main doors, and it was supposedly placed in position by Artemis herself when the architects could not devise a method to lift it. However, Pliny described in detail how the builder raised the enormous beams into position over the columns on the temple facade. He said that this was done by "- filling bags of plaited reeds with sand and constructing a gently graded ramp which reached to the top of the capitals of the columns. The beam was dragged up and then, little by little, the workers emptied the lowest layer of bags, so that the fabric (beam) gradually settled into its right position." (*Natural History,* Book XXXVI. 21.98.) The immense architrave beam can also be seen on the many coins which show the temple facade.

Ephesos was strategically located on the Aegean coast, and it served as the main terminal port on the trade route from the east. The Ephesians became very wealthy from their involvement as middlemen in the trade and commerce which passed through their city. Also, in ancient records, Ephesos was mentioned as an industrial center well known for metal working, perfume manufacture, and wine making. As well, the city was famous for its banking institutions. It is worth noting that Ephesos was one of the few Roman provincial cities permitted to strike its own silver and gold coinage. This privilege was probably conferred because of the city's commercial importance and great wealth. Supposedly, the Temple of Artemis, utilizing its enormous treasury and its many priests as clerks and accountants, became a renowned merchant bank. Today, we could say that it functioned as the "Central Bank of Asia" for the Graeco-Roman world. It is recorded that all the surrounding Asiatic city-states deposited their money in the Temple of Artemis for investment and safekeeping. One can easily imagine the ancient temple precinct, the porch, and all the spaces between the columns filled with the stalls of bankers, money changers, jewellers, and brokers, all speaking several languages and conducting business with the foreign merchants who came to the city by both land and sea. Through this international commerce, the city developed into a cosmopolitan community which enjoyed a mixed culture of Asiatic, Roman, and Oriental religious beliefs overlaid with a veneer of Greek culture.

The Temple of Artemis also acquired a reputation for being a place of refuge or asylum. In the local myths, the Amazons were given refuge in the temple, and statues of these legendary warriors appeared in the pediment to commemorate this event. The statues of four armed Amazons can often be seen in the pediment of the temple facade on the coins. See Sear GIC 1409 above. History records an occasion when the children of the Persian king Xerxes I were granted safe asylum in the temple after he was defeated by the Greeks in 479 B.C. However, this law of temple sanctuary was often violated. Alexander the Great had two of his slaves, who had been granted refuge there, forcibly removed from the temple and put to death. Also Mark Antony, in 36 B.C., seized Arsinoe, the younger sister of Cleopatra VII, from the sanctuary of the temple and had her executed.

The famous temple building lasted until A.D. 262, when it was destroyed by the invading Goths. It was then rebuilt as a shrine on a much smaller scale, and was completed some time near the end of the 3rd century. The worship of Diana/Artemis continued for many years at Ephesos, and was finally suppressed in A.D. 401 when Saint John Chrysostom had the shrine razed to the ground. The large stones from the demolished temple were reused in several later buildings, and many of the temple's columns were taken to Constantinople by Justinian I, 527-565, to be used in the interior of his famous church, the Santa Sophia. However, the deeply rooted and lasting memory of Artemis continued to play a part in the development of religious beliefs at Ephesos. Traditionally, it is believed that the Virgin Mary did not remain in Jerusalem, but accompanied Saint John to Ephesos and died there. Also, it is an historical fact that the very first church dedicated to Saint Mary was founded in Ephesos, and there, in A.D. 431, an Ecumenical Council overruled the objections of conservative church elders and conferred on Mary the official title "Mother of God." The feast of her assumption was assigned to August 15, the same date as the annual pagan festival to Diana/Artemis, another virgin divinity of an older but not completely forgotten religion.[9] From then on, clay images of the holy Virgin Mary were sold to Christian pilgrims in the very market places of Ephesos where silver images of the pagan Artemis were once peddled to ancient tourists.

---

[9] *The Loom of History,* by Herbert J. Muller, Harper and Brothers, New York, 1958, page 140.

Chapter 5

Cities on Coins

It has been said that without cities there would be no civilization, no society, and no culture. This broad, general statement may be disputed by modern social scientists, but cities did play a very important part in the development of early ancient history. The Bible mentions a city in Genesis, its very first chapter. After Cain murdered Abel, he was banished to the Land of Nod, where he founded a city named after his son, Enoch. Biblical scholars consider the Cain and Abel story to be a parable about the early struggle between settled farmers and wandering herdsmen, or between civilized people and nomadic raiders. In this confrontation, farmers gave up roaming and remained in one place in order to sow and reap their crops. They gathered together for mutual protection, and eventually to share expertise and specialized tasks, thereby creating agricultural settlements which later developed into cities. These early cities required that people cooperate with each other, and this was the beginning of the social environment that we call civilization. In fact, the word "civilization" comes from the Latin word *civis,* meaning "city-dweller." The earliest cities known to archaeologists may date from the eighth millennium B.C., a date that coincides with the beginning of organized, primitive farming settlements in lower Mesopotamia. It is believed that one of the earliest cities was the pre-pottery Neolithic biblical city of Jericho, established sometime before 7,000 B.C. when the massive walls and remarkable stone defensive towers were built.[1]

The use of a rectangular grid plan for laying out city streets was invented by the ancient Babylonians before the 5th century B.C. However, Aristotle (*Pol. II,* 1267b, 21) credits an architect from Miletus named Hippodamos for inventing the gridiron system and the social order that it enforced on the people living in cities. Hippodamos supposedly designed his own city, Miletus, the city of Thurii in Italy in 443 B.C., and the port of Athens, Piraeus, in 466 B.C., using the right-angle grid as a plan.[2] The orthogonal street plan was further developed by the Greeks, who passed it on to the Romans through the Etruscans. Roman engineers, using surveying methods and tools invented by the Etruscans, laid out the entire area of their empire in squares called *centuriae* (centuries) because they were intended to contain 100 small, subsistence farmsteads. These century parcels were 2,400 feet (728 m) square. An *oppidum* (a city) or a *castrum* (a fortress) was established at some of the main north-south and east-west intersecting lines of these large squares. The boundary lines of the squares became the main streets of the city, called the *cardo* for the east-west and the *decumanus* for the north-south road. The intersection of these streets was emphasized by making it into the civic center of the city, with the forum, temples, basilica, and the main market areas located at the four corners. When a city was not flat, the street grid pattern and the location of the walls were modified to fit onto the terrain and natural contours of the site.

---

1 *Encyclopedia of Archaeological Excavations in the Holy Land,* Vol. II, by M. Avi-Yonah, Prentice Hall, New Jersey, 1976, page 554.
2 *A History of Science,* Vol. I, by George Sarton, The Norton Library, New York, 1952, page 294.

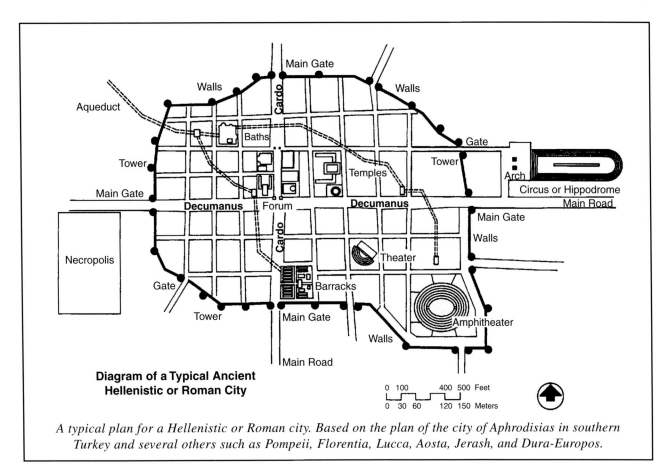

**Diagram of a Typical Ancient
Hellenistic or Roman City**

Main Gate

Walls

Aqueduct

Cardo

Walls

Baths

Tower

Gate

Tower

Main Gate

Temples

Arch

Circus or Hippodrome
Main Road

Decumanus Forum **Decumanus**

Main Gate

Cardo

Walls

Necropolis

Theater

Gate

Barracks

Tower

Main Gate

Walls

Amphitheater

Main Road

0 100   400 500 Feet

0 30 60   120 150 Meters

*A typical plan for a Hellenistic or Roman city. Based on the plan of the city of Aphrodisias in southern
Turkey and several others such as Pompeii, Florentia, Lucca, Aosta, Jerash, and Dura-Europos.*

Early cities were always fortified, and
the principal activity of city architects and
engineers was the construction of walls,
towers, and gates to ward off attackers.
But the invaders had their own architects,
who responded to the city's defenses by
inventing new siege machines such as battering rams and assault towers. The ancients
eventually developed a round defensive
tower for their walls because the corner
stones of a square tower were extremely
vulnerable to battering rams. The main
gates were also reinforced because they
were the weakest point in the fortifications.
Most gateways were protected by massive
towers, ditches, drawbridges, and portcullis
type barriers, and archaeologists who exca-
vate Bronze and Iron Age cities are always

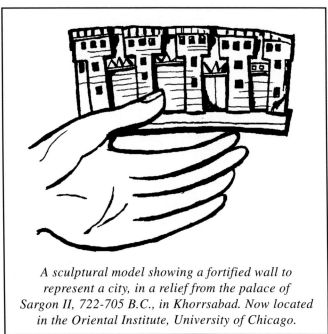

*A sculptural model showing a fortified wall to
represent a city, in a relief from the palace of
Sargon II, 722-705 B.C., in Khorrsabad. Now located
in the Oriental Institute, University of Chicago.*

impressed by the gates' heights, widths, and solid construction. It is worth noting that, in ancient
artwork, cities were always symbolically represented by their walls and gates, the most easily
recognized feature of a fortified settlement.

Numerous cities are pictured on ancient coinage, and they are always shown as walled, with
massive ramparts, gates, and towers. The best examples of these coins were struck in the Roman
empire during the 2nd and 3rd centuries A.D. Sometimes only the prominent main gate and

An AE30 of the city of Augusta Traiana in Thrace, struck by Caracalla, A.D. 198-217. The city is represented by its enormous, powerful gate and its crenelated tower fortifications. Sear GIC 2491.

An AE35 struck by Gordian III, A.D. 238-244, in the city of Marcian-opolis in Thrace. This city was founded by Trajan and named after his sister Marciana. The coin shows the entire city, walls, towers, and gate, with a temple and cult image at the center. BMC Greek 3, 39.

See plates, coin 12.

An AE35 struck by Severus Alexander, A.D. 222-235, in the city of Amaseia in Pontus. It shows the entire city in elevation view as a series of facades one above each other. Clearly seen are the mountain outcrops, walls, gates, towers, temples, and statues. Von Aulock 44.

defensive towers are shown on a coin to depict the entire forti-fied city. See Sear GIC 2491.

Many of the cities in the eastern provinces of the Roman empire had been founded in early history, and over a long period of time they acquired enormous fortification walls of which the citizens were justly proud. The cost of constructing these walls, encompassing the entire city, must have been prohibitive. As coinage often functioned as an advertisement for the city's wealth and security, coins showing a powerful and impregnable defensive system would be very desirable as propaganda. Three cities that employed exceptional architectural coinage to illustrate their power and strength were Amaseia in Pontus and Marcian-opolis and Bizya in Thrace. See the coins below.

Other city architectural coins were also used as propaganda devices to promote religion or piety among the inhabitants of the area. These coins concentrated on the religious edifices located in the city, or on the temples and shrines of the deities that were patrons and protectors of the community. On these coins, the artists also emphasized the topography of the city site by depicting mountains, rivers, or other landscape elements as part of the composition. These natural features served as a background scene for the architecture and also to reinforce the cult worship that usually took place there. Many of the city gods were nature deities served by sacred caves, trees, or other natural elements such as rivers and lakes. The best examples of these types of city religious coins were struck by Neapolis in Samaria and Pella in Syria, both cities of the Roman Decapolis, a league of ten cities in Palestine/ Syria. See Sear GIC 2052.

The most remarkable design for a city religious coin was produced for Neapolis in Samaria, near modern day Nablus. This coin combines a plan or map of the site, showing the two summits of Mount Gerizim, rock outcrops, stairs, and rivers, along with the facades of buildings, temples, altars, and shrines built by the biblical Samaritans and later reconstructed and dedicated to the god Zeus by the emperor Antoninus Pius. The eastern coin engravers, probably Greeks, were daring artists and were not averse to taking a chance when designing a coin. Often these city views are rendered with innovative, three dimensional graphics techniques, in order to show the details of the structures and landscape which normally would not be seen in traditional views. This artistic improvisation is usually very creative, and suggests that great artistic freedom was given to the engravers by the authorities in control of the mints. See Sear GIC 1506.

The most spectacular and historic city-view coin that promoted a religious cult is one that shows the walls and the famous acropolis of the city of Eryx in Sicily. The coin is a Roman Republican denarius struck by C. Considius Nonianus in 62 B.C. (Syd. 886). Eryx was the legend-

An AE35 struck by Philip I, A.D. 244-249, at the city of Bizya in Thrace. It shows the entire city, with much detail, using an oblique drawing view from above. The walls and all the towers are clearly rendered, and much attention is paid to the gate and its sculpture. BMC Greek 3, 91.

An AE36 struck by Commodus, A.D. 177-192, at the city of Pella in Syria. The mountainous site is clearly depicted by the rocky foreground. Sear GIC 2052.

An AE33 struck by Antoninus Pius, A.D. 138-161, to commemorate his dedication of the temple to Zeus on Mount Gerizim in Neapolis, Samaria. Details of the temples, shrines, altars, and landscape are visible in this view, which combines a plan of the site with the facades and an axonometric of the buildings. Sear GIC 1506.

38

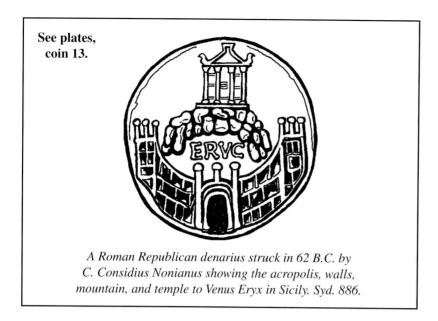

See plates, coin 13.

A Roman Republican denarius struck in 62 B.C. by C. Considius Nonianus showing the acropolis, walls, mountain, and temple to Venus Eryx in Sicily. Syd. 886.

ary son of Aphrodite/Venus and Poseidon/Neptune who was killed by Hercules in a contest of strength. Supposedly, he had built a temple to his mother on this mountaintop in Sicily. The ancient temple of Venus in Eryx was famous as a citadel, but also for the temple prostitutes who took part in the cult's rituals. One day of the year was given over to licentiousness in the temple, and all the female members of the cult, regardless of social status, had to prostitute themselves to strangers. The cult of Venus Erycina was introduced into Rome during the Second Punic War, 218-201 B.C., even though many Romans disapproved of the cult practices. A temple for Venus Erycina was built in Rome in 181 B.C., but was located outside the Servian city wall, so that the debauched customs of the cult would not corrupt the citizens. Vitruvius, in his writings (Book I, Chap. VII, 1), recommended that all temples to Venus be placed outside the city walls or in the disreputable harbor area, in order to keep the cult away from the impressionable matrons and the youth of the city.

Cities were depicted on many other ancient coins, and these indicate how important the civic structures were to ancient civilizations.

Chapter 6

Picture Postcards from the Acropolis

Today, when people say the word "acropolis", they mean only one place—the famous ancient citadel of Athens. The word acropolis is made up of two Greek words, *acro* for the top of, and *polis* for city. This steep-sided hill in the center of Athens is renowned as the site of several Greek architectural masterpieces. The most famous building is the celebrated Parthenon, a temple to Athena, the daughter of Zeus and the tutelary goddess of the city. The Greek word *parthenos* means "the virgin", and in this case it refers to the legendary purity of Athena. The Parthenon, built in 447-436 B.C., is the finest of all ancient Greek temples, and it is considered to be the paramount example of the Doric style of architecture. From several inscriptions found on the site we know that the architects who designed the Parthenon were named Iktinos and Kallikrates, usually spelled in Latin as Ictinus and Calicrates.

The Parthenon was constructed according to the rules of the classical proportioning system, but to further enhance its beauty, the edges of the columns, steps, and beams were made to curve slightly outwards. This was done as an optical refinement to eliminate the visual distortion caused by long, straight, parallel lines, which seem to sag or bend in the middle. The temple is so beautiful that it is considered to be the finest example of ancient architecture in the world. Some of the surviving marble sculptures that adorned the temple's frieze and pediment can be seen in the Elgin Marbles gallery in the British Museum in London.

Most people believe that the Parthenon is the only important structure on the Acropolis, but there are several other remarkable buildings located there. The Temple to Athena Nike (Victory), sometimes called Nike Apteros (Wingless Victory) because of a wingless statue of Victory it contained, is a tiny architectural gem of the Ionic style. It was built in 427-424 B.C. and was designed by Kallikrates, the architect of the Parthenon. Also sited on the Acropolis is the Erechtheion, 421-405 B.C., considered to have been the finest Ionic style building in Greece. From an inscription, we know it was designed by an architect named Mnesciles. Attached to the Erechtheion is the famous Caryatid porch, or portico, with its six supporting columns made to resemble the gowned figures of Greek women. Also built on the Acropolis were the Propylaea, the ceremonial entrance buildings to the citadel, built in 449 B.C. Dominating the citadel was a thirty-foot (9 m) high, gilded bronze statue of Athena Promachos (the Champion) sculpted by the famous sculptor Pheidias. This famous and skillful artist also created the "chryselephantine" statue of Athena Parthenos located inside the sanctuary of the Parthenon. Chryselephantine is an adjective that describes a statue made of gold and ivory. The sun glinting off the tip of the spear or the helmet of the colossal statue of Athena Promachos supposedly acted as a beacon for ships approaching Athens by sea.

The city of Athens, as the main center of Hellenistic culture, was highly respected by many foreign kings and emperors. They donated artwork and temples to the city, embellished the citadel, and added new buildings to the hillside on the south side of the Acropolis. History records that the grecophile Roman emperor Hadrian was a patron of the arts, and adorned and refurbished several parts of Athens. Some of the more significant additions to Athens, made over the years, were the enormous Theater of Dionysos, a temple to Ascelepius, the Stoa of Eumenes II, and another large theater called the Odeion of Herodes Atticus. Eumenes II was the king of Pergamum in 197-160

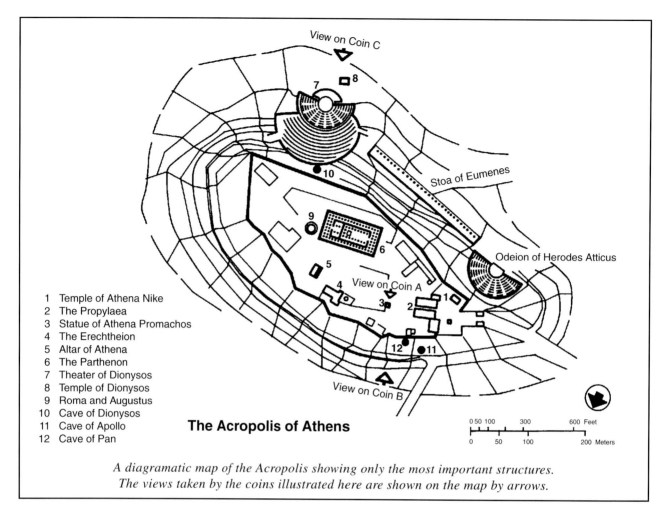

1 Temple of Athena Nike
2 The Propylaea
3 Statue of Athena Promachos
4 The Erechtheion
5 Altar of Athena
6 The Parthenon
7 Theater of Dionysos
8 Temple of Dionysos
9 Roma and Augustus
10 Cave of Dionysos
11 Cave of Apollo
12 Cave of Pan

The Acropolis of Athens

A diagramatic map of the Acropolis showing only the most important structures.
The views taken by the coins illustrated here are shown on the map by arrows.

B.C., and he contributed many buildings to the cities of Rhodes, Delphi, and Athens. Herodes Atticus was a philanthropic Greek-born senator and consul of Rome. He was a friend of Hadrian, and he honored his emperor by contributing a building to Athens. Also, in early Roman imperial times, a small, round, Ionic temple, dedicated to Roma and Augustus, was built on the Acropolis just behind the Parthenon.[1]

The Acropolis is a flat-topped mound rising 512 feet (155 m) above the city. It is precipitous and can only be approached on foot from the narrow and steep west side. It was originally a late Bronze Age fortress containing a palace, massive fortification walls, and gates. In the 8th century B.C. it became the religious center for the city, and a rough altar and a small temple to Athena were constructed on its highest points. In 480 B.C. the Persians, under Xerxes I, sacked Athens, destroyed the citadel, and burned all the buildings. A short time later, Athens experienced its greatest cultural epoch under the leadership of Pericles, and work began to restore the burned-out Acropolis. When the Persian threat was finally removed in 449 B.C., the citadel was designated as a national war memorial, and most of the great buildings were erected after that date.

The Acropolis became famous early in its history. It was always on the itinerary of ancient tourists who came to gawk at the beautiful, multicolor temples, the amazing sculptures and paintings, and of course, at the crowds of other tourists from exotic countries, dressed in outlandish clothing, who wandered around the buildings both day and night. Naturally, these tourists needed picture postcards to take home as souvenirs of their visit, and the Athenians, beginning probably in

---

[1] For the best architectural descriptions of these buildings, see *A History of Architecture,* by Sir Bannister Fletcher, republished by Butterworths, London, 1981, pages 110-120.

the time of the Roman emperor Hadrian, A.D. 117-138, satisfied this need by striking bronze coins that showed the architectural marvels of the city. With a little imagination, we can visualize the numerous stalls on the Acropolis and in the Stoa selling small statues of the main deities of the city, Athena, Apollo, Dionysos, and Pan, along with paintings or coins showing views of the Acropolis. Many of these coins can be co-related to the descriptions of the monuments

Coin A. An AE22 struck in the 2nd to 3rd century A.D., showing the bust of Athena on the obverse and the statue of Athena Promachos located on the Acropolis on the reverse. This image of Athena is thought to represent the actual statue. Sear GIC 4850. See the map for the view taken by the coin.

of Athens given by Pausanias, the geographer and travel writer, who wrote a popular tourists' guide book of Greece. For example, a detailed report on the colossal, armed statue of Athena Promachos is given by Pausanias in Book I, 28.2. This statue appears on the bronze coin illustrated here exactly as described by Pausanias (Sear GIC 4850).

Athens was a quasi-autonomous city in the Roman empire, and was given the privilege of striking its own coinage, which did not have to show the portrait and name of the emperor or any member of the imperial family. Instead, these coins always carried the bust of the goddess Athena, wearing a crested Corinthian helmet and the Aegis, her magical protective cloak. During the reigns of Hadrian and the Antonines, Athens struck enormous quantities of bronze coins, and several of these displayed the spectacular monuments on the Acropolis.

The most impressive coin struck in Athens, probably for the tourist trade, is one that shows a view of the entire Acropolis from the north (Sear GIC 4855). This coin is one of the most fantastic architectural coins in the Roman Provincial series. All the important buildings are shown on this coin, in an innovative three-dimensional composition where the buildings are depicted by frontal views on a pseudo-plan of the site. Clearly seen above the retaining wall, from left to right, is a small temple, perhaps the round Ionic Temple to Roma and Augustus, the Erechtheion with a solid stone side wall, the huge statue of Athena Promachos, and the Propylaea

Coin B. An AE22, struck at Athens in the 2nd to 3rd century A.D., showing a view of the Acropolis and its buildings from the north. Sear GIC 4855. The obverse shows the usual bust of Athena wearing a Corinthian helmet. See the map for the position of the view taken by this coin.

Coin C. An AE22 struck at Athens in the 2nd to 3rd century A.D., showing a panoramic view of the Acropolis and the theater of Dionysos on the southern side. Sear GIC 4854. The obverse portrays the bust of Athena as on Coins A and B. See the map for the position of the view taken by this coin.

buildings or the temple of Athena Nike at the top of the stairs. Many historians claim that the solid walled structure actually represents the colonnaded Parthenon, but the engraver was not skillful enough to show the columns. Also shown on the coin are the grottos of Pan and Apollo in the rocks below the wall, and the monumental staircase of the sacred way leading up to the entrance. These coins are usually found in worn or corroded condition, and the fine detail of the buildings cannot be easily recognized or appreciated.[2]

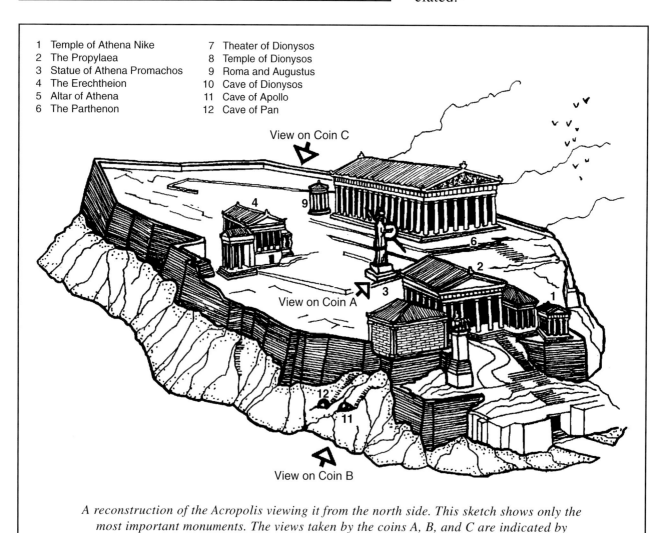

1 Temple of Athena Nike
2 The Propylaea
3 Statue of Athena Promachos
4 The Erechtheion
5 Altar of Athena
6 The Parthenon
7 Theater of Dionysos
8 Temple of Dionysos
9 Roma and Augustus
10 Cave of Dionysos
11 Cave of Apollo
12 Cave of Pan

View on Coin C

View on Coin A

View on Coin B

A reconstruction of the Acropolis viewing it from the north side. This sketch shows only the most important monuments. The views taken by the coins A, B, and C are indicated by arrows which co-relate this sketch to the plan and three coins shown on the preceding pages.

---

[2] See *Coins and Their Cities,* by Martin Price and Bluma Trell, published by V.C. Vecchi and Sons, London, 1977, page 68, for full color illustration of the best examples of coins B and C presently available.

Undoubtedly the most outstanding example in this series of Athenian coinage is one that shows the retaining wall and slope of the south side of the Acropolis, with the theater of Dionysos in the foreground (Sear GIC 4854). These coins reveal a panoramic view of the site that is unsurpassed on ancient coinage. The large theater of Dionysos is faithfully depicted with its sections of seats. Above the theater are the caves in the rocks, which represent the sacred grotto of Dionysos. The immense retaining wall of the Acropolis is shown surmounted by, at the left, the Propylaea entrance building, the Parthenon in the center, and another small temple at the right, perhaps the Temple to Roma and Augustus that was later erected by the Romans.

These city-view coins are so accurate that they could have been used as maps by tourists to find their way around the Acropolis and its surroundings. A comparison of the scenes shown on the coins with the reconstruction drawing of the north side of the Acropolis, shown on page 42, indicates that the artists who designed and engraved the coins were truly masters of their art.

Today, the Acropolis of Athens is considered to be one of the most important antiquities in the world. The coins, illustrated on pages 41 and 42, show that it contained a remarkable collection of monuments, and that these were widely advertised, especially in the 2nd century A.D. In history, Athens was called the "School of Hellas", that is, the fountainhead from which all Greek knowledge flowed. It was also considered to be the birthplace of democracy. As the Acropolis was the symbol of the entire city, these picture postcard coins can be regarded as great architectural/ numismatic mementoes of the glory that once was ancient Athens.

Chapter 7

The Temple of Jerusalem

The biblical Temple of Jerusalem is the most written about religious building in the history of mankind. In the words of the prophet Isaiah, *56:7*, "- it is a house of prayer for all peoples"—and so it is revered by Jews, Christians, and Muslims. But principally it is the unique, sacred emblem of the Jews. More than any other symbol, it represents the spiritual center and focal point of their faith and the very essence of their religion and history. Any new attempt to describe or reconstruct the Temple in literature may be superfluous, because so much has been written about it by many well-qualified authors. However, recent research and the details of the Temple on coins indicates that perhaps some significant elements have been overlooked.[1]

The silver tetradrachms, called shekels, struck for Simon Bar Kokhba (Bar Kosiba), usually with the legends "Jerusalem" or "For the Freedom of Jerusalem," are the only coins that show the facade of this famous temple. These coins were struck during the Second Jewish War against the Romans in A.D. 132-135. The shekels show the Temple as a Hellenistic, tetrastyle structure with a barrier fence in front, but instead of the usual statue of a pagan deity standing in the center, a shrine or chest, perhaps the Ark of the Covenant, is shown inside. This same representation of the Temple can be seen on gold glass bowls found in the Jewish catacombs of Rome.[2] A similar temple image can also be seen on a wall painting in the famous 3rd century A.D. synagogue found at Dura Europos in Syria,[3] and on floor mosaics located in ancient synagogues at Khirbet Susiiya and at Beth Shean in modern Israel.[4]

A drawing of the wall painting at Dura Europos, painted in the 3rd century A.D., showing the Temple of Jerusalem as a Hellenistic type of building.

The representations of the Temple seen on these coins, paintings, and artifacts actually show the edifice built by Herod the Great in 20 B.C., and not the earlier temple constructed for King Solomon, 970-931 B.C. The original Temple of Jerusalem, called the "First Temple", was built with the help of the Phoenician king, Hiram of Tyre, who provided most of the materials and the skilled craftsmen. This First Temple was greatly influenced by Tyrian art and culture, and it incorporated many architectural features normally associated with Phoenicia. These included the flat roof, the crenelated decorations at the roof edge, and the two large, prominent columns, like

1 *Coin and Temple,* by Alice Muehsam, Leeds University Press, Leeds, 1966, the most comprehensive study of the architectural representation of the Temple on ancient coins, is considered to be out of date.

2 *The Coinage of the Bar Kokhba War, Typos VI,* by Leo Mildenberg, Verhlag Sauerlander, Frankfurt, 1984, page 34.

3 *The Discovery of Dura-Europos,* by Clark Hopkins, Yale University Press, New Haven, 1979, page 155. Also in *Coins and Their Cities,* by Martin J. Price and Bluma L. Trell, V.C. Vecchi and Sons, London, 1977, page 178.

4 *Vision of the Temple,* by Helen Rosenau, Oresko Books, London, 1979, page 30.

monoliths or obelisks, at the entrance. The construction of Solomon's Temple began in 966 B.C. and was completed in 959. Three different biblical texts describe its size and appearance. These passages are, *Ezekiel, 40-46*, written in 593-571 B.C., *I Kings, 6-8*, documented about 550, and *II Chronicles, 2-4*, formalized around the 4th century B.C. All three biblical accounts record different dimensions for the structure, the largest being given in II Chronicles. However, all these statistics indicate that the temple building was quite small. Historians remind us that the Temple was not meant to be a space in which people assembled. It was the "House of the Lord" and His dwelling place. Worshippers gathered in the courtyards outside the Temple, and even the high priest entered the inner sanctuary only on one day of the year, on Yom Kippur, the Day of Atonement. The smallness of the building may also have been dictated by the maximum structural span, about 33 feet (9 m), permitted by the wooden roof beams made from the cedars of Lebanon.

The building consisted of three high chambers, with 13 small store rooms on each of three storeys around the sides. The innermost chamber was the "Dvir", the sanctuary or the "Holy of Holies". This room enclosed the Ark of the Covenant and it was separated from the other rooms by heavily embroidered veils. It was described as a cube in shape, 20 cubits in size. There are several dimensions given for this biblical cubit, but the one recognized as having been used in the Temple measured one foot, eight inches (.5 m) in length. This would make the Dvir a cube 33 feet (10 m) long, wide, and high. The middle chamber was called the "Hechal," the hall or Holy Place, which contained the golden candelabrum, incense altars, and the table of the shewbread. It was 66 feet (20 m) long by 33 feet (10 m) wide. The front area was the "Ulam," the porch or vestibule. It was 16 feet (5 m) long by 33 feet (10 m) wide.[5] The size and form of this biblical plan set the pattern for all the succeeding holy temples. The dimensions and style of Solomon's Temple, dictated by the Lord himself, became the law and were sacrosanct.

The two famous columns at the entrance of the Temple were cast in solid bronze by an architect/artist from Tyre, with the same name as the king, Hiram. They were set each side of the doorway, and were the only freestanding columns used in the First Temple. The walls alone carried the weight of the roof. These columnar monuments were so important that their names were recorded in the Bible, Jachin on the right, and Boaz on the left. The meaning and the origin of these pillars is unknown, but they have been variously described by scholars as obelisks, fire altars, incense altars, symbolic trees of life, or a gateway to the sun.[6] Some scholars claim that Jachin and Boaz were pre-biblical, early Bronze Age pagan gods still remembered and revered by the people and commemorated by these monuments, but this theory cannot be verified by any archaeological or historical evidence. The columns were noted in *I Kings 7:15* as being 18 cubits or 30 feet (9 m) high, and in *II Chronicles 3:15* as being 35 cubits or 58 feet (17.5 m) high. At either dimension, they were massive, remarkable bronze castings for their day, at least 6 feet (1.8 m) in diameter.

That the religious tradition of Jachin and Boaz was sacred and continued to be remembered in Israel can be seen on a coin struck at Ashkelon in the late second century A.D. Ashkelon was a wealthy port city that struck coins for over 600 years, from 375 B.C. to A.D. 235. This coin (Sear GIC 2274), struck under the Roman emperor Septimius Severus, A.D. 193-211, shows two large Phoenician style columns each side of a series of doorways or entrances to a temple dedicated to Phanebalos. This name is the Greek transliteration of "Pane Ba'al," the face of the Ba'al, a common name for the goddess Tanit, who was a Phoenician deity inherited by the cosmopolitan residents of

---

[5] *The Temple of Jerusalem,* by Joan Comay, Holt, Rinehart and Winston, New York, 1975, page 48.
[6] *The Temple of Jerusalem*, as above, page 51.

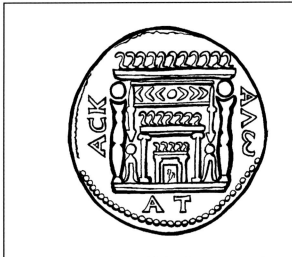

An AE25 struck at Ashkelon by Septimius Severus, A.D. 193-211. It shows the entranceways to the temple of Phanebalos and the two large columns flanking the doorway. Sear GIC 2274 and BMC Greek 27.136, 231.

Ashkelon from the people that originally founded the city. She was eventually transformed into the goddess Atargatis, equivalent to the Greek Aphrodite, and was worshipped in many eastern countries. Coins with this same gateway or entrance reverse were also struck by Antoninus Pius, A.D. 138-161, see *BMC Greek, 27. 191.*

The most discernible architectural detail on this coin is the columns placed each side of the main entranceway. They closely resemble the Phoenician, so-called *lotus-form* columns that some scholars believe were the same shape used for Jachin and Boaz in the original Solomonic Temple. Recently, a small statue of a Phoenician lotus-form column, made of gold and wood, was found in excavations at Biblos, in modern day Lebanon. Its shape and form closely matches the columns shown on the coins of Ashkelon.

To compliment the bronze columns, a large altar, accessible by a ramp, was placed in front of the entrance to the Temple. Near this altar was "The Molten Sea", an enormous bronze bowl or laver of water, over 16 feet (5 m) in diameter.

In 587 B.C. Jerusalem was conquered by the Babylonian armies of King Nebuchadnezzar and the Temple of Solomon was destroyed. The bronze columns and the Molten Sea were cut up and melted down to make weapons. The great First Temple had existed for 372 years. The normal Babylonian policy was to avoid future problems by re-settling captive peoples far away from their homeland, and most of the Judaeans were taken to Babylon as exiles. In 539 B.C., the Per-

A 12th century B.C. Phoenician, wood and gold, lotus-like colonette statue believed to be similar in appearance to Jachin and Boaz, found at Biblos, Lebanon.

A conjectural reconstruction of the First Temple of Jerusalem, built for King Solomon, and showing the two Phoenician style columns named Jachin and Boaz which dominated the facade.

sian king Cyrus the Great conquered the Babylonians and became the ruler of their empire. According to the Bible, after consolidating his power, Cyrus issued a decree permitting the return of the Jewish exiles to their land and the rebuilding of the Temple of Jerusalem (*Ezra I: 2-4*). He even restored the artifacts plundered from the Temple by Nebuchadnezzar, and contributed a sum of money to pay for the reconstruction. Two waves of exiles, freed by Cyrus, immediately returned to Jerusalem. These people were led by prominent Persian/Judaean aristocrats named Sheshbazzar and Zerubbabel. After some delays, caused by political problems with neighbouring people, the building was completed in 515 B.C. This was the second temple on the holy site. It was less imposing than the Temple of Solomon, and some historians even claim that it was a makeshift building, but it served to create a national and religious center for the new community rebuilding Jerusalem.[7] In 445 B.C., when Artaxerxes I was king of Persia, larger groups of exiles from Babylon, led by Nehemiah and later by the prophet Ezra, returned to Jerusalem, completed

the construction of the city walls, and embellished the Temple. This second temple survived for the next 450 years. It witnessed the invasions of Alexander the Great, the Ptolemies of Egypt, the Seleukids of Syria, the Judaean Hasmoneans, the Parthians, and the Romans. The Temple was actually plundered and desecrated by the Syrian king Antiochus IV, in 168 B.C., and by the Roman general Pompey in 63 B.C., but the structure itself was not damaged.

Herod the Great, 40 B.C. -A.D. 4, the Roman client-king of Judaea, was the descendant of an Idumaean family converted to Judaism by the Hasmoneans. In order

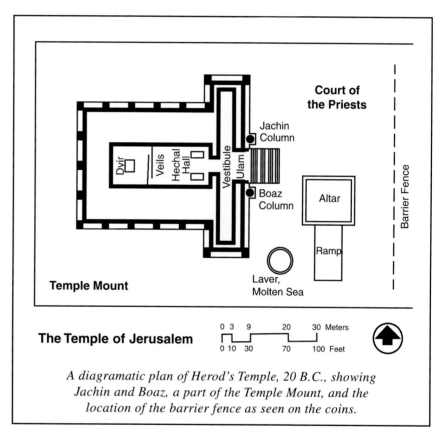

A diagramatic plan of Herod's Temple, 20 B.C., showing Jachin and Boaz, a part of the Temple Mount, and the location of the barrier fence as seen on the coins.

to ingratiate himself with the Jewish people, he began an extensive building program to glorify Jerusalem. He extended the platform of the Temple Mount and rebuilt the Temple to a much larger size. As the Temple appears to have been totally reconstructed at this time, it should be properly called the "Third Temple", but historians continued to call it the Second Temple, perhaps to diminish the accomplishments and reputation of the hated King Herod. In his new construction, Herod managed to exceed the codified, traditional size of the First Temple of Solomon by referring to and using the larger dimensions and heights quoted in *II Chronicles, 3.4*.

Herod is reported to have made the porch of the Temple extremely high, so that the facade would be very monumental and visible from afar. He also clad the entire building in white, polished marble with golden decorations, and added contemporary Ionic columns or pilasters typical of

---

[7] *Herod the Great,* by Michael Grant, American Heritage Press, New York, 1971, page 152.

those used on the temples of his time. The building lost its Phoenician, eastern appearance and began to look more like a typical Hellenistic structure. It must have been considered a marvellous sight in the Greco-Roman world, because the emperor Augustus is recorded as warning his grandson, Gaius, not to be tempted into visiting the Temple on a trip to the east.[8]

This new, Hellenistic appearance is evident from the descriptions of the Temple given by the Jewish/Roman historian Flavius Josephus, in his writings titled *The Jewish War* and the *Jewish Antiquities*.[9] Also, the radical change from Phoenician lotus-form to Hellenistic Ionic-style columns can be clearly seen on the shekels struck by Bar Kokhba during the Second Revolt, A.D. 132-135. Some of these early coins, probably engraved by skillful Greek artists, show an Ionic temple facade, but with a typical eastern flat roof. See Sear GIC 5647. Other shekels, made later by less skillful artists, use a cruder set of symbols to represent the architectural features, but the Hellenistic style is still unmistakable.

The Temple facade on a shekel of Year 2, A.D. 133-134, The Coinage of the Bar Kokhba War, by Leo Mildenberg, coin 14, or Sear GIC 5647.

One exceptional detail that appears on the later Bar Kokhba tetradrachms struck in the years 134-135 (see Mildenberg 93) is a wavy line above the columns. The best and most recent theory to explain this symbol has been proposed by Lawrence D. Sporty.[10] Dr. Sporty suggests that this line is a representation of the golden vine with clusters of grapes that was placed on the architrave around the top of the building. Josephus describes such a decoration in two separate places in his writings. He said that ". . . above it (the entrance) those golden vines, from which depended grape-clusters as tall as a man." (*The Jewish War*, Book V, Ch. V), and ". . . under the cornice, spread a golden vine with grape-clusters hanging from it." (*Jewish Antiquities*, Book XV, Ch. XII). As Josephus, a member of the Judaean priestly class, saw the Temple first-hand before its destruction in A.D. 70, we probably can trust his words on this matter.

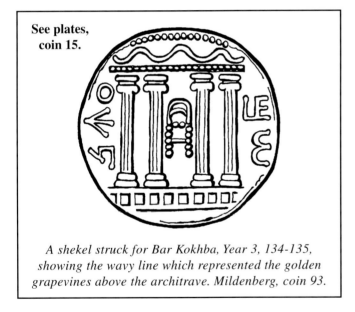

A shekel struck for Bar Kokhba, Year 3, 134-135, showing the wavy line which represented the golden grapevines above the architrave. Mildenberg, coin 93.

An accurate model, reconstructing ancient Jerusalem before the destruction of A.D. 70, has been built on the grounds of the Holyland Hotel in modern Jerusalem. This model shows the Temple, with Ionic style pilasters attached to the walls and a decoration of large, golden vines and

---

8 *The Twelve Caesars,* by Suetonius, translated by Robert Graves, Augustus, 93. Penguin Books, London, 1979.

9 *The Works of Josephus,* translated by W. Whiston, updated version by Hendrickson Publishers, Massachusetts, 1987.

10 "Identifying the Curving Line on the Bar-Kokhba Temple Coin," by Lawrence D. Sporty, in *Biblical Archaeologist*, Spring, 1983, pages 121-123.

clusters of grapes on the architrave.[11] However, this reconstruction does not include any indication of the two traditional, freestanding columns Jachin and Boaz. This omission can be found in all of the existing scholarly descriptions and reconstructions of Herod's Temple, and no explanation is ever given as to what happened to the two columns. Historians fully accept that the Temple of Solomon was the codified prototype for the succeeding designs, therefore, elements as important and mystically traditional as the two main columns would never have been omitted from the new temple design. We know that Herod was a grecophile and he adopted Hellenistic culture and ideals. He used Greek styles and motifs in his buildings and he employed Greek inscriptions or symbols on his coinage. But even a despot as powerful as Herod would not have dared to disregard the venerable, religious legacy of Jachin and Boaz. Herod may have used some scriptural arguments to convince the priests of the Temple to accept two massive Ionic columns, overlaid with gold, to replace the Phoenician style Jachin and Boaz when he built the porch area twice as high as it had been previously. Most likely, these became the only two freestanding, round columns in the structure, the others being attached to the walls as rectangular pilasters. This would have set them apart and stressed their symbolic importance.

A reconstruction of Herod's Temple showing the Hellenistic design and two mighty, freestanding Ionic columns representing Jachin and Boaz. Drawn from details of the coins.

The First War or Revolt of the Jews against Roman domination began in A.D. 66. After four years of terrible conflict, the Romans defeated the Judaeans and captured Jerusalem. Herod's Temple was destroyed by the legions of Titus in the final assault in A.D. 70 and was never rebuilt. Sixty-two years later, the Second War against Rome broke out during the reign of Hadrian. The engravers of the Bar Kokhba shekels portraying the Temple had probably never seen the building. Burnt out and razed to the ground, not even one stone remained upon another. Few survivors of the First War were still alive, and they would be over 70 years old, with only dim, childhood memories of its appearance. With faulty recollections, but with some knowledge of what the great temples in the Roman empire looked like, the coin artists produced their idea of a close approximation of the Second Temple using a Hellenistic, Ionic tetrastyle temple as their model. But in the disruption and haste of wartime conditions, they produced only a symbolic representation of the structure without any attempt to clearly delineate important details, such as the two columns, Jachin and Boaz, and this abbreviated or simplified composition was used on all the coins. However, all this would not have mattered very much, because when the Second War for freedom was lost, the Jewish community was banished from Jerusalem and forbidden to visit the Temple Mount. Then the Temple of Jerusalem transcended its physical form and became a purely spiritual symbol, a "Temple of Hope", implanted forever in the souls and prayers of the exiled and dispersed Jews.

---

11 See also *Ancient Jewish Coinage, Vol. 2,* by Ya'akov Meshorer, Amphora Books, New York, 1982, page 143 for a description of the use of this decorative element in Jewish coinage.

Chapter 8

The Temple of the Paphian Aphrodite

Paphos is an ancient city on the west coast of the island of Cyprus and, in legends, it was considered to be the birthplace of the goddess Aphrodite. This divinity was the Greek interpretation of the Canaanite/Phoenician goddess Astarte, who also spawned the Babylonian Ishtar and the Arabian Athtar. Originally a fertility deity, she was later transformed into Venus, the Roman goddess of love. The earliest worship of Astarte was probably brought by the Phoenicians to their trading posts on Cyprus, and it then spread through Crete, Sicily, and Greece, where the Greeks renamed the deity Aphrodite. Homer describes Aphrodite as the daughter of Zeus and an obscure, feminine divinity named Dione. This explanation did not satisfy the common people, so a bizarre myth about her origins was created by Hesiod, the Greek poet, in the 8th century B.C.[1] According to Hesiod, Cronos, at the instigation of his mother, Gaea, castrated his own father, Uranus, the first ruling deity in mythology, and cast the severed member into the sea. The organ floated on the water, producing a white foam from which Aphrodite arose. The ocean winds carried her on a seashell along the coast of Crete, and she arrived on the shores of Cyprus at Paphos, where she emerged naked from the sea. Her name, Aphrodite, supposedly came from the Greek word for foam, *aphros.*[2]

Aphrodite had several epithets or titles which identified her functions or status in mythology. She is Aphrodite Cyprian, from Cyprus; sometimes Paphian, from Paphos; Urania, the celestial sky goddess; Pandemonos, of the common people; occasionally Porne, of the prostitutes and courtesans; or Pontia, of the sea.[3] She was a goddess of great physical beauty; the famous, armless sculpture called the Venus de Milo is a statue of her later image. Aphrodite was admitted to the Greek pantheon—as recorded by Hesiod—early in history, and became a very popular deity, worshipped throughout the ancient world. Famous cult centers for Aphrodite existed in Cythera, Corinth, Ephesus, Abydos, Byblos, Sardis, Pergamum, Athens, and of course, Paphos.

The city of Paphos is first mentioned as being connected to Aphrodite by Homer in the *Odyssey,* VIII, 361-2, but it was well known long before Homer's time. It may have been founded as early as the 18th century B.C., because it was recorded as having paid tribute to the Egyptian pharaohs in 1600 B.C.[4] Sometime before the 12th century B.C., the Phoenicians built the first sanctuary for the worship of Astarte, later to become Aphrodite, on Cyprus.[5] Paphos was a famous port-of-call for traders in ancient times because of the copper mined nearby and the timber cut from the surrounding forests. Legends record that a hero of the Trojan war, named Agapenor, founded a new city adjacent to the old citadel of Paphos in the 9th century B.C. This new, enlarged city later assisted Alexander the Great in his siege of Tyre in 332 B.C., and a mint located at Paphos struck Alexandrian coinage. In the history books, the temple complex to the cult of Aphrodite at Paphos was considered to be an architectural marvel, and it later became

---

1 *Theogony,* by Hesiod, translated by H.G. Evelyn-White, Loeb Classical Library, Harvard University, Cambridge, 1936.
2 *New Larousse Encyclopedia of Mythology*, Hamlyn, London, 1959, page 130.
3 *Myths of the Greeks and Romans,* by Michael Grant, Mentor Books, New York, 1962, page 101.
4 *Paphos,* by Andrea C. Phylactou, Zavallis Press, Cyprus, 1977, page 1.
5 *The Phoenicians,* by Donald Harden, Pelican Books, London, 1971, page 53.

the site of a famous oracle. As the city prospered, it became a great cosmopolitan religious center containing many cult sanctuaries and temples to a variety of religions. It is recorded that the apostle St. Paul, on his first missionary voyage in the middle of the first century A.D., preached in a synagogue located in Paphos (*Acts* xiii. 6).

In A.D. 69 Titus, on his way to Judaea from Rome, stopped off in Paphos to consult the oracle about his future. The Roman historian Cornelius Tacitus, A.D. 55-120, recorded this event in his books and fully described the famous temple of Aphrodite. He said that "– the form under which the goddess is adored, is a form found in no other place. – – It is forbidden to pour blood on the altar; the place of sacrifice is served only with prayers and pure flame, and although the place of sacrifice stands in the open air, it is never wet with rain. The image of the goddess does not bear the human shape; it is a rounded mass rising like a cone from a broad base to a small circumference. The meaning of this is doubtful."[6]

Plan of the temple complex of the Paphian Aphrodite in Cyprus.

An AE18 struck for Drusus, before A.D. 23, showing Jupiter Salaminios (of Salamis) holding a patera and scepter. At the right is the temple of Aphrodite at Paphos, shown in the typical, pseudo three-dimensional style emphasizing the forecourt. Sear GIC 342.

This unusual temple and the strange image of Aphrodite in Paphos appears on many coins struck by the Roman emperors, from Augustus, 27 B.C., to Caracalla and Geta, A.D. 212. These are here referenced by numbers in Sear GIC, and are as follows. Struck by the city of Paphos: Augustus, 105; Drusus, 342; Vespasian, 731; Trajan, 1065; Septimius Severus, 2251; and Caracalla, 2635. Struck by the city of Sardis: Hadrian, 1186. Struck by the city of Byblos: Macrinus, 2963. Pergamum and several other eastern cities also struck coins which showed their own local temples of Aphrodite.

---

6 *The Histories,* by Tacitus, translated by A.J. Church and W.J. Brodribb, *The Great Histories Series,* Washington Square Press, New York, abridged version, 1964. Book II, 2-3.

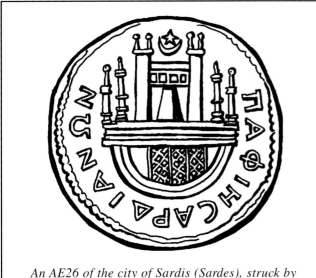

An AE26 of the city of Sardis (Sardes), struck by Hadrian, A.D. 117-138. It shows the temple of the Paphian Aphrodite, perhaps in Paphos, but probably a temple located in Sardis. Sear GIC 1186.

An AE26 of Paphos, struck by Trajan, A.D. 112-117, showing the temple complex of Aphrodite. Sear GIC 1065.

The temple appears on most coins as an open structure with a very large, semicircular forecourt. A good illustration of this temple appears on a later coin struck under Hadrian, A.D. 117-138. See Sear GIC 1186. This coin shows a large court before the temple, and incense burners, used for the cult rituals to Aphrodite, are shown on each side of the building. The temple structure is impressive, and as Tacitus said, resembles the construction of no other known temple in the ancient world. It was built in a "tripartite" form, with three distinct parts to the facade. This temple form and style is common in the east and was frequently used by the Phoenicians. However, the unusual, cone-like sacred stone of the goddess, located centrally in the temple, requires some explanation. The historian W.R. Halliday states that the Greek goddesses Aphrodite, Artemis, and Athena, were derived from a Bronze Age, Asiatic, pre-Hellenic mother-goddess of nature. The places of worship for these fertility deities were in natural settings such as caves, meadows, or shrines placed in the open air. He says that "In cult, the divinity was represented, not by a statue, but by a sacred tree or by a pillar, which was sometimes surmounted by the sacred double axe. To this 'Fetish' the goddess was summoned – – and her advent is often represented by the device of a dove settling upon the pillar."[7] On several coins, such a dove can be seen on the temple roof. See Sear GIC 2251.

The later coins of the Severan emperors employed a type of one point perspective to present the semicircular forecourt in three dimensions. This court area may have been an important feature of the temple precinct because the cult of Aphrodite set aside one day of the year as a festival, when female congregants and temple priestesses had to prostitute themselves. Historical descriptions indicate that the process of men selecting the women took place in a court in front of the temple.[8] Earlier coins of Trajan, however, use a type of pseudo two-dimensional engraving to show the court area in plan, combined with the temple facade in elevation. See Sear GIC 1065. The skill of Trajan's engravers was not equal to the subject matter, and the portrayal of the temple complex became sterile and diagramatic.

---

[7] "The Gods of Ancient Greece," in *The Wonders of the Past,* Vol. 2, edited by J.A. Hammerton, G.P. Putnam's Sons, New York, 1924, page 270.

[8] *The Sacred Fire, the Story of Sex in Religion*, by B.Z. Goldberg, Horace Liveright, New York, 1932, page 164.

However, most numismatists comment on the clear rendering of the joints and paving slabs in the court area shown on the coins struck by Septimius Severus and Caracalla. This type of detail, if read properly, defines and accurately explains the construction of the court area. See Sear GIC 2251.

The joints between the paving stones in the court are emphasized by being engraved with a double line. This technique makes them appear to be more important than single line, material joints between the slabs, and these joints may be drainage channels that are left as open spaces between the paving stones. Tacitus reported that the court, "– though it stands in the open air, it is never wet with rain." This is a sensational journalistic statement hinting at

An AE33 of Septimius Severus, A.D. 193-211, struck in Paphos, showing the temple of Aphrodite in marvellous detail. The double line, vertical joints between the paving slabs can be clearly seen. Sear GIC 2251.

some magical phenomenon, but it is also a technically naive description of a well drained, open court. Had Tacitus been scientifically inclined, he might have examined the pavement more closely and then been able to explain the purpose of the joints.

Undoubtedly, the sacred court was constantly crowded with worshippers and pilgrims, and large puddles of rainwater would make the ceremonies uncomfortable. The ancients were well acquainted with sophisticated drainage systems, and they often drained large marshes and swamps with channels, canals, and ditches. Also, the Forum in Rome had a highly developed sewer system from as early as 100 B.C., and a main drain, the Etruscan Cloacina Maxima, kept the area dry even when the Tiber periodically overflowed its banks. The joints in the paving of the court at Paphos must have been drainage slots, into which the rainwater flowed and then ran to nearby cisterns. A very similar method is used to drain large, paved courts today. Paving slabs are laid with wide, open joints over a thick bed of coarse gravel, and the gravel layer acts as a drainage plane through which the water runs. Rain flows off the slabs, through the joints, and into the gravel layer, where it is carried off to sewers. From archaeological excavations, and from several literary sources, we know that the ancients could control water drainage on large paved areas.

On the same coins struck by the Severans, three circular elements are always shown on the right side of the court area. In their description of this coin, Sear GIC 2251, numismatists propose that these are additional round altars for open-air offerings.[9] It can be suggested that these are the cisterns used to collect the rainwater from the courtyard, and perhaps this water was saved for use in some fertility ritual to Aphrodite, or for washing the altars. By coincidence, three is also a magic number in many religions, and three cisterns containing water used for ceremonial purposes may have been just as important as the tripartite divisions of the temple facade.

The architectural composition of the temple to Aphrodite, shown on many coins struck at Paphos and other eastern cities, gives some insight into the ritual practices of this cult. Some of this information can be verified by the writings of ancient authors, and the coins then become an accurate historical record of the cult mysteries and the design or construction of these remarkable temples to Aphrodite.

---

9 *Coins and their Cities,* by Martin J. Price and Bluma L. Trell, V.C. Vecchi and Sons, London, 1977, page 147.

Chapter 9

The Temple of Apollo at Didyma

The writers who made up the traditional list of the "Seven Wonders of the World" were probably influenced by the religious, cultural, and political biases of their times. This may be proven by the one famous monument that was omitted from their catalog only because it was located in a city that was not politically prominent in those days. This was the temple of Apollo, called the Didymaion, at Didyma in Ionia, and by all accounts it was a fabulous structure. It could be called the Eighth Wonder of the Classical era. It was certainly the largest temple ever built in the Greco-Roman world. Also, the foremost modern reference books on ancient architecture name this temple as the largest and best example of the Ionic architectural style.[1] The sun deity Apollo may not have been in favor when the "Seven Wonders" were chosen, or maybe he was outranked and eclipsed by Zeus and Artemis, the two deities whose statue and temple did appear on the list of "Wonders."

The Greek name Didyma comes from the expression for "twin", probably in honor of Apollo, the twin brother of Artemis. Didyma was a small city located on the Aegean coast, 11 miles (17.6 km) south of the important metropolis of Miletus, now Palatia in Turkey. Today the site of Didyma is occupied by a tiny village called Yenihissar, where the partially reconstructed temple of Apollo is the main tourist attraction. Herodotus, 484-420 B.C., mentions the oracle at the temple of Apollo in Didyma and calls it the temple of the Branchidae (*History of Herodotus*, Book I, Chapter 157). The Branchidae were the native people of the area, who took their tribal name from the Branchides, the family of priests serving in the first temple of Apollo at Didyma built in the 6th century B.C. This archaic temple at Didyma was destroyed by the Persians in their war with the Greeks in 494 or 480 B.C., and the Branchidae were deported to the distant Persian province of Sogdiana in present day Afghanistan. The descendants of these Ionian Greek exiles were totally annihilated, for some unknown reason, by Alexander's soldiers when they occupied this remote area in 328 B.C.

Alexander the Great commanded that a new temple to Apollo be built at Didyma in 330 B.C. to replace the one destroyed by the Persians. At that time, Didyma was an obscure city dominated and controlled by Miletus, and the new religious center of Didyma was linked to Miletus by a paved road, a sacred way, lined with sculptures of divinities.[2] Earlier, a famous statue of Apollo called the Apollo Didymaeus had been sculpted for the first temple by the famous Greek artist Canachus of Sicyon. It had been removed by the Persians as plunder, but was restored to the new temple by Seleucus I, 312-280 B.C., who ruled over most of the old Persian empire after the death of Alexander.

The new temple of Apollo in Didyma was a gigantic building, 188 feet (57 m) wide by 389 feet (118 m) long.[3] It was built in the contemporary Ionic style, and Vitruvius reported that it was

---

[1] See *History of Architecture,* by Sir Banister-Fletcher, Butterworths, London, 1987, page 134, and *Key Monuments of the History of Architecture,* by H.A. Millon and A. Frazer, Harry N. Abrams Inc, New York, page 80.

[2] *Illustrated Encyclopedia of the Classical World*, by M. Avi Yonah and I. Shatzman, Harper and Row, New York, 1975, page 159.

[3] *Fodor's Turkey*, David Mackay Co. Inc., New York, 1992, page 228.

"decastyle" and "dipteral."[4] This means that it had 10 columns (deca) across the front, and two rows (di) of 21 flanking columns (the pteron) forming a colonnade along the sides. This is the largest arrangement of columns ever attempted by Greek or Roman architects. There were only a few decastyle temples built in all of the ancient world; the most notable ones were located at Didyma, Heliopolis in Syria, and in Rome. The columns of the Didymaion were 6.5 feet (2 m) in diameter and 63 feet (19 m) high, and these were considered to be the tallest and most slender structural members ever used in Greek architecture. In comparison to the Didymaion, the famous temple of Artemis at Ephesus, selected for the original list of the "Seven Wonders of the World," was only octastyle, with eight columns across the front and 20 along the sides. Also, the Artemision's columns were 6 feet (1.8 m) in diameter, but only 58 feet (17.5 m) high. From the modern excavations at Ephesus, the temple to Artemis was proven to be only 163 feet (49 m) wide by 342 feet (103.5 m) long, covering an area twenty percent smaller than the temple of Apollo.

Because of its great size and marvellous detail, the temple to Apollo at Didyma became famous in its own time. Like the great medieval cathedrals of Europe, it took centuries to build, and it was not fully completed by A.D. 17 when it was shaken by an earthquake. It is assumed that it was substantially completed by A.D. 40, but in the excavations of the remains at Didyma, it was discovered that several of the newest columns had never been carved with the traditional flutes, indicating that the temple was not even completed when it collapsed in the 15th century A.D.

Vitruvius reported that the design of the Didymaion was "hypaethral", meaning that the cella, or central sanctuary building, was roofless. The temple at Didyma was also very unusual in other ways. The cella was open to the sky, as befitted a temple dedicated to a sky/sun deity, but the floor was also lowered to make an interior, sunken court reached by a monumental

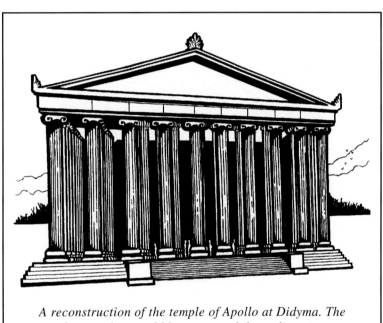

A reconstruction of the temple of Apollo at Didyma. The sculptures that would have covered the pediment area and the architrave beam over the columns are not shown.

flight of stairs. In this courtyard was another freestanding temple, the oracle shrine, called a *naiskos*, approximately 30 feet (9 m) wide by 50 feet (15 m) long. Its facade had four columns (tetrastyle), and contained the fountain or spring of the oracle and the famous cult statue of Apollo. This oracle was famous and as highly respected as the oracle at Delphi. Under the courtyard was a network of stone corridors, which may have been used to magnify the voice of the priest, who uttered the words of the oracle through a hole in the floor. The tunnels could have functioned as echo chambers that distorted the speech and produced a ghostly sound in the sanctuary. The column capitals and bases were highly decorated with intricate designs, embellishing the usually simple and elegant Ionic style. Also, two interior stairs led up to the roof, suggesting that the attic space over the portico was used for religious ceremonies or as the priests' living quarters.

---

4 *De Architectura, the Ten Books on Architecture,* by Vitruvius, translated by Morris H. Morgan, Dover Publications, New York, 1960, pages 77-78.

56

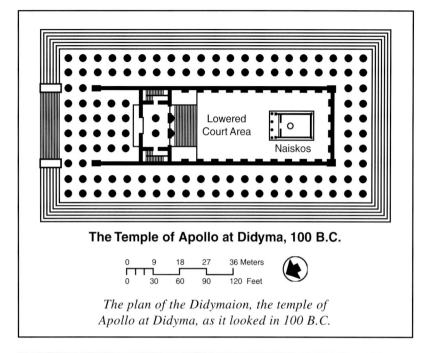

The Temple of Apollo at Didyma, 100 B.C.

| 0 | 9 | 18 | 27 | 36 Meters |
| 0 | 30 | 60 | 90 | 120 Feet |

The plan of the Didymaion, the temple of Apollo at Didyma, as it looked in 100 B.C.

An AE32 struck at Miletus under Gordian I, Gordian II, and Balbinus in A.D. 238, showing the naiskos of the temple of Apollo at Didyma. The famous cult figure of Apollo Didymaeus, made by Canachus of Sicyon, is also shown, holding a stag in one hand and his famous bow in the other. Price and Trell, fig. 239, page 134. This rare coin is located in the collection of the Bibliotheque Nationale in Paris, France.

The site of the temple at Didyma was excavated by German archaeologists from 1906 to 1939. They discovered widely scattered ruins, the result of an earthquake which tumbled the structure sometime in 1493. Also, the excavators found many of the columns and building blocks still lying on the floor of the temple, and re-erected them to create a partial reconstruction that can still be seen today. The main door was over 18 feet (5.5 m) wide, but a stone sill at the door was 26 feet (7.8 m) long, 6 feet (1.8 m) wide, and protruded 3 feet (.9 m) up from the temple floor to create a stage-like platform on which priests performed rituals or delivered oracles. Side passages of the temple were roofed over with stone barrel vaults, the earliest use of this type of construction, long believed to have been invented by the Romans sometime in the 1st century A.D.[5]

Unfortunately for numismatists, this colossal temple of Apollo at Didyma was never depicted on ancient coins. However, the interior oracle shrine or naiskos, enclosing the spring and the cult image of Apollo Didymaeus, was shown on the rare joint coinage of Gordian I, Gordian II, and Balbinus struck at Miletus in A.D. 238.[6] From these coins, the naiskos appears to have been an impressive structure in its own right, with an arched beam called an "arcuated lintel" over the door, and four frontal Ionic columns that were spirally fluted. The arcuated lintel and the spirally fluted columns betray an eastern architectural influence on the shrine, perhaps from Persia or Syria.

The architectural style of the temple to Apollo was outstanding, and it influenced the large, later temples built in Hellenistic and Roman cities. For example, the enormous temple dedicated to Venus and Roma, built by the emperor Hadrian in Rome, undoubtedly imitated the scale and style

---

[5] *The Greek Stones Speak,* by Paul MacKendrick, Mentor Books, New York, 1966, page 294.
[6] This rare coin is illustrated in *Coins and Their Cities,* by M. Price and B. Trell, V.C. Vecchi and Sons, London, 1977, page 134.

of the Didymaion. This temple was slightly smaller than the Didymaion, 175 feet (53 m) wide by 350 feet (106 m) long, but it was the only decastyle temple built in Rome. It had 10 columns across the front and 20 along the sides, but the side colonnade consisted of only one row of columns. Space was left in the aisle for the missing second row, presumably to be erected at a later time. Vitruvius calls this arrangement for a colonnade "pseudodipteral." Also, the column capitals on the temple to Venus and Roma were carved in the ornate Corinthian style, not the Ionic as used on the Didymaion. The grandiose temple to Venus and Roma appears on sestertii of Hadrian, RIC Hadrian 783, and of Antoninus Pius, RIC Antoninus, 622.

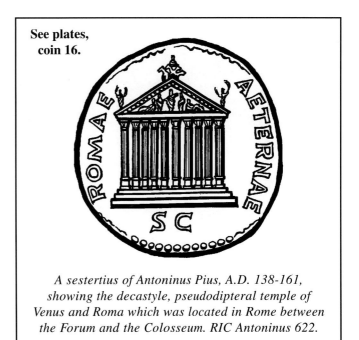

See plates, coin 16.

A sestertius of Antoninus Pius, A.D. 138-161, showing the decastyle, pseudodipteral temple of Venus and Roma which was located in Rome between the Forum and the Colosseum. RIC Antoninus 622.

Many art historians claim that one of the largest temples ever built in the Greco-Roman world was the famous temple to Jupiter located in the Syrian colony of Heliopolis, now Baalbek, 40 miles (64 km) from modern Beirut in present day Lebanon. Probably inaugurated in the 1st century B.C., this temple was dedicated to the local Semitic sun deity Ba'al Biqah, or Ba'al Haddad, who later became assimilated with the Roman god Jupiter. This temple had the reputation of being enormous because it was very tall, located in a very large temple precinct, and raised up on a 23 foot high podium consisting of three massive stone steps. This platform, called the "trilithon" because of the three steps, contained monolithic stones that were 64 feet (19 m) long by 14 feet (4.2 m) wide, and weighed an astonishing 1,200 tons.[7] The lofty podium of the temple can be clearly seen today at the site, and also on the Roman provincial coins of Heliopolis that illustrate this temple on their reverses. See Sear GIC 3962.

Today, the spectacular and well preserved ruins of the Baalbek temple attract tourists from all over the world. The temple was decastyle, with 10 columns across the front, but only 19 along the sides. However, there was only one row of these columns in the colonnade, making the temple pseudodipteral, similar to Hadrian's temple to Venus and Roma, and therefore less grand than the temple of Apollo at Didyma. The columns at Baalbek were 7 feet (2.1 m) in diameter and 65 feet (19.7 m) high. In plan, the dimensions of the temple were 160 feet (48.5 m) wide by 300 feet (91 m) long.[8] This is a considerably smaller area than the temple of Apollo at Didyma or the temple of Ve-

The Temple of Jupiter at Baalbek, Lebanon

| 0 | 9 | 18 | 27 Meters |
| 0 | 30 | 60 | 90 Feet |

Plan of the temple of Jupiter at Baalbek, Lebanon.

7 "Baalbek: Splendid in its Ruins", by R. Curle, in *The Wonders of the Past,* edited by J.A. Hammerton, G.P. Putnam's Sons, New York, 1923, page 127.

8 *Roman Architecture,* by Frank Sear, Cornell University Press, Ithaca, 1982, page 247.

See plates, coin 2.

The temple of Jupiter at Baalbek shown in axonometric view, on an AE25 of Septimius Severus, A.D. 193-211, struck at the colony of Heliopolis. Sear GIC 2265. The heavy trilithon podium of the temple can be seen on the coin. The same temple, shown with exactly the same three-dimensional view, can be seen on coins of Philip I, A.D. 244-249, Sear GIC 3962.

nus and Roma in Rome, but the columns were the tallest of any temple in the world. Coins of Heliopolis show the temple using an axonometric (trimetric), three-dimensional view seen from above. The temple structure is shown on the coins with 10 columns across the front, sometimes only nine are visible, but with only 17 columns along the side, although there were 19. The accuracy of the engraving may be questionable, but the coin does verify that the temple of Jupiter had fewer columns than the Didymaion.

These enormous and impressive Greek and Roman temples prove that religion played a large part in the daily lives of the ancients. However, in those days as in modern times, the size of a temple was taken to indicate the importance of the deity it was consecrated to, or the power and wealth of the ruler who dedicated it. If we apply these criteria to the temple of Apollo, we would have to say that the oracle at Didyma was an important religious phenomenon, the people of the area around Miletus were wealthy and influential, and that the founders of the temple, the Branchidae and later Alexander the Great, fully deserved their prominent places in history. In justification of the fame attributed to this temple, the Didymaion influenced the styles of religious architecture in ancient and medieval societies. This influence was long lasting, even for thousands of years after the oracle of the shrine dried up and the mysteries and rituals of Apollo were long forgotten.

Chapter 10

The Pharos of Alexandria

The original list of the "Seven Wonders of the World" was first made in the 3rd century B.C. as a guide for travelers sightseeing in the Hellenistic world. The catalog is mentioned in a poem written by Antipater of Sidon, who lived in Alexandria in the 2nd century B.C. A second listing of world wonders was published 100 years later by Philo of Byzantium, but both of these early lists did not include the Pharos of Alexandria. The Pharos was first recorded as a "Wonder" by Gregory, Bishop of Tours, A.D. 538-594, but he also included Noah's Ark in his choices.[1] Only three of the marvels of the final list, the Temple of Artemis at Ephesus, the Statue of Zeus at Olympia, and the Pharos of Alexandria, were illustrated on ancient coinage, however, the Pharos was so outstanding a structure that it became a theme for coins struck by several ancient countries.

The word Pharos was the old name of an island lying opposite the harbor at Alexandria, and this name was later given to the lighthouse built on its shore. The word *pharos* later became the proper noun for lighthouse in several languages: *pharus* in Latin, *faro* in Spanish and Italian, and *phare* in French. Also, until recent times, the word pharos was used to mean a lighthouse in poetic English. This great beacon tower was commissioned by Ptolemy I Soter, and completed in the reign of his son, Ptolemy II Philadelphos, 285-247 B.C., probably in 279. It was a part of a plan to expand the harbor facilities at Alexandria. The lighthouse was supposedly designed by the Greek architect Sostratos of Cnidos, but this is disputed by some historians, who claim that Sostratos may have been a wealthy courtier or merchant living in Alexandria who donated money to construct the tower. An inscription with his name, purportedly found on the structure, and all the other written documents except for those of Pliny the Elder, do not make the status of Sostratos absolutely clear.[2] The Pharos, made of white marble, was between 135 to 600 feet (41 to 182 m) high, depending on which ancient author you believe. Pliny the Elder, A.D. 23-79, our usual source for scientific information about the ancient world, reported that the Pharos cost 800 talents to build, but he does not mention its height. He said that the king magnanimously permitted the architect to place his own name on the structure. Pliny also said that the function of the lighthouse was to provide a beacon at night, which gave warning of nearby shoals and directed ships to the entrance of the harbor, and that such lighthouses existed at the Roman ports of Ostia and Ravenna.[3]

The Pharos was built in a "wedding-cake" or telescope style, with tiers placed one on the other and reducing in size as they rose. Most historians agree that the building consisted of three tiers: a square shape at the bottom, an octagonal building in the middle, and a circular one at the top. A lantern structure above this supposedly contained the fire beacon, and the lantern was surmounted by a bronze statue of Poseidon. Other sources claim that the statue was of Ptolemy or of Zeus. At

---

1 *The Seven Wonders of the World,* by Michael Ashley, Fontana Paperbacks, London, 1980, page 274.

2 "The Pharos at Alexandria", by Peter A. Clayton, in *The Seven Wonders of the World,* edited by P. Clayton and M. Price, Routledge Publishers, London, 1988, page 143.

3 *Natural History*, by Pliny, Book XXXVI, xviii, 83, translation by D.E. Eichholz, Loeb Classical Library, Harvard University Press, Cambridge, 1962, page 65.

each level, there was a broad balcony decorated with a railing of bronze and marble statues. On the lowest level, statues of Triton, the son of Poseidon, were placed at the corners. The demi-god Triton was usually represented as a human with the lower body of a fish, and he is portrayed blowing a long conch shell trumpet.

The Pharos was constructed with a central core of stone supporting the upper tiers, and a stairway or ramp wound around this core up to the top. A thick, exterior marble wall was built around the stairs to give the building its shape, and these walls were pierced with windows to give light to the stairs. Ancient writers say that the stonework of the lighthouse was held together with clamps of lead, placed in slots at the end of the blocks. It is reputed that at least 100 spacious rooms were contained in a low building that surrounded the tower's base. By tradition, the 72 Hebrew scholars who wrote the Septuagint, the Greek translation of the Old Testament, for Ptolemy II were separately housed in these rooms at the Pharos.

The Greek geographer Strabo, 64 B.C.-A.D. 21, described the harbor and the Pharos of Alexandria, and documented the information that Pliny probably used in his report.[4] Flavius Josephus, the Jewish/Roman historian, who is considered to be a fairly reliable source, described some of the architecture of his own times and compared the Pharos with the tower of Phasael, built by Herod the Great in Jerusalem. Josephus said that they were very similar in form and shape. He also stated that the height of the Phasael tower was 90 cubits, or 135 feet (41 m), but this seems to be very low for the famous Pharos.[5]

Most historians believe that the lighthouse at Alexandria was just over 300 feet (91 m) high. Also, this is considered by modern engineers to be the maximum height for any ancient, stone, load bearing structure with a reasonable base size. The pyramid of Cheops at Giza, the tallest structure of antiquity, is about 480 feet (145.5 m) high, but it has a very broad base, 756 feet (229 m) to a side. If the Pharos was higher than 300 feet, ancient writers would certainly have compared it to the height of the nearby and well-known pyramids. The actual shape of the Pharos was probably derived from earlier Babylonian tower-temples, which were always tiered and very lofty. The Pharos later became the prototype for the minarets in Moslem mosques and the spires of Christian churches.[6] Examining the existing reconstruction drawings of the Pharos, one may also see it as the model for our early skyscrapers, which were built in tiered or wedding-cake form. All things considered, the Pharos was undoubtedly the tallest structure built in Hellenistic and Roman times.

The Pharos gave birth to many legends, even before it was even completed. To bring materials and workers to the site, a causeway called the *Heptastadion* was built to join the island to the mainland. It was almost one mile (1.6 km) long, and a minor wonder in its own right. Over the years, accumulating silt widened this land bridge, and it is now a heavily populated quarter of modern Alexandria. Moslem writers claim that a polished metal mirror was used to reflect the light of the beacon far out to sea. Some even say that this mirror was used to flash messages from the tower to the mainland.[7] The city of Alexandria was the principal center for research in science and technology at that time. In the 4th to 3rd centuries B.C., it was home to many scientists, including Euclid, the father of modern mathematics; Archimedes, noted for his mechanical inventions; Eratosthenes, who deduced that the earth was round and calculated the circumference of the world; and Hipparchus, the astronomer who discovered the precession of the equinoxes.

4 *Geography,* by Strabo, XVII.
5 *The Wars of the Jews,* by Josephus, Book V, Chapter 4, 4, translated by W. Whiston, John C. Winston Co., Philadelphia, 1929, page 782.
6 *Ancient Times, A History of the Early World,* by J.H. Breasted, Ginn and Co., Boston, 1944, page 529.
7 *Coins and Their Cities,* by M. Jessop Price and Bluma L. Trell, V.C. Vecchi and Sons, London, 1977, page 181.

These great men taught or studied at the "seat of the muses," the *Museum* which was located near the Pharos. To such great scientists or their disciples who lived afterwards, the invention and application of reflecting mirrors for use on the lighthouse would have been child's play.

In the legends of the Arabs who conquered Egypt in the 7th century, the Pharos was thought to contain the treasure of the Ptolemies. The later Arab writers also mention an immense mirror (lens) at the tower's summit which could give a view of distant cities, even as far as Constantinople. They also claim that this mirror could be used to concentrate the sun's rays onto distant enemy ships and set them on fire. Plutarch, A.D. 50-125, was the first ancient writer to suggest using a lens or mirror to make fire. He mentions that the fire in the temple of Vesta in Rome had to be rekindled with the pure rays of the sun reflected from a concave mirror.[8] The mirror on the Pharos was supposed to have been made of transparent stone, perhaps quartz but probably glass. Egypt was one of the most productive and technologically developed glass manufacturing countries in the ancient world.

The Arabs continued to use the lighthouse for many years, until it was damaged by earthquakes and fell into disrepair. A major earthquake in 956 destroyed much of the upper portion of the structure. In 1323 another earthquake toppled the remains of the tower into the sea.[9] A fifteenth century Islamic fort, the Kait Bey, which still stands today, was built on the site of the Pharos using some of the surviving stonework. In 1995, underwater archaeologists discovered a number of statues, columns, and stone blocks from the Pharos in the sea opposite the walls of the Islamic fort.[10]

A Spanish Moor named Al-Idrisi was the famous cartographer of the Norman king, Roger II of Sicily. He traveled through Egypt in around 1115, and recorded that the Pharos was 600 feet high. Another Moorish traveler, Yusuf ibn-ash-Shaykh, visiting Alexandria in 1165, mentioned that a mosque had been built on the top of the ruins of a still standing Pharos.[11] Another Arab traveler, Abou Haggag Youseff ibn-Mohammed el-Balawi, visited the Pharos in 1166 and made the most detailed report, complete with measurements, of the remaining structure. Although the dimensions he gave were inconsistent, he accurately described the construction of the tower as made up of three tiers, a square base 190 feet (57.5 m) high, an octagon shaped mid tier 92 feet (28 m) high, and the cylindrical top 24 feet (7.2 m) high. This made the total height of the tower 306 feet (92.7 m). Abou Haggag used a knotted string with a stone on the end to make these measurements. He also said that the entrance door was high up on the tower, accessible by a long ramp built on arches, and this feature can be clearly seen on some of the ancient coins that illustrate the Pharos.

Abou Haggag entered through the door and investigated the building around the base of the tower, which he said contained 67 rooms. He claimed that the lighthouse base itself was only 28 feet (8.5 m) to a side, but this is very small for a structure that he reported as being 306 feet high.[12] This base dimension only makes engineering sense if the 28 feet represents the distance the tower projected out from the corner of the low building at the ground level, and this suggests an offset or asymmetrical massing for the tower in relation to the ground building. This presents a picture quite different from the traditional reconstructions of the Pharos, which always show the tower located symmetrically in the center of the low building. However, the offset tower does agree with

8 *Parallel Lives, Numa Pompillius,* by Plutarch, translation by Dryden, revised by A.H. Clough, Vol. I, Little Brown and Co. Boston, 1888, page 140.

9 "The Pharos of Alexandria," by J.A. Brendon, in *Wonders of the Past,* Vol. II, J.A. Hammerton editor, Putnam, New York, 1923, page 505.

10 "The Discovery of the Pharos of Alexandria," in *Minerva* magazine, Vol. 7, No. 1, Jan./Feb., 1996, page 5.

11 *Great Cities of the Ancient World,* by L. Sprague de Camp, Dorset Press, New York, 1972, page 289.

12 A good translation of his report is given in "The Pharos at Alexandria", by Peter Clayton, as above, page 153.

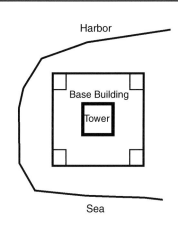
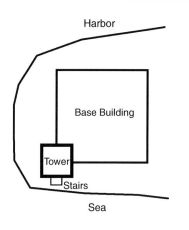

A diagramatic plan of the traditional symmetrical reconstruction of the Pharos complex. After Thiersch, 1909.

A diagramatic plan of a proposed new reconstruction of the Pharos complex showing an asymmetrical massing.

An AE18 of Corinth, struck under Commodus, 177-192, showing an elaborate lighthouse of perhaps eight tiers, probably a copy of the Pharos. Cohen 1077 or Price and Trell, fig. 147.

An AE25 struck at Heracleia Pontica in Bithynia under the emperor Gallienus, 253-268, showing a three tiered lighthouse in one-point, aerial perspective, with a square tier at the bottom, octagonal in the middle, and circular at the top. Sear GIC 2442.

the representation of the lighthouse shown on the coins of Alexandria. The illustration here shows the two conjectural plans for the Pharos complex of buildings.

The Pharos became the prototypical lighthouse in the ancient world, and was copied by many cities for their own harbours. These imitations are shown on several coins, including those struck in Heracleia Pontica in Bithynia under Gallienus, A.D. 253-268, Aegeae in Cilicia under Trajan Decius, 249-251, Berytus in Phoenicia under Septimius Severus, 198-211, Panormus in Sicily under Commodus, Corinth in Greece under Commodus, 177-192, and Laodicea in Syria around A.D. 150. The Pharos itself appears on many Roman coins struck in Alexandria.

The majority of coins showing the Pharos were struck in Roman Alexandria during A.D. 81 to 192 by the emperors Domitian, Trajan, Hadrian, Antoninus Pius, and Commodus. Some of these also show the goddess Isis Pharia (Faria), the Isis of the Pharos. There was a temple to Isis located near the lighthouse, and this proximity established Isis as the protector of the Pharos. The details of the lighthouse are extremely clear on these coins, and they confirm some of the descriptions given by ancient writers.

Coins depicting the Pharos frequently show several circular elements placed near the top of the tower. Many scholars interpret these as being shorthand versions of rectangular windows, where the engraver drilled a simple circle in the die rather than painstakingly cutting a rectangle. Others claim they are votive shields hung from the tower to commemorate some military victory. See Milne 2683. A more recent theory makes a strong case for the circles being windows of a circular shape, from which missiles and arrows could be showered down onto enemy ships attacking the harbour.[13] Undoubtedly, the mighty Pharos was also part of the harbour fortifications, but circular windows were notoriously difficult to construct in thick masonry walls. This could only be done using a wooden centering as a form for the arches until the keystones were placed. This construction method is complicated and slow, requiring the precise fitting of the small stones into the awkward spaces left by the massive rectangular blocks used for the walls. Even today, this is a difficult task for experienced masons. At any rate, the theory falters because archers and catapults operate just as efficiently from rectangular openings as they do from circular windows. Also, due to the forces of gravity, missiles projected from great heights are only effective against targets which are close to the building. Repelling ships from a tower became practical only in the Middle Ages, with the invention of gunpowder and cannon, and in most

See plates, coin 17.

A billon tetradrachm of Alexandria struck under Commodus, 177-192, showing a galley sailing past the Pharos. Sear GIC 2067, and Milne 2683.

See plates, coin 18.

A bronze drachm of Alexandria, struck under Antoninus Pius, 138-161, showing Isis Pharia holding an inflated sail before the Pharos. Milne 2004.

documented cases, the ancients preferred to fight off raiding ships with other ships or from the shore.

The circular elements on the tower are sometimes shown on coins alongside or mixed in with rectangular openings, so they are obviously not a timesaving or shortcut technique for engraving windows. See Milne 2004. It is tempting to suggest that they are the metal mirrors so often mentioned by Arab writers. Such mirrors, mounted on the corners of the tower, at slightly different angles from each other, would act as reflectors to flash the sun's rays far out to sea at various times of the day. Even when low-lying mist hid the shoreline, the mirrors could capture the sun's rays from above the fog and make an effective beacon. Wood fuel for beacon fires was scarce in Egypt, which lacked forests, and actually, on most voyages, mariners preferred to sail only in the daytime. Therefore, some ingenious device was necessary to make the lighthouse an effective beacon even in the daylight. Mirrors reflecting the sun may have provided

---

[13] See Price and Trell in *Coins and Their Cities*, as above, page 181.

the solution. However, a small oil fire magnified by a mirror or lens may also have been used at twilight or at nighttime.

Taking into account the form of the Pharos shown on the coins, and the detailed account by the Arab traveller Abou Haggag, it may be safely concluded that the Pharos was a tower of three tiers, with a stairway to an entrance above the ground level. The tower was located at the corner of a low, ground level building containing many rooms, which may have been used as a fortification or palace. This low building is not shown on coins because it was secondary to the prominent tower of the lighthouse, and would not fit onto the small area provided by the coin's surface. Also, in the three-dimensional views used on the coins, most of the ground level building would fall behind the tower and not be visible. On some of the coins, a slight swelling of the base of the tower may represent the visible part of this low building.

It is possible that the Pharos lighthouse had rectangular windows to give light to the stairway and round metal mirrors attached to the corners to act as sun-reflecting beacons. The existing reconstruction drawings of the Pharos were done by H. Thiersch in 1909, G.G. Woodward in 1916, and A. Forestier (after M. Gaston Jondet) in 1920. All these rely on early scholarship, and most are adaptions of the original drawing made by H. Thiersch.[14] Based on the information presented by the coins, and by a new interpretation of the circular elements shown on the coins, a different, new reconstruction of the Pharos is possible. The tower would be located prominently at the corner of and projecting out from a large, low building. A monumental stair or ramp led up to the tower's entrance. There would be several round, metal reflecting mirrors placed in a high position at the corners of the lighthouse.

This drawing conforms with the illustration of the Pharos on the coins, and it provides for a logical explanation of the round elements. However, we will have to wait for the discovery of more conclusive archaeological evidence, perhaps now lying in the sea, before consigning the older reconstructions to the wastebasket.

See plates, coin 19.

A bronze one-half drachm of Hadrian, 117-138, showing the Pharos tower with all its details, including statues of two Tritons blowing horns. Milne 1381. The same reverse was also struck by Antoninus Pius, Milne 1841. These coins show distinctly a mix of circular and rectangular openings on the tower.

See plates, coin 20.

A bronze drachm of Hadrian, 117-138, showing Isis Pharia holding a billowing sail before the Pharos. The slight swelling of the tower's base at the right may represent the visible part of the base building. Milne 1440.

14 The most readily available illustrations of the reconstruction drawing of the Pharos proposed by H. Thiersch can be found in the popular book *The Greek Stones Speak,* by Paul MacKendrick, St. Martins Press, New York, 1962, page 338, and in "The Pharos at Alexandria," by Peter Clayton, in the book *The Seven Wonders of the World*, page 144.

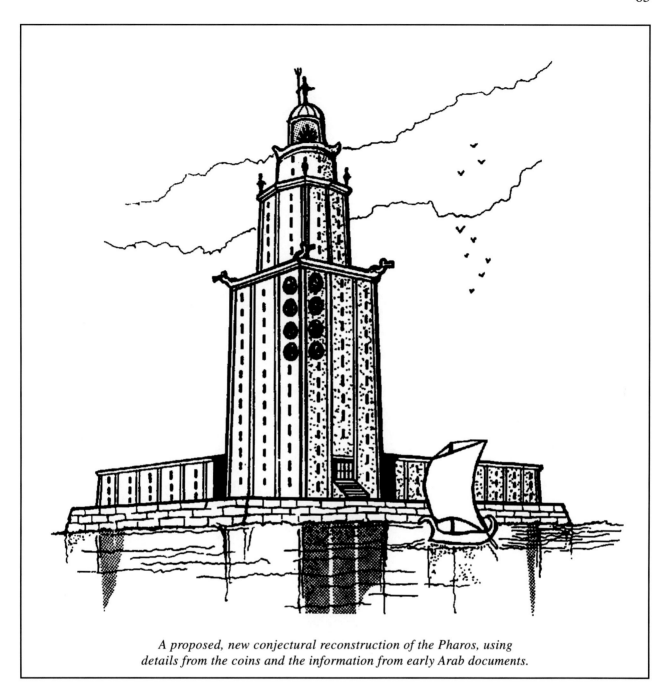

*A proposed, new conjectural reconstruction of the Pharos, using
details from the coins and the information from early Arab documents.*

Chapter 11

The Mausoleum of Halikarnassos

The majestic tomb of Mausolos (also spelled Maussollos), 377-353 B.C., built in the city of Halikarnassos (Halicarnassus in Latin) in Caria, was also one of the "Seven Wonders" of the classical world. It gave the word *mausoleum* to our language, yet of these seven famous monuments, it is the one least understood. Roman writers such as Vitruvius and Pliny the Elder wrote about the Mausoleum at Halikarnassos, and referred to it by actually using the words "one of the Seven Wonders of the World". As far as we know, only the Statue of Zeus, the Temple of Artemis, and the Pharos at Alexandria were depicted on ancient coinage, but it is possible that the Mausoleum at Halikarnassos may have been represented indirectly on some coins.

Mausolos was the ruler of Caria, and also the Persian satrap or viceroy of the surrounding areas. In around 362 B.C., he enlarged his personal domain by taking over Ionia, Lycia, and the islands of Rhodes and Cos. Mausolos then moved from his ancestral city of Mylasa and established a new capital at ancient Halikarnassos, present day Bodrum on the Aegean coast of Turkey, in order to obtain a good harbor for his warships. He was constantly fighting off invasions by the Greeks, who were excellent mariners, so he built a battle fleet patterned after the ships of his enemies. Mausolos married his sister, Artemisia, and founded a dynasty which lasted until Caria was conquered by Alexander III, the Great, in 333 B.C. Apparently, he began the construction of his own tomb around 365 B.C. On his death in 353 B.C., his wife Artemisia became the ruler of the kingdom, and a popular legend related that she consummated her succession to the throne by drinking her cremated husband's ashes mixed with wine. But she also hired many famous artists to complete the grand tomb, and Mausolos was buried in it after her death in 350 B.C.

This immense tomb was so elaborate and magnificent that it became famous all over the classical world. According to Vitruvius, the structure was made of hard, burned clay brick covered with a highly polished stucco which glistened like glass or polished marble. Vitruvius also commented on the building's many sculptures, made by the great Greek artists Leochares and Timotheus, and he noted that the structure was "classed among the Seven Wonders of the World".[1]

Pliny the Elder, writing in A.D. 74, left us the most detailed description of the Mausoleum. He said that the tomb was decorated with sculptures by four famous Greek artists–Scopas, Bryaxis, Timotheus, and Leochares, each one working on a different wall. Pliny stated that these marvellous and colossal statues made the edifice into one of the Seven Wonders of the World. Relying on secondhand information, Pliny recorded that the building was rectangular in plan, with the sides 120 feet (36 m) and 100 feet (30 m) long, for a total perimeter of 440 feet (132 m). He also said that the tomb consisted of three parts: a lofty podium or base about 60 feet (18 m) high, a colonnaded section made up with 36 Corinthian columns, and above this a pyramid of 24 steps. The top was surmounted by the sculpture of a four-horse chariot, called a quadriga. From the ground to the chariot measured 140 feet (42.5 m). Pliny stated that the quadriga group was sculpted by a fifth

---

[1] *De Architectura, the Ten Books on Architecture,* by Vitruvius, Book II, Chpt. VIII, 10-11, translated by M.H. Morgan, Dover Publications Inc., New York, 1960, page 54. This edition also contains an illustration of the reconstruction of the Mausoleum made by Friedrich Adler in the 19th century, page 55.

artist named Pythis.[2] This sculptor may have been the famous Pythios, mentioned by Vitruvius as having been the architect of the Mausoleum.

In 333 B.C., Halikarnassos was destroyed by Alexander the Great to prevent the Persians from using it as a naval base on the Aegean Sea. After Alexander's death, the city was rebuilt and taken over by one of Alexander's successors, Antigonus Monophthalmos (the One Eyed), and subsequently by Lysimachus in 301 B.C. These kings were followed in 281 B.C. by the Ptolemies, and then the Seleucid kings, who finally relinquished the city to the Romans in 64 B.C. For administrative purposes, the Romans placed Halikarnassos under the rule of the nearby island city-state of Rhodes. The Mausoleum survived during these turbulent centuries with only the usual damage caused by the ravages of time, minor earthquakes, and the theft of some of the sculptures by passing conquerors. Sometime before the 12th century A.D., a major earthquake destroyed most of the superstructure of the tomb and toppled the stepped pyramid and colonnade to the ground. In 1402, the crusader Knights of St. John took possession of Halikarnassos and built a fortress, called the Castle of St. Peter, near the harbor. The crusaders used the cut stones taken from the ruined Mausoleum to build their castle walls, and burnt the marble sculptures to make lime for the mortar. In 1522, when the Sultan Suleiman the Magnificent was preparing to drive the crusaders out of Turkey, the Knights tore up the remaining ruins and foundations of the Mausoleum to obtain more stones to strengthen their fortifications. While doing so, they supposedly discovered a large underground chamber and a stone sarcophagus. As night had fallen, they stopped working and returned to the safety of their castle. In the morning they discovered that the local tribesmen had broken into the tomb and robbed the coffin; only a few fragments of gold cloth and some small gold ornaments remained.

The Knights had preserved some of the magnificent sculptured panels of the tomb by building them into the walls of their new castle. Twelve stone panels showing the mythological war between the Greeks and the Amazons were retrieved in 1846 from the ruined crusader fortress by Lord Stratford de Redcliffe, the British ambassador to Turkey. These were sent to the British Museum, and can be seen today in the famous Mausoleum Room. The assertion by Vitruvius that the structure was made of brick proved to be incorrect, because the Knights of St. John had used thousands of green lava stones, obviously plundered from the Mausoleum, to build the walls of their fort. Later excavations revealed that the tomb had been faced with white marble, and that the sculptures were colored, in the Greek style, with blue, red, yellow, and gold paint.

In 1856, the English archaeologist Sir Charles Newton began an extensive new excavation of the Mausoleum site. He uncovered most of the ruins, and found several sculpted lions and many other fragments of statues, including a part of the chariot group and two larger-than-life size statues, supposedly of Mausolos and Artemisia. From 1966 to 1977, a Danish team of archaeologists re-excavated the Mausoleum site and discovered the fragments of the destroyed sarcophagus, including some gold ornaments overlooked by the tomb robbers in 1522. The Danish team also discovered 550 fragments of sculpture missed by the English excavators in 1856.[3]

Many scholars have made reconstruction drawings of the Mausoleum at Halikarnassos. These include: Maerten van Heemskerck, a famous 16th century artist who specialized in classical subjects; Nicholas Hawksmoor, 1690, a pupil of the famous English architect Christopher Wren; and A.J. Stevenson working for the British Museum. Recently, an accurate illustration based on the archaeological excavations was made by Geoffrey B. Waywell.[4] In 1974 and 1988, the Danish

2 *Natural History,* by Pliny, Book XXXVI, Chpt. IV, 30-31, translated by D.E. Eichholz, Loeb Classical Library, Cambridge, 1962, Vol. X, page 23.
3 "A Tomb to Wonder At," by Chris Scarre, in *Archaeology* magazine, September/October, 1993, page 32.
4 "The Mausoleum at Halicarnassus," by Geoffrey B. Waywell, in the book *The Seven Wonders of the Ancient World,* edited by Peter Clayton and Martin Price, Dorset Press, New York, 1989, page 119.

A reconstruction of the Mausoleum at Halikarnassos, based on the most recent illustrations, but simplified and redrawn to emphasize the construction and the architectural form.

archaeologist Kristian Jeppesen, who led the excavations of 1966-1977, made two models of possible reconstructions. All these drawings and models rely on the ancient description given by Pliny the Elder and scholarly conjectures based on the archaeological discoveries. The most up-to-date drawings show the building adorned with large statues and friezes. A sculpted relief panel of a war between the Greeks and Persians is shown on the lowest level near the ground. More free-standing statues are located on the intermediate levels. A frieze of the mythical war between the Amazons and Greeks is assumed to have been placed below the colonnade. Thirty-six large statues of Mausolos, Artemisia, and their relatives or ancestors are located between the columns. Fifty-six sculpted lions march around the top edge of the colonnade, and the quadriga, placed on a sculptured plinth, surmounts the pyramid roof. Left unanswered by these reconstructions is the question as to who was driving this chariot. Statues of the god Apollo were found among the sculptures recovered at the site, and as he appears to have been the only deity represented on the Mausoleum, he may have been the driver of the quadriga, or perhaps it was Mausolos himself.

It has been said by art experts that the design of this tomb was an attempt to combine the architectural fashions of Greece, Egypt, and Persia, and that several types of this amalgamated style can be found in Caria. Because the Mausoleum at Halikarnassos became so famous in the ancient world, we would expect some representation of it to appear on the local coinage. However, the coins struck by the descendants of Mausolos and by the later rulers of the city do not display any illustrations of the magnificent monument. Instead, the local coins usually show the god Zeus in his Carian form, carrying a double axe. This axe was a fetish associated with Zeus, and the axe's Greek name, Labrys, gave this form of the deity the surname "Labraundos." We know that Zeus was an early Carian sky deity, and that the Greeks adopted him from the native tribes when they settled on the coast of Asia Minor.[5] Also commonly shown on coinage struck by the descendants of Mausolos was the god Apollo (Helios in the east), usually portrayed by a three-quarters, front facing bust. See

---

5 *Botsford and Robinson's Hellenic History,* revised by D. Kagan, 5th edition, Macmillan and Co., London, 1969, page 45.

Sear Greek 4954. This common appearance of Apollo on the coinage may indicate that the city state of Rhodes, which frequently used exactly this same bust of Apollo on its coins, had a great political, economic, and religious influence on Halikarnassos from the earliest of times.

It is often noted that the Romans borrowed most of their art and culture from other civilizations. They were known to have freely adopted, and often improved upon, the artistic forms of the nations they conquered. The second century A.D. traveler, geographer, and guide-book author Pausanias said that

The coinage of Halikarnassos struck by the dynasty of Mausolos. This is a silver tetradrachm of Mausolos, 377-353 B.C., showing the face of Apollo, with Zeus Labraundos on the reverse. Sear Greek 4954.

the Mausoleum at Halikarnassos "was of such a size and so marvellous in its construction that even the Romans have been utterly astounded by it and have used the word mausoleum for their own grandiose tombs."[6] If this statement was true, then it is possible that some representation of the Mausoleum may have appeared on Roman coins. However, the only architectural element on Roman coinage which resembles the reconstruction of the Mausoleum is the so-called "funeral pyre" first seen on the consecration coins struck for Diva Faustina I by Antoninus Pius after A.D. 141 (RIC Antoninus 1135 and many others).

The Roman funeral pyre seen on these coins, called a *rogus* in Latin, is usually labelled as "enigmatic" by numismatic scholars. It is shown as a four storeyed building with a two level colonnade, filled with statues and surmounted by the four-horse chariot or quadriga. When it is used on consecration coins for deified empresses, a biga replaces the quadriga. The chariot was considered to be a vehicle frequently used in the apotheosis, that is, the deification of the dead emperor or empress. The numismatic identification of this structure as a funeral pyre led to some dispute among historians, but it is firmly based on an historical description of such structures used for the deification of emperors. Herodian, a Greek/Roman historian of A.D. 165-255, said that in the apotheosis of an emperor, "a square structure was erected, constructed exclusively of large logs, in the form of a chamber. The whole structure was filled inside with firewood and adorned on the outside with coverlets interwoven with gold, ivory statues, and colorful paintings."[7] Herodian also reported that the structure consisted of four chambers, one on top of the other and reducing in size as they rose. The body was placed in the second highest chamber, covered with gifts, spices, and incense, then cremated. The architectural form of the pyre shown on the Consecratio

See plates, coin 21.

A Consecratio sestertius of the deified emperor Divus Antoninus Pius, struck by his successors, Marcus Aurelius and Lucius Verus, after A.D. 161. Clearly seen are the masonry colonnades of the structure that may represent a funeral pyre. RIC Marcus Aurelius 1266.

6 *Description of Greece,* by Pausanias, translated by W.H.S. Jones, Loeb Classical Library, Cambridge, 1918.

7 *History of the Period after Marcus Aurelius,* by Herodian, IV, ii, translated by C.R. Whittaker, Loeb Classical Library, Cambridge, 1961, page 377.

coins agrees in many ways with Herodian's description. However, some scholars argue, correctly, that the structures on the coins seem to be made of stone, not wooden logs. The coins distinctly show masonry colonnades and arches on the facades of the monuments. See RIC Marcus Aurelius 1266.

The realization that this building was made of stone led to an early proposal that the structure was actually meant to represent the mausoleum of Hadrian. This enormous tomb was a multi-tiered structure built in Rome after A.D. 130. It was never commemorated on any Roman coins, but we know from the inscriptions on the walls that the ashes of Antoninus Pius, Faustina I, Marcus Aurelius, Lucius Verus, Commodus, Julia Domna, Septimius Severus, Caracalla, and Geta were actually placed in this tomb built for Hadrian.[8] It exists today, although greatly altered by medieval renovations, as the Castel Sant' Angelo on the bank of the river Tiber in Rome. Hadrian's tomb was cylindrical in shape, colonnaded, and with many statues. However, the hypothesis that the funeral structure shown on the Consecratio coins is Hadrian's mausoleum has been dismissed by most historians because of the irreconcilable differences in architectural detail. A newer theory proposes that the funeral pyre was actually a masonry building used as an *ustrinum*. The word ustrinum is the Latin term for a crematorium. This may be a more plausible argument, but it has not convinced the majority of numismatists, who tenaciously cling to the label "funeral pyre" or rogus in all their descriptions of these coins.

An objective examination of the building shown on the Consecratio coins reveals a very close resemblance to the drawings of the reconstructed Mausoleum of Halikarnassos. Also, archaeological excavations in Rome, some as early as 1703, have revealed the remains of such stone structures, perhaps used as crematoria by the Antonine emperors.[9] The ruins of the so-called "Ustrinum Antonini" were discovered near the Column of Antoninus Pius on the Campus Martius, and it is believed to

Monuments on the Campus Martius

Plan of the area of the Campus Martius, where the crematoria and memorial columns of Antoninus Pius and Marcus Aurelius were discovered.

See plates, coin 22.

The Column of Antoninus Pius shown on a sestertius of Marcus Aurelius. The legend DIVO PIO identifies the column as belonging to the deified Pius. RIC Marcus Aurelius 1269.

8 *Hadrian and the City of Rome*, by Mary Taliaferro Boatwright, Princeton University Press, Princeton, 1987, footnote 29, page 170.

9 *The Ruins and Excavations of Ancient Rome*, by R. Lanciani, Bell Publishing, New York, reprint 1979, page 508.

be the crematorium building used for Faustina I, Antoninus Pius, Lucius Verus, and Faustina II. In 1908, a second structure, described as the ustrinum of Marcus Aurelius, was excavated near the site of the Ustrinum Antonini. This area of Rome was already the site for the memorial columns of Antoninus Pius and Marcus Aurelius, so it is logical that the crematorium would be located there.

An ustrinum building also appears on the Consecratio coins of Divus Marcus Aurelius, and later on the coins of Commodus and Pertinax.[10] Surprisingly, all these structures appear to be almost identical. It seems possible that these edifices were influenced by and patterned after the famous Mausoleum of Halikarnassos, or after some grand tomb in Rome which was constructed as a copy of the famous tomb of Mausolos. See RIC Commodus 662.

During the reign of Septimius Severus, A.D. 193-211, a new crematorium may have been built, or one of the earlier ustrina was reconstructed. On the Consecratio coins of Severus a spectacular building of five, not four, tiers appears. See RIC Caracalla 4908. It also resembles the Mausoleum at Halikarnassos, but has been embellished with more sculptures and drapery, probably reflecting the ostentatious taste of those later times. This same building shows up on the consecration coins of Caracalla struck by Severus Alexander, (RIC Severus Alexander 719), and it may have been a dynastic crematorium used by several of the succeeding emperors. The last representation of this crematorium appears on a consecration sestertius of Valerian II, struck by Gallienus after A.D. 255 (RIC Gallienus 35).

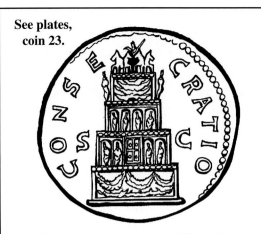

See plates, coin 23.

A Consecratio sestertius of Divus Marcus Aurelius struck by his son, Commodus, after A.D. 180. It shows the same crematorium building as the one depicted on the coins of Antoninus Pius. RIC Commodus 662.

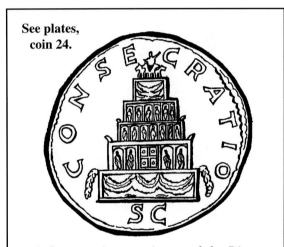

See plates, coin 24.

A Consecratio sestertius struck for Divus Septimius Severus by Caracalla, after A.D. 211, showing the five-tiered, heavily decorated ustrinum. RIC Caracalla 490B.

Unfortunately, the identification of all these structures as ustrina is questionable; no written proof exists. Many historians argue that they were not crematoria by pointing out that the heat of the pyre inside would probably destroy the marble stonework, statues, and sculpture. They propose instead that these structures were actually memorial buildings marking the location of the outdoor, traditional wooden funeral pyre.[11] However, Dio Cassius, the Roman historian, compares the funeral pyres to "towers" (*Dio Cassius* 75.5.3) and Herodian, the expert on cremation ceremonies, likens them to "lighthouses" (*Herodian* 4.2.8). The buildings shown on these coins do indeed resemble the stepped or telescope shaped towers and lighthouses of the Roman world.

If one accepts the consensus of numismatic opinion that the monument on the Consecratio coins

---

[10] *The Monuments of Ancient Rome as Coin Types,* by Philip V. Hill, Seaby, London, 1989, page 102.
[11] *Hadrian and the City of Rome,* as above, page 226.

72

is a traditional rogus or wood log funeral pyre and not a stone mausoleum, then different and other evidence that the Mausoleum of Halikarnassos was portrayed on Roman coins must be found. Turning to more recent research about architecture on coins, Martin Price and Bluma Trell, in *Coins and Their Cities*, mention a whole new category of buildings which they say appeared on ancient coinage.[12] They call these structures *"tower-altars,"* and illustrate them by showing several coins from Persis, Ephesus, and Etenna in Pisidia. These newly classified monuments are very large altars or shrines which look like elaborate temples. Price and Trell say that these shrines are indirectly related to the "stepped funeral pyre" buildings shown on the reverses of Roman coins, but offer no examples or comparisons, nor do they elaborate on this point. Then they tease the reader by saying "The relationship between the tower-altar-shrine and a tomb shrine such as the Mausoleum at Halicarnassus is now the subject of fascinating speculation." There are no further comments, references, or footnotes for this provocative statement. However, I can suggest a coin that I believe shows a "Tower-Altar-Shrine" which by its form may be connected to the Mausoleum at Halikarnassos.

This coin is a bronze, 38 millimeters in diameter, struck at Amasia in Pontus under Severus Alexander in A.D. 226-227. See Sear GIC 3275. The reverse is described as a large altar, sur-

A bronze coin of Severus Alexander, struck at Amisia in Pontus in A.D. 226-27, showing a tower-altar-shrine. Sear GIC 3275.

mounted by an eagle, above which appears Helios in a facing quadriga. This building may have been a well-known, ancient shrine or tower-altar consecrated to Zeus. The eagle is an exclusive attribute of the king of gods, and we know that a ceremonial chariot was often dedicated to Zeus. The famous chariot at Gordium, according to a legend, was erected by King Midas of Phrygia as a thank-offering to Zeus.[13] The yoke of this same chariot was tied with the puzzling Gordian Knot, which Alexander the Great supposedly unraveled by cutting with his sword.

The tower-altar shown on this coin of Amasia appears to resemble the rogus shown on the Roman Consecratio coins and also the reconstruction of the Mausoleum of Halikarnassos. The coin artists of Pontus may have transformed the stepped pyramid of the Mausoleum roof into an eagle, by artistically transcribing the steps or jagged edge of the roof pyramid into the similarly jagged wing tips of the bird. Also, Dio Cassius said that during an imperial cremation, a caged eagle was released to carry the emperor's soul upwards to heaven (*Dio Cassius* 56.42.3). The chariot, the vehicle for apotheosis and also sacred to Zeus, is shown on the coin surmounting the eagle, similar to the way it is placed on the roof of the Mausoleum. For this reason, one may argue that the architectural form of the tower-altar-shrine had been adapted from the shape of the Mausoleum at Halikarnassos. This could resolve the question of the unknown rider in the chariot on top of the Mausoleum. It may have been Zeus, the deity with whom Mausolos identified, or the son of Zeus, Apollo/Helios, who is shown in the quadriga of the tower-altar on the coin. The statue in the chariot may even have been that of Mausolos himself, dressed and equipped as either of these two gods.

[12] *Coins and Their Cities, Architecture on the Ancient Coins of Greece, Rome and Palestine,* by Martin J. Price and Bluma L. Trell, V.C. Vecchi and Sons, London, 1977, page 38.
[13] *The Will of Zeus,* by Stringfellow Barr, J.B. Lippincott Co., New York, 1961, page 398.

There is little concrete evidence for any of these suppositions, and consequently no conclusions as to the appearance of the Mausoleum can be drawn from the Roman coins. Despite this, it is reasonable to believe that such a sumptuous tomb, made famous by writers as early as 250 B.C., and included by ancient authors in a list of the "Seven Wonders of the World," must have had some influence on the artistic style of, and the social taste in, the funeral architecture of those times. Even though it may not appear directly on coins, the Mausoleum at Halikarnassos undoubtedly served as the inspiration for the design of many Roman tombs, and perhaps most of the imperial crematorium buildings.

PART III

ENGINEERING AND ARCHITECTURE ON COINS

Chapter 12

Roman Highways

The ancient Romans were great road builders. Many of their highways, called *viae* in Latin, have lasted for centuries, and some of these routes are still used by modern nations in Europe, Asia, and Africa. The earliest paved road systems were developed by the Persians and the Carthaginians sometime before 600 B.C., and the Romans learned road-building techniques from these earlier civilizations. The Greeks had dabbled with the concept of constructing roads, but built few of them because Greece consisted of many independent city states, usually unfriendly to each other, and roads connecting them together were not desirable. Also, because Greece consisted of many islands and a lengthy mainland coastline, the Greeks used the sea as their principal highway. A few ceremonial Greek roads were constructed, but these were mainly "sacred ways" used for religious processions to the major temples.[1] The more practical Romans saw highways as instruments of dominion and commerce. They used them primarily for military purposes, to get armies and supplies to the provinces and frontiers as quickly as possible, but they also recognized roads as being useful for political, commercial, and social or intellectual interchange.

Roads eventually connected all of the many corners of the Roman empire. The whole network of paved highways built by the Romans was estimated to be 50,000 miles (80,000 km) long.[2] The length of the secondary, unpaved road system, supplementing the highways, was at least an additional 200,000 miles (320,000 km). These distances were recorded on a golden milepost, actually a gilt bronze column, called the *Miliarium Aureum*, that was placed in the Forum Romanum by Augustus around 20 B.C., and the miles from Rome to all the major provincial cities were engraved on it.[3] Most of the first Roman highways were named after the consul or censor responsible for their construction, and these so-called *consular roads* were often built on top of pre-Roman paths or trails. For example, the Via Salaria, the salt road, named for the salt pans of the Tiber, and the Via Latina, named after the central Italian tribes, were both well-worn trails long before Rome emerged as a great power and converted them into paved roads.

Roman roads were extremely well built, and the construction methods used would impress most modern day highway engineers. The Latin phrase for building a road was *munire viam*. Munire means literally to build a wall, and that was, in fact, what the Romans did; they built a heavy wall recessed into the ground, the top of which functioned as a roadway. First a trench, called a *fossa* in Latin, was dug into the ground. The floor of this trench was then consolidated by tamping or rolling. Then the road's foundation, made up of lime mortar or sand and called the *pavimentum*, was laid down. Next came the *statumen,* or first bedding course, made up of fist-sized stones cemented together with mortar. This course could vary from 10 inches to two feet (250-600 mm) depending on the density and condition of the ground. The second course, called the *rudus*, was laid down with 9 to 12 inches (200-300 mm) of concrete, made of cement and aggregates of sand and ceramic potsherds. The third course was a layer of concrete called the *nucleus*. This was 12 inches (300 mm)

---

1 *The Greeks and Romans, Their Life and Customs,* by E. Guhl and W. Koner, reprint by Bracken Books, London, 1989, page 71.
2 *Roman Life,* by Mary Johnston, Scott, Foresman and Co., Chicago, 1957, page 329.
3 *Rome of the Caesars,* by Leonardo B. Dal Maso, Bonechi-Edizioni, Rome, 1970, page 29.

thick at the edge of the road, and 18 inches (450 mm) at the crown or center to provide a camber so that the rainwater would drain to the sides. Finally, the *summum dorsum*, or top course, was placed. This was made up of polygonal shaped, hard paving stones made from selce, a flint material, or of basalt, a type of volcanic rock. These pavers were carefully fitted at the joints, and were sometimes laid into the still wet concrete of the nucleus.

Secondary roads were not paved with stones, but only topped with a thick bed of consolidated gravel. The paved highway surface was from 15 to 20 feet (4.5-6 m) wide, while secondary roads varied from 12 to 16 feet (3.6-4.8 m). Stone curbs were set at the edges of the roadway, and a footpath for pedestrians was often placed on one side. Milestones were provided to mark the distance from Rome, and hostels or inns and government post houses for couriers and their horses were conveniently located at reasonable distances along the highways. This idea was borrowed from the Persians, who were the first nation to establish a postal system for the royal mail.

The main highways flowing into Rome were constructed during the Republic. Among the oldest was the Via Latina, built in 370 B.C., connecting Rome with the Alban hills, the ancient homeland of the Romans. The renowned military highway, the Via Appia, called by early historians the "Queen of Roads," was started in 312 B.C. by the censor Appius Claudius, who also built an aqueduct for Rome at the same time. He used thousands of enslaved criminals and defeated soldiers to construct these public works, often working them to death. The Appian Way ran south from Rome to Capua, and later was extended to Tarentum, modern Taranto, and then to Brundisium (Brindisi) in the heel of Italy. It was 333 miles (532 km) long, and in order to construct it, the builders had to overcome many natural obstacles by filling in marshes, bridging over rivers with viaducts, and tunneling through hills. The Romans tried to build their roads as straight as possible, however, many had to follow the natural contours of the land or the slopes of hills. Some historians claim that the Romans needed to build very straight roads because the front axles of their transport wagons were rigidly fixed and could not turn, but this may be only speculation.[4]

The Via Valeria, started in 303 B.C., ran east from Rome towards the Adriatic Sea. It was later extended north along the coast to join up with the Via Flaminia, the route to Ariminum, present day Rimini. The Via Aurelia, constructed about 241 B.C. by the censor Aurelius Cotta, ran north from Rome along the coast to Genua (Genoa), and was later extended to Nicaea, present-day Nice. The Via Flaminia was constructed in 220 B.C. by the consul Gaius Flaminius, and ran north from Rome to the city of Ariminum, on the Adriatic coast. Joining Rome to the coastal city of Populonia was the Via Clodia, built sometime in the 3rd century B.C. In 187 B.C., the Via Aemilia, named after the general Lucius Aemilius Pallus, began at Ariminum and extended the Via Flaminia to Placentia, modern Piacenza, and then went on to the northern provinces beyond the Alps. The Via Cassia, 154 B.C., actually a branch of the Via Aemilia, proceeded north from Rome to Arretium and Pisae (Pisa). The Via Annia was built in 153 B.C. from Florentia, present-day Florence, went north to Bononia (Bologna) and then to Patavium, modern Padua. In 148 B.C., the Via Postumia was built in northern Italy from Genua eastwards to Verona, and on to Aquileia, near present-day Trieste. The Via Egnatia and Via Gabinia were also built in 148 B.C. to connect the ports on the east coast of the Adriatic Sea to the interior.[5] A highway was built in 132 B.C. from Capua south to Rhegium (Reggio di Calabria), in the toe of Italy on the straits of Messana, opposite Sicily. Some historians label this highway the Via Popilia, others call it the Via Annia. The debate over this road's proper name has not yet been resolved.

In the following years, the highway network was extended to include the Via Domitia, started in 121 B.C. and named after Gnaeus Domitius Ahenobarbus. It started where the Via Aurelia

---

4 *The Mute Stones Speak,* by Paul MacKendrick, 1st edition, St. Martin's Press, New York, 1960, page 300.
5 *History of Rome,* by Theodor Mommsen, Philosophical Library, New York, 1959, page 318.

terminated at the city of Nicaea and carried on to the provinces of Gaul and Spain. Also, a main highway was built along the coastline of Sicily to link the cities of Panormus, Messana and Syracuse. Eventually, this growing network of paved roads connected Rome with York in Britain, Vienna in Austria, Thessalonica in Greece, Damascus in Syria, and Egypt in North Africa.[6] Other, shorter paved highways linked Rome with the densely populated urban centers which grew up nearby. The Via Ostiensis provided access to the important port at Ostia at the mouth of the Tiber. The Via Tiburtina joined Rome to the urban center at Tibur (Tivoli), and the Via Tusculana ran south to the city of Tusculum. The Via Nomentana, a short highway, ran northeast to the city of Nomentum, and an important highway, the Via Salaria, to the Tiber river. The Via Portuensis was later built from Rome to the new port north of Ostia called Portus. All in all, 11 of these main roads entered Rome, and as many as 18 minor routes linked up with these highways at the gates of the city. By Imperial times, as proclaimed by an anonymous 14th century proverb, "all roads lead to Rome."

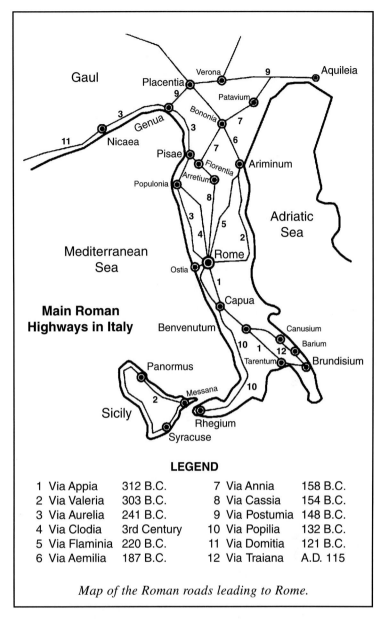

Main Roman Highways in Italy

LEGEND

1	Via Appia	312 B.C.	7	Via Annia	158 B.C.
2	Via Valeria	303 B.C.	8	Via Cassia	154 B.C.
3	Via Aurelia	241 B.C.	9	Via Postumia	148 B.C.
4	Via Clodia	3rd Century	10	Via Popilia	132 B.C.
5	Via Flaminia	220 B.C.	11	Via Domitia	121 B.C.
6	Via Aemilia	187 B.C.	12	Via Traiana	A.D. 115

Map of the Roman roads leading to Rome.

In laying out their highway system, the Romans first established colonies in newly conquered areas of Italy and Gaul, then extended the roads to connect them to Rome. For example, the city of Ariminum was founded in 268 B.C., and the Via Flaminia was built, joining it to Rome, in 220 B.C. These great highways were normally constructed by the army when the soldiers were not on campaign or at war, but many were also built by levees of citizens or slaves from the towns along the thoroughfare. Normally, the state paid the costs of building the roads out of the treasury or from the spoils of war. Gaius Gracchus, the tribune and reformer of 123-122 B.C., is mentioned by Plutarch as having built many paved roads when he was in power, "in a straight line and crossing over valleys with viaducts, for their usefulness as well as their beauty and elegance."[7] Maintenance costs were paid out of the taxes imposed on nearby cities and communities, but also by toll charges set on the people using the highways. Sometimes, the emperor or some wealthy Roman paid for the reconstruction of a road system out of his own purse. Also, Augustus encouraged his victorious generals to use a part of their plunder to pay for these public works. A dedicatory inscription was

6 *Caesar and Christ, the Story of Civilization,* Part III, by Will Durant, Simon and Schuster, New York, 1944, pages 77-78.
7 *Plutarch's Lives, Gracchus 7.* Vol IV, by A.H. Clough, Little Brown and Co., 1888, page 539.

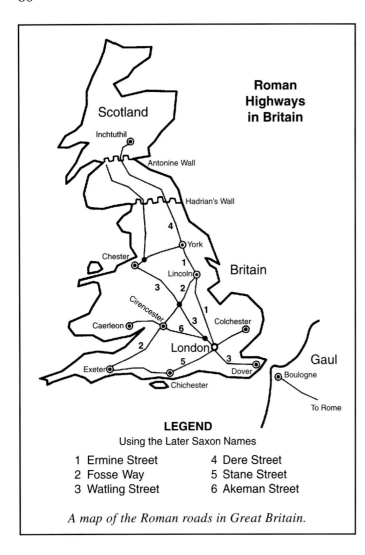

Roman Highways in Britain

Scotland

Inchtuthil

Antonine Wall

Hadrian's Wall

4

York

Chester

1

Lincoln

Britain

3 2

Cirencester

1

Caerleon

3

6

Colchester

2

London

5

3

Exeter

Dover

Gaul

Chichester

Boulogne

To Rome

LEGEND
Using the Later Saxon Names

1 Ermine Street 4 Dere Street
2 Fosse Way 5 Stane Street
3 Watling Street 6 Akeman Street

A map of the Roman roads in Great Britain.

See plates, coin 25.

Two rare "Munitae" denarii of Augustus, struck in 18-17 B.C., showing the triumphal arches dedicated to Augustus for his road building activities. RIC Augustus 142, showing the two arches, and RIC Augustus 144, showing the quadriga.

usually placed on a milestone or on a *cippus*, a round, column-like stone monument, at the edge of the road to honor the person who paid for the construction. Such monuments and inscriptions are found in countries all along the Roman highway system. Many of these, dedicated to Tiberius, were found in Spain, and one for Vespasian was found near Smyrna. Several more dedicated to Trajan have been discovered in Dacia, Arabia, and near the Via Appia in Italy. Several milestones mentioning Hadrian have been found in Egypt, Spain, and North Africa. One inscription to Hadrian found on the Via Appia states that the emperor had rebuilt this section of the highway, for 15.75 miles (25 km) in A.D. 123, and he contributed a sum of 1,147,000 sestertii to the amount of 569,100 sestertii collected by the local landowners to pay for the cost.[8]

Suetonius, in his book *The Twelve Caesars, Augustus,* 30, states that the emperor Augustus repaved the Via Flaminia as far as Ariminum at his own expense, and called upon men who had been awarded triumphs to spend their prize money on repairing the other highways. Augustus not only repaired the highways, but also rebuilt many of them, and erected new bridges and viaducts to improve the traffic flow. These acts are commemorated on a spectacular and rare series of aurei and denarii, RIC Augustus 140-144, which were struck in 18-17 B.C. at a mint in Spain, perhaps in the city of Colonia Patricia. All of these coins carry the legend QVOD VIAE MVN(ITAE) SVNT, meaning in translation "For having caused the highways to be built." One coin in this remarkable series shows the emperor in a quadriga of horses, on an arch over a viaduct of a highway, and being

8 From the "Corpus Inscriptionum Latinarum," Vol IX, No. 6075, quoted in *Roman Civilization Source Book II,* by N. Lewis and M. Reinhold, Harper Torchbooks, New York, 1966, page 154.

crowned by Victory. Another coin shows two triumphal arches with equestrian statues, and two trophies of arms on the arcade of a highway viaduct.

A different series of MVNITAE, or road-building coins, was struck in the name of Augustus by his moneyer, the triumvir L. Vinicius, at Rome in 16 B.C. One of these rare denarii, RIC Augustus 359, shows a beautiful triumphal arch, perhaps erected at Ariminum or on the road outside of Rome, to commemorate the emperor's repair of the Via Flaminia and other viae. The reverse of another of these denarii, RIC Augustus 360, shows the bust of the emperor on the obverse and a round monument, or a cippus, on the reverse with the inscribed legend S.P.Q.R. IMP. CAE QVOD. V M.S. EX. EA. P.QIS AD. A. DE in six lines. This cippus illustrates the type of monument used

as a milepost along the highways. The legend is thought to be the abbreviation for SPQR IMPERATORI CAESARI QVOD VIAE MVNITAE SVNT EX EA PECVNIA QVAM IS AD AERARIVM DETVLIT, meaning "The senate and the people of Rome (dedicate this) to the emperor, for having caused the highways to be built with the money he procured from the state treasury." The most elaborate denarius of this series, RIC Augustus 362, shows an equestrian statue, probably of Augustus, in front of the gate and walls of a city, perhaps Ariminum or Rome. The reverse shows a cippus with the same legend as the coin mentioned above.

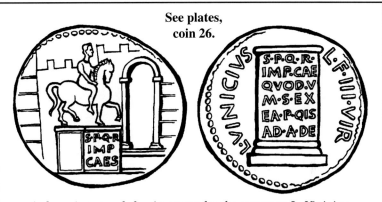

See plates, coin 26.

A denarius struck for Augustus by the moneyer L. Vinicius, in 16 B.C., which shows an equestrian statue in front of a city gate, and a commemorative cippus with the famous road building legend. RIC Augustus 362.

The emperors succeeding Augustus recognized the importance of the highway network and kept it in good repair. In later years, Trajan improved the Via Appia by building a new highway from Benvenutum to Brundisium by way of Canusium and Barium, but parallel to the Appian Way. This new highway was named the Via Traiana after the emperor.[9] This road is commemorated in the reliefs on the Arch of Benvenuto, one of the most beautiful Roman triumphal arches still in existence, and the Via Traiana is also honored on the coins struck by Trajan in A.D. 114-117. These show a female

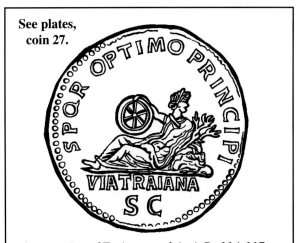

See plates, coin 27.

A sestertius of Trajan struck in A.D. 114-117 to commemorate his new highway, the Via Traiana, paralleling the Via Appia. RIC Trajan 639.

personification of the highway reclining and holding a wheel in her lap. The wheel represents the extensive cart and carriage traffic carried by the new road. The legend VIA TRAIANA appears below the figure, and it gives a positive identification of the highway being commemorated. This coin was struck in most of the denominations. The aureus is RIC Trajan 266, denarius RIC 267, sestertius RIC 636-640, dupondius RIC 641, and the As is RIC 639.

9 *The Lives of the Later Caesars,* by Anthony Birley, Penguin Books, London, 1976, the chapter on Trajan, page 46.

Even after the Roman empire had collapsed, medieval armies still sought out these well de-fined but hidden roadways and used them to invade the surrounding countries. Today, when archaeologists report the discovery of a remnant of these lost highways in some remote and distant place, we are reminded that the ancient roads functioned as powerful "chains of stone," linking together the widespread Roman empire in the same way that the 19th century railroads of North America served as unbreakable "ribbons of steel" to tie together the distant frontiers of a new world.

Chapter 13

Harbors

The city of Rome, at the height of its power, was the greatest of all the ancient market places. Manufactured products and raw materials were brought to the city from every corner of the known world; slaves from Greece and Asia, silk from China, gold from Thrace, wood from Gaul, cotton and gems from India, purple dye from Phoenicia, figs and dates from Judaea, iron from Noricum, and frankincense from Arabia. The most important commodity was grain shipped from Egypt and North Africa. This supply of grain was called the *Annona*, literally the "annual produce," and it was distributed free to the citizens of Rome, whose staple food was bread. Annona, personified by a woman holding ears of grain, is portrayed as the "harvest of grain" on the reverses of many coins. She is often coupled with Ceres, the goddess of crops or agriculture, and both are shown with the prows of the ships which carried the grain to Italy, or the container, called a *modius*, used to measure portions of cereal. Publius Aelius Aristides, A.D. 117-185, the most celebrated rhetorician of his time, delivered a famous public speech in A.D. 150, titled "To Rome." In this panegyric he praised the Roman emperor and mentioned all the marvellous, international goods brought to Rome as an illustration of the magnificence, grandeur, and wealth of the Roman empire.

The Roman maritime trade required highly developed harbors to receive the ships and process their cargos. In Republican times, the main port for Rome was located at Puteoli, modern Pozzuoli, in the Bay of Naples, 150 miles away. Road transportation was expensive and often unreliable, so small ships picked up the goods at Puteoli, sailed north along the coast, then up the Tiber River to unload at the docks in Rome. During the stable reign of Augustus, 27 B.C.-A.D. 14, the population of Rome increased substantially, and the supply of grain brought from Puteoli became inadequate. A new, larger port became necessary at a location closer and more directly connected to Rome. The coast of central Italy on the Tyrrhenian Sea did not have any natural harbors, so a new port, close to Rome, had to be man-made, and that required extensive, costly construction. The old small port in Ostia at the mouth of the Tiber River seemed to be the most logical choice for such a harbor, and both Julius Caesar and Augustus considered this site for a new port, but abandoned the proposal because of the extremely high costs involved. The emperor Claudius, A.D. 42-54, revived this scheme, and construction work on a new harbor north of the town of Ostia and linked to the Tiber began in A.D. 42.

Ostia was originally a coastguard station or fort (*castrum*), founded around 349 B.C. to protect the mouth of the Tiber and the river access to Rome. In about 80 B.C., Ostia was provided with extensive fortification walls by Sulla, and was given the status of a commercial port town, receiving goods to be trans-shipped to Rome. In those days, the suburbs of Ostia also served as a summer, seaside resort for the wealthy people of Rome, only 18 miles (29 km) away. This small harbor on the Tiber catered mostly to small, commercial ships and to pleasure craft. Building a larger port in the marshlands north of Ostia was considered to be so impractical that the civil servants grossly exaggerated the costs in order to discourage the emperor. But Claudius recognized the importance of a regular supply of grain to Rome and would not be deterred. He took personal charge of the project and began the construction.

84

Workers cut a large basin into the swamps 2 miles (3 km) north of Ostia and constructed a canal from the Tiber to this new harbor. This canal today is a branch and second mouth of the Tiber located at present-day Fiumicino, near the modern airport of Rome. For protection of the harbor, engineers built two breakwaters jutting out into the sea. To construct these, the engineers dropped large rocks into the sea, and poured concrete around them using pozzuolana, a natural cement that can harden under water. The concrete breakwaters were then built on these foundations and faced with limestone. For parts of the breakwater, ships were sunk and filled with rubble and concrete. Suetonius reported that a large, famous ship was sunk as a part of the north mole, and was used as the base of an immense lighthouse which was said to rival the legendary Pharos of Alexandria.[1] Depictions of the new lighthouse often appear in mosaics and sculptural panels found at Ostia, and they show a typical Roman lighthouse structure of the usual "telescope" or tiered shape. This consists of three layers of building, arranged as a tall tower, large at the bottom and small at the top. Purportedly, a fire on the roof served as the beacon, which could be seen far out at sea.

The large ship used as the foundation for the lighthouse had been constructed during the reign of the emperor Caligula, A.D. 37-41, to carry an obelisk from Heliopolis in Egypt to Rome in A.D. 40. This obelisk can still be seen in front of St. Peter's in the Vatican. Pliny the Elder said that the ship required 300 rowers to propel it, and that the obelisk weighed 330 tons.[2] Archaeological excavations of the breakwaters at Ostia have revealed the outline of Caligula's ship, and it measures 240 feet (72.7 m) long, an exceptional length for ships of those days.[3] When the port was completed, the grain ships from Egypt and North Africa bypassed Puteoli and sailed directly to Ostia. These grain ships were renowned for their size and carrying capacity; they would have been the ancient equivalent of our modern day, oil carrying "super tankers." The most famous of these ships was named the *Isis*, after the Egyptian grain goddess. It was reported to carry 1,200 tons of cargo and be able "to feed everyone in Attica for a year."[4] The *Isis* was 180 feet (54.5 m) long, 50 feet (15 m) wide, and 44 feet (13 m) high from keel to deck. People flocked to the harbor when these grain ships arrived in order to admire their gigantic size and to watch the unloading, which took several days. Most grain cargos in those days were carried in *amphorae,* the large clay jars used as storage containers and packing cases. A dumping place for broken and discarded amphorae in the ancient port of Rome on the Tiber now forms a large hill called the "Monte Testaccio," or Hill of Sherds. This hill is five-eighths of a mile (1 km) in circumference and over 100 feet (30 m) high. Modern excavations of the broken amphorae in this hill provided archaeologists with a wealth of information about Rome's foreign trade.[5]

Claudius did not strike any coins to commemorate the building of this port, perhaps because it was not fully completed in his short reign. The succeeding emperor, Nero, A.D. 54-68, continued Claudius' measures to assure a constant supply of grain to Rome, and he struck coins to designate the new, completed port as the main grain terminal at Ostia. We can judge the size and importance of this new port, and perhaps its inadequacy in design, by a report of Tacitus, the Roman historian, that in A.D. 62 a violent storm sank 200 vessels at anchor in the harbor's roadstead.[6]

Nero's commemorative coins show the port in great detail by using an unusual type of graphic view. The circular harbor is drawn in plan, and then the buildings around it are flopped down so that

[1] *The Twelve Caesars, Claudius* 20, by Suetonius, translated by Michael Graves, Penguin Books, London, 1979.
[2] *Natural History*, Book XXXVI. xiv. 70-75, by Pliny, translated by D.E. Eichholz, Harvard University Press, Cambridge, 1962.
[3] *The Magic of Obelisks*, by Peter Tomkins, Harper and Row Publishers, New York, 1981, page 9.
[4] Lucian of Samosata wrote a satire in A.D. 165 titled *The Ship* in which he describes these immense grain ships. *The Ship, i - ix.*
[5] *Archaeology of Ancient Rome*, by Anthony King, Crown Publishers Inc., New York, 1982, page 37.
[6] *The Annals of Imperial Rome*, Book XV. xviii. 3, by Tacitus, translated by Michael Grant, Dorset Press, London, 1980.

their facades can be seen. This is a clever adaption of a one-point perspective to clearly show all the elements of the harbor. Several varieties in the design of this rare and famous coin were struck during those years. On these various coins, from seven to twelve ships are shown in the port, and they are an historical illustrated catalog of the different types of commercial ships used by the Romans. The buildings are shown in great detail, and the arched structure on the right side may be a group of vaulted warehouses located at dockside or, more likely, it is a depiction of the innovative breakwater of the port. Roman naval engineers had devised a special type of breakwater constructed on arches. These arches held back the heavy waves, but the openings permitted the ocean currents to enter the harbor

See plates, coin 28.

A rare sestertius of Nero, struck in A.D. 57, showing the Claudian port near Ostia. This coin commemorates Nero's acts to assure a steady supply of grain to Rome. RIC Nero 178-183.

and flush out the accumulating debris and silt.[7] As the arches on the coin are shown sitting directly in the water, they may represent an accurate portrayal of this ingenious structure. Neptune is shown seated at the entrance to the harbor, appropriately holding his attributes, a rudder and a dolphin. A large statue of the emperor placed on an elaborate pedestal, at the top of the coin, dominates the port. The abbreviated legend is AVGVSTI POR OST, which can be translated as "The Augustan Port of Ostia." See RIC Nero 178-183.

By A.D. 100, the port at Ostia was too small to meet the growing needs of an enlarged Roman population, and the emperor Trajan began to expand the harbor facilities. Pliny the Younger described how Trajan built a new commercial port at ancient Centum Cellae, now Civitavecchia, north of Ostia.[8] We also know from other sources that he constructed a harbor at Ancona, on the Adriatic, and enlarged the Claudian port at Ostia. A coin struck in A.D. 103 commemorates this harbor work. Earlier numismatists, such as H. Cohen and S.W. Stevenson, believed that

this coin depicted the port at Civitavecchia, but excavations at Ostia revealed an inner harbor basin with a hexagonal plan and surrounding buildings exactly as shown on this coin. The distinct hexagonal basin can still be seen today; it is now a large pond, on the private Torlonia estate located alongside the Tiber River. Dio Cassius, A.D. 155-230, the Roman historian, described this new harbor at Ostia and recorded its name as Portus, the "Port." He explained that it was built, primarily, to assure a better supply of grain to Rome, in all seasons

See plates, coin 18.

A sestertius of Trajan struck in A.D. 103, showing a hexagonal plan of the new harbor called Portus. RIC Trajan 471.

[7] *A History of Seafaring,* by Joseph W. Shaw, George F. Bass editor, Thames and Hudson, London, 1972, page 97.

[8] *The Letters of the Younger Pliny* Book VI, No.31, by Pliny, translated by B. Radice, Penguin Classics, London, 1960, page 181.

and weather.[9] The port was originally called the "Portus Ostiae," and then later the name was changed to the "Portus Romae," the Port of Rome. By the time of Dio Cassius' description, the port had grown so large that it became an independent city probably called "Portus."

The artist who engraved this coin chose an unusual graphics technique to depict the port in great detail. The hexagonal dock area is drawn in plan, the buildings, temples, and warehouses are drawn as fallen down facades in perspective, and the two buildings in the foreground, perhaps temples, are rendered with an axonometric (isometric) method. This combination of three pictorial techniques is common in Roman art, and in this case it produced an exceptional composition. Three ships are shown in the basin, and two statues on pedestals between the buildings. The abbreviated legend is PORTVM TRAIANI, which can be translated as "The Port of Trajan."

The construction of these ports had a great influence on the Roman economy. The ports provided the commercial facilities to encourage foreign trade and, as large scale public works, they provided employment for the people. Stamped bricks found by archaeologists give some indication of the importance of these construction projects. Bricks were usually stamped with seals giving the name of the factory making the brick, the name of the owner of the kiln, or the name of the consuls under whose term the bricks were made. Very rarely were the bricks stamped with the name of the building in which they were used. Bricks stamped with building names have been found in only three Roman structures. These buildings were the "Castra Praetoria," the praetorian camp headquarters at Rome; the "Portus Augusti," the Claudian harbor at Ostia; and the "Portus Traiani," Trajan's port.[10]

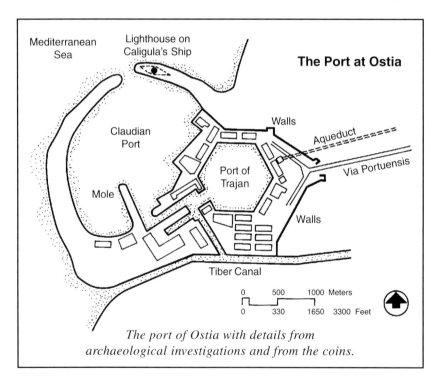

The port of Ostia with details from archaeological investigations and from the coins.

The hexagonal harbor basin built by Trajan was connected directly to the Tiber River by a canal, so that small river ships could transport cargo directly to Rome. The new port contained many warehouses, shipping offices, repair shops, buildings for port authorities, guards, and even a palace for the prefect of the port. It also contained temples, hotels or hostels, baths, restaurants, and brothels. As it was an international harbor, many foreign merchants from Syria, Greece, Gaul, Africa, Egypt, and Spain established wharves, storehouses, and offices in the harbor area or in Ostia, where they were also permitted to erect temples to their native religions. Archaeologists have discovered temples to Bacchus, Isis, Ceres or Magna Mater, Serapis, Mithras, and even the ruins of early Christian churches around the harbor area. In 1963, when constructing a new expressway from Ostia to Rome, workers discovered the ruins of a synagogue in the ancient port. While it is known that a large community of Jews lived in Rome as early as the 2nd century

9 *Roman History*, LX. xi. 1-4, by Dio Cassius, Penguin Classics, London, 1963, page 10.

10 *The Ruins and Excavations of Ancient Rome*, by R. Lanciani, Bell Publishing Co., New York, reprint of the 1897 edition, 1967, page 40.

B.C., and that there are Jewish catacombs and written records of 11 different synagogues, this is the only synagogue building ever discovered in Italy. The foundations of the original synagogue date to the first century A.D., while the last, unique and imposing building dates from the 4th century. Archaeologists discovered that the synagogue contained an annex with several rooms, probably used as a hostel by visiting merchants.[11]

The Roman empire surrounded the Mediterranean Sea, and all the nations under imperial domination traded with the merchants of Rome. Excellent harbors existed in almost all these ancient maritime countries, and many of them struck coins that proudly exhibited their own port facilities. Some of the most out-

A rare AE30 of the city of Caesarea Germanica in Bithynia, struck under the usurper Pescennius Niger, A.D. 193-194, showing a view of the port. Price and Trell, fig. 57, page 40.

standing of these coins were struck in Corinth, Phoenicia, Egypt, Greece, and Asia Minor. A remarkable coin of the colonial city of Caesarea Germanica in Bithynia, showing a view of the harbor, is typical of many of the coins struck by the seaport cities in the provinces. The coin engravers used an unusual technique, combining a plan of the circular harbor basin with an oblique projection of the main temple in the port. Breakwaters, lighthouses, statues, and a ship with its sail furled are also shown.

A more abstract composition of a harbor view was used by the city of Side in Pamphylia. This port city is mentioned often in historical documents as a large trade center or emporium for the eastern area. The circular harbor basin is shown in plan, with a ship entering through the breakwater. The warehouses on the wharves at the edge of the port are shown as typical arched structures, but lying flat so that their facades can be recognized. The whole design fits well into the round shape of the coin blank and compliments the circular band of the inscription around the edge.

As Rome declined, foreign trade moved to other harbors on the Mediterranean and Adriatic. The port of Ostia, finally abandoned in the 5th century A.D., silted up and was covered over by the expanding delta of the Tiber River. The site of the ancient port is now located one mile (1.6 km) from the sea coast. Most of the harbor is buried under Rome's international airport, the Leonardo da Vinci at Fiumicino, and on some of the runways, modern airplanes taxi over buried, ancient wharves and sunken ships. It is interesting to note that a twentieth century, international transportation terminal was built on top of a similar first century transportation center; poetic proof that the foundations of the present are often built on the history of the past.

A rare AE28 of Side in Pamphylia struck under the emperor Gallienus, 253-268, showing an abstract view of the circular harbor. Price and Trell, fig. 481, page 220.

11 *Judaism in Stone, The Archaeology of Ancient Synagogues,* by Hershel Shanks, Harper and Row Publishers, New York, 1979, pages 162-168.

Chapter 14

Aqueducts

Water is one of those basic necessities of life that we take for granted because it is so readily available: just turn on a faucet. But in ancient days, obtaining an adequate supply of good water was a daily concern. The people in early urban centers dug wells, collected rainwater in cisterns, or used existing springs, rivers, and lakes. Many ancient cities were established on a particular site only because there was a large amount of potable water nearby. As these cities grew, they had to draw on more distant sources of water. The science of collecting and controlling water resources was probably developed very early in Egypt, where the harnessing of the flood from the Nile was very important to sustaining life. The oldest known water conveying structure, a masonry aqueduct, was built by the Assyrians under Sennacherib, 705-681 B.C. Parts of this 900 foot (273 m) long system were discovered during archaeological excavations near Nineveh in 1933.[1] The early Greeks also constructed some primitive stone channels to carry water from mountain streams into their cities, but it was the Romans who invented the science of hydraulic engineering and developed water supply systems, called *aquae* in Latin. The remains or ruins of Roman aqueducts are found all over the Roman empire, from Persia to Spain and from North Africa to Great Britain.

A once popular theory claimed that the Roman empire declined because the population suffered from chronic lead poisoning, and were so weakened by this condition that they were unable to resist the barbarian invasions. This poisoning was blamed on the lead pipes used by the Romans as conduits for their drinking water. Today, we know that this theory was exaggerated. The Romans did use lead pipes in their water systems, but they were fully aware of the possibility of this metal contaminating the water. The architect Vitruvius explained the dangers of using lead pipes for water supply in his writings. He dedicated one whole book to water, and in it he reiterated the apparently well-known Roman rule that drinking water should always be conducted in clay pipes and not in lead because of the poisonous qualities of this metal.[2] Also, he accurately described the causes and symptoms of lead poisoning, which he observed among the workmen who inhaled lead fumes in the refineries. The Romans used many lead pipes and fittings in their plumbing systems, but not enough to poison the entire population. Furthermore, chemically untreated water is "hard," or saturated with minerals, and after a short period of time the insides of pipes become coated with a lining of calcium carbonate, which would isolate the water from the lead. Because of the formation of this mineral lining, lead pipes were considered to be quite safe until this century, and were used to conduct water up until 1930, when they were replaced by galvanized iron and later by copper piping. Today, the small amount of lead in the solder used to join copper piping is still considered to be detrimental to our health, and is of some concern to public health officials.

Modern historians know that the decline of the Roman empire was caused by a multitude of complex, interrelated political, demographic, and socio-economic problems. If many Romans suffered from lead poisoning, it was because they used cooking and drinking vessels which

---

[1] *Ancient Times, A History of the Early World,* by James Henry Breasted, Ginn and Co., Boston, 1944, page 192.
[2] *The Ten Books on Architecture,* Book VII, Chpt. VI, 10-11, by Vitruvius, translated by M.H. Morgan, Dover Publications, New York, 1960, page 246.

contained lead, or they added large quantities of "white lead," an oxide of this metal, to their vinegar-like, cheaper wines in order to sweeten them.

To obtain a steady supply of good water, Roman engineers devised complex water systems, some of which still stand and are used today. These ancient systems consisted of several parts. A large source of water and a reservoir to contain it was the prime component. Preferably this was a spring, river, or lake located higher up above the city, so that gravity-flow could be used to convey the water. A water channel, built at a very slight slope or gradient and lined with waterproof lime plaster, carried the water. This channel was built through obstacles such as mountains by tunneling, or it was carried over valleys by bridge structures. Such a bridge was usually constructed with arches, and was called an *arcuatio* in Latin. This is the architectural feature we commonly associate with the word "aqueduct" today. In the early aqueducts, the stone arches were made of large blocks of stone, accurately fitted and laid up without any mortar. Metal clamps were used instead of cement to hold the stones together. Later aqueducts were built with cheaper construction methods, using masonry faced concrete or brick.

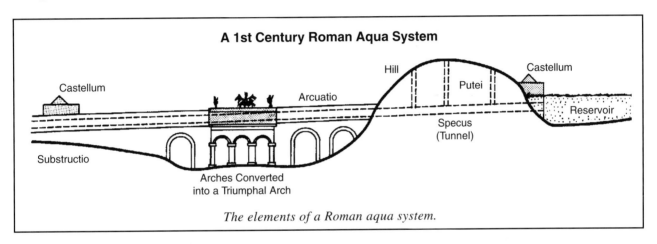

The elements of a Roman aqua system.

The tunnel used to carry a water channel through a hill was called a *specus,* or a "cave" in Latin. Vertical shafts called *putei* or "wells" were dug down to the specus in order to provide access during construction and for later maintenance work. The putei also functioned as valves, to relieve the water pressure which built up when large amounts of water passed through the tunnel. On level ground, the water channel was set on a low wall structure called the *substructio.* An aquae ended in the city at a distribution building, called a *castellum,* or at a water tower, which fed the fountains, bath buildings, and private houses. Sometimes an ornate fountain structure, called a nymphaeum, was built at the end of the water system. Overflow water which exceeded the capacity of the distribution point was carried into the city's sewer system and was used to flush it out. A castellum also functioned as an intermediate distribution terminal, or as a sluice gate to control the flow of water along the length of the aqua system.

The distribution castellum usually had a large holding tank with three pipes placed in a vertical row. The upper pipe fed the private houses and estates. The middle pipe supplied the public buildings and baths. The lowest pipe in the reservoir provided water to the public fountains, so that even when there was a drought or water shortage, the common people would not go thirsty. Also, the pipes could be placed at angled positions in the aqua channel to control the amount they received from the flow of water. A pipe angled toward the flow would receive the largest quantity of water. At the source reservoir, a special castellum was used to house several large tanks, which allowed the sand and mud to settle and to purify the water.[3]

3 *Engineering in the Ancient World,* by J.G. Landels, University of California Press, Berkeley, 1978, page 40.

The earliest city of Rome was well supplied with water from many local springs and from the Tiber River. The Etruscan kings of Rome had built fountains or pools, such as the Lacus Curtius and the Lacus Juturnae, to contain and hold the free-flowing springs in the Forum area. Later, these kings built some primitive masonry aqueducts to bring water into the city from outlying springs. However, the main source of water, the Tiber, was also used as a sewer, and by 312 B.C. the river and springs became inadequate for drinking water. The first of eleven aquae to bring water from the nearby mountains to Rome was built by the censor Appius Claudius. This structure was named the Aqua Appia in honor of its famous builder. It was 11 miles (17.5 km) long, all of it below ground in a tunnel except for about 300 feet (91 m) carried on an arcuatio. In 272 B.C., the second underground aqua, called the Anio Vetus (the Old Anio, to differentiate it from a later aqueduct, the New Anio), was built to bring water from the Anio River in the Apennine hills. In 144 B.C., the senate commissioned Quintus Marcus Rex to repair the existing aquae and to build a new one (Pliny, *Natural History,* Book XXXVI, 121). This new aqueduct was an above ground, masonry structure called the Aqua Marcia, after its builder, and it brought water to the buildings on top of the Capitoline Hill.

A Roman Republican denarius was struck in 56 B.C. by Marcius Phillipus, a descendant of Q. Marcius Rex, to commemorate the building of the Aqua Marcia. Shown on the obverse was the head of Ancus Marcius, and on the reverse of the coin is an equestrian statue on an arched aqueduct. The legend AQVA MAR, an abbreviation for Aqua Marcia, appears inside the arches. The Marcia

See plates, coin 29.

A denarius of Marcius Phillipus struck in 56 B.C. to commemorate the Aqua Marcia. Sydenham 919.

family claimed descent from Ancus Marcius, the fourth Etruscan king of Rome, who supposedly was one of the first rulers to bring water to Rome by means of an aqueduct. The equestrian statue on the reverse is probably that of Quintus Marcius Rex, the consul who built the Aqua Marcia in 144 B.C. This coin honored both of the illustrious ancestors of Marcius Phillipus and their great contribution to the water supply of Rome.

The Romans were a very practical people, and when the aqueduct's arches began appearing in the middle of the main streets and intersections of Rome, some bureaucrats saw a short-cut method for creating "instant" triumphal arches. They converted the arcade part of the aqueduct into a monumental arch by adding triumphal decorations and embellishing the structure with statues and inscriptions. This secondary use of aqueduct arches is recorded on a Republican As of C. Marcius Censorinus, another descendant of Q. Marcius Rex. Struck in 88 B.C., it shows two arches of the Aqua Marcia, with the statue of Victory in one arch and the entire prow of a warship, used as a trophy, in the other. We do

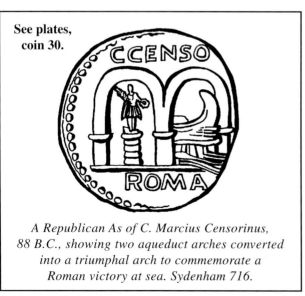

See plates, coin 30.

A Republican As of C. Marcius Censorinus, 88 B.C., showing two aqueduct arches converted into a triumphal arch to commemorate a Roman victory at sea. Sydenham 716.

not know where this monument was located, but the statue and the ship's prow commemorated some Roman victory at sea.

The construction of aquae in Rome was usually financed by the spoils of war or the tribute received from defeated nations. The Aqua Marcia was reputedly paid for with the loot taken in the wars with Carthage and Corinth, and cost 180,000,000 sesterces.[4] The fourth and last aqueduct built during the Roman Republican period was called the Aqua Tepula, from the Latin word *tepidus,* meaning lukewarm or tepid. This name accurately described the temperature of the water provided by this aqua system. It was completed in the year 125 B.C. by the censors Cn. Servilius Caepio and L. Cassius Longinus. A part of it was built on top of the water channel of the Aqua Marcia so that the new construction was carried by the older arcade of arches. In 33 B.C. Agrippa, the son-in-law and associate of Augustus, enlarged the Tepula by building a new aqueduct called the Aqua Julia, after Julius Caesar, and merging it with the Tepula so that in some places, three water channels were placed on the same arcuatio. Also, the combining of these two water sources improved the quality and temperature of the water delivered by the aqueduct. Two more new aquae were constructed under Augustus, the Aqua Virgo in 19 B.C., to deliver water to the thermae or baths built by Agrippa, and the Aqua Alsietina in 2 B.C., which supplied poor quality, undrinkable water to a new ceremonial lake, the Naumachia, and also for the irrigation of the large orchards, located on the west bank of the Tiber. Augustus also added a branch aqueduct, called the Aqua Augusta, to the Aqua Marcia in 5 B.C. to extend this supply of water into the enlarged city center.

The emperor Caligula, A.D. 37-41, began two aqueducts which were finished by his successor, Claudius, in A.D. 47 and 52. The most magnificent one, called the Aqua Claudia, supplied water for the imperial palaces located on the Palatine Hill. Its ruined arches, along with the remains of six other aqueducts, can still be seen in Rome today at the Porta Maggiore, the ancient Porta Praenestina. This portal was the arch of an aqueduct that was converted into a triumphal arch, and then later built into the fortification walls of Rome as a gateway. The other aqua, named the Anio Novus, the New Anio, was the second aqueduct taken from the Anio river, and it delivered the largest volume of water to Rome. It consisted of eight miles (12.8 km) of arches, some of them built 100 feet (30 m) above the ground. The water channel of the Anio Novus ran for its last seven miles (11 km) on the same arches that carried the Aqua Claudia, a feat of engineering which proved that Roman builders had completely mastered the construction of aqueducts. These architects and engineers were probably military men, because only army professionals had the knowledge and experience needed to design and supervise the construction of such complex structures.

The emperors of the first century, perhaps as a cost-cutting measure or for reasons of expediency, fully adopted the earlier Republican custom of converting some of the arches of the aqueducts into triumphal arches. This was done especially with arches located in prominent thoroughfares or road intersections of the city. For example, Claudius converted part of the arcuatio of the Aqua Claudia into a triumphal triple arch where it entered Rome at the Porta Praenestina mentioned above. It was embellished with a pediment and niches, called *aediculae* or little temples, which acted as shrines for the statues of deities.[5] The walls of the water channel on top of this triple arch became the attic area, and they still show a memorial inscription to Claudius, and legends of Vespasian and Titus, who later restored or re-dedicated this triumphal arch.

During the next two centuries, several emperors restored and built extensions to the many aquae of Rome. For example, Trajan extended the Aqua Marcia to the Aventine Hill and enlarged the Aqua Anio Novus. The rebuilt and enlarged older aquae were given compound names, such as the

4 *The Mute Stones Speak,* by Paul MacKendrick, St. Martin's Press, New York, 1960, page 320.
5 *Roman Architecture,* by Frank Sear, Cornell University Press, New York, 1982, page 93.

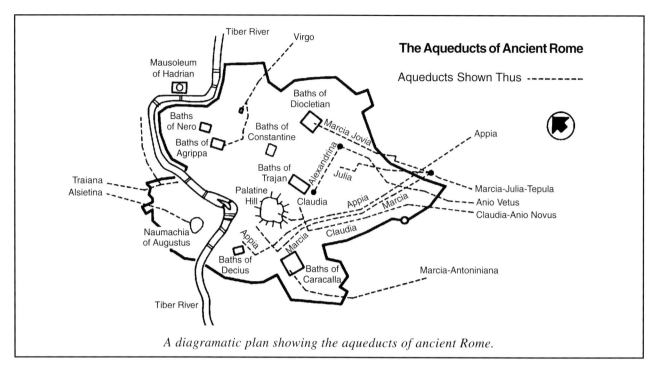

A diagramatic plan showing the aqueducts of ancient Rome.

Name	Constructed By	Date
Appia	Appius Claudius	312 B.C.
Anio Vetus	M. Curius Dendatus, F. Flaccus	272-269
Marcia	Q. Marcius Rex	144-140
Tepula	Cn. S. Caepio, L. C. Longinus	125
Julia	M. Agrippa	33
Virgo	M. Agrippa	19
Alsietina	Augustus	2 B.C.
Claudia	Caligula, Claudius	A.D. 38-52
Anio Novus	Caligula, Claudius	38-52
Traiana	Trajan	109
Marcia-Severiana	Septimius Severus	196
Marcia-Antoniniana	Caracalla	212
Alexandrina	Severus Alexander	226
Marcia-Jovia	Diocletian	A.D. 305

See plates, coin 31.

A sestertius of Trajan, struck A.D. 104-111, showing an arch of the Aqua Traiana, or as other numismatists suggest, a castellum of the aqueduct. The statues on the arch suggest a building or triumphal arch rather than an arcuatio. The river Tiber is seen reclining below. RIC Trajan 607. Also struck in Asses, RIC 463, 608, and as a dupondius, RIC Trajan 609.

Marcia-Severiana, constructed by Septimius Severus in 196, the Marcia-Antoniniana, extended by Caracalla in 212, and the Marcia-Jovia, rebuilt by Diocletian in 305. In A.D. 109, the emperor Trajan constructed a totally new aqua, the Aqua Traiana, as part of his extensive building program to restore and enhance Rome. This aqua ran from the Lago Bracciano to the Trastevere quarter on the west bank of the Tiber, and also supplied water for Trajan's newly constructed thermae or bath buildings. This new aqua is commemorated on coins of Trajan, for example on sestertii, RIC 607.

Probably the last aqua built to service Rome was the Aqua Alexandrina, constructed during the reign of Severus Alexander, A.D. 222-235. The ruins of the arcuatio of this aqua can still be seen today in the Piazza Vittorio Emanuele in Rome. It was actually a large addition to and reconstruction of the old Aqua Anio Vetus and the Aqua Julia, but it was so extensive that it was recognized as an entirely new system. The structure was almost 14 miles (22.5 km) long, and supplied water to the fountains and baths built by Severus for the convenience of a greatly enlarged Roman population. The most impressive terminal for an aqua system was a monumental, temple-like fountain, dedicated to the water nymphs and called a nymphaeum. Such a fountain ended the Aqua Alexandrina, and it was supposedly portrayed on the reverse of an As struck by Severus Alexander in A.D. 226, RIC 450. This coin is one in a series struck by this emperor to celebrate the architecture of his extensive and important building activities in Rome. In early years, this structure was thought to be

a representation of the Thermae of Alexander, which were the baths of Nero restored by Severus Alexander, but most numismatists now recognize it as a new nymphae. The semicircular fountain area can be seen in the foreground, with the arcuatio represented by an arcade behind it and a temple shown at the rear. Many statues of nymphs adorn the entire structure and it is surmounted by a statue of the emperor in a quadriga.

A rare As of Severus Alexander, struck in A.D. 226, showing the Nymphaeum Alexander in Rome, RIC Severus Alexander 450. Also struck as a denarius, RIC 59.

Some of the most famous Roman aqueducts were built in the distant provinces. One of these, called by the local people the "Puente del Diabalo," the Devil's Bridge, is located at Segovia in Spain. Medieval Spaniards, who gave it this name, believed that only some supernatural power could have constructed such an enormous stone structure without using mortar. It was built in the time of the emperor Trajan, and is 164 feet (50 m) high, with two tiers of arches, one on top of the other. This aqueduct still supplied some of the water for Segovia up until the mid 1950s, but today the structure is in disrepair, suffering from the affects of modern pollution and the vibra-tions caused by the vehicular traffic nearby. The most beautiful and highest Roman aqueduct, the "Pont du Gard," still stands over the river Gardon near Nimes, ancient Nemausus, in France. Built in the

1st century A.D., perhaps by Agrippa, it is a spectacular, triple tiered, arched structure, 180 feet (54.5 m) high and famous throughout the world. The water system is over 31 miles (50 km) long, and the masonry water channel is inclined accurately at a slight slope of 1 in 3,000, so that it falls only 57 feet (17 m) over its entire length.

Impressive remains of Roman aqueducts can still be seen today near the ancient cities of Carthage, Smyrna, Caesarea Maritima in Israel, Cherchel in Algeria, Timgad, and at many other locations.

The Pont du Gard as it looks today.

An AE22 of the city of Buthrotum in Epirus, struck under the emperor Nero, A.D. 54-68, Cohen 441, showing the aqueduct. Cohen wrongly attributed the coin to Mauretania, but correctly identified a coin of Augustus, Cohen 742, showing the same aqueduct, as coming from Buthrotum. The above coin can also be seen in a book by Jean Mazard, the Corpus Numorum Numidiae Mauretaniaeque, *page 200, coin no. XI.*

An AE25 of the city of Anazarbus in Cilicia showing an arched arcuatio. Three buildings, probably castellum, appear above the arches. Struck during the reign of Severus Alexander, A.D. 222-235. Coin no. 1450, plate 98, in the Sylloge Nummorum Graecorum, Switzerland I. *Another example of this coin with a variation of the aqueduct design and a single castellum appears in Price and Trell, fig. 8, page 46, and also on page 50.*

Some of these provincial cities struck coinage which proudly pictured their own aqueducts. The city of Buthrotum in Epirus, present-day Albania, struck a series of aqueduct coins from the times of Augustus to the emperor Nero which showed an impressive two tiered, arched arcuatio. These coins were originally attributed to Babba, a city in Mauretania, North Africa, because large quantities of them were found in that location, but numismatists now believe that the mint at Buthrotum produced them. See Cohen 441.

Another beautiful depiction of an aqueduct can be seen on coins of the city of Anazarbus in Cilicia, present-day southern Turkey. This coin, struck during the reign of Severus Alexander, A.D. 222-235, shows an ornate arcuatio with three triangular roofed structures above. These may be shrines decorating the arches and converting them into a triumphal monument, or they may be a representation of a castellum building acting as a sluice gate or distribution tank for the aqua.

All of the emperors carefully administered and frequently reconstructed the aquae so that the water systems survived for many years. It is only because of this policy of maintaining the water supply that we know so much about aquae. Sextus Julius Frontinus, a senator, soldier, writer, and ex-governor of Britain, was appointed *Curator Aquarum,* in charge of the Roman water supply, by Trajan in A.D. 97. He wrote two books in which he describes all that he knew about the aquae.[6] He intended these books to be a guide for the administrators who succeeded him, and he recorded his observations in great detail. Of particular interest is his description of the illegal practices of the supervisors and workers, usually slaves, attached to the aquae. They frequently sold unauthorized connections from the water system to wealthy land owners and householders. Frontinus calls these illegal connections "punctures," and apprehended culprits were fined the enormous sum of 100,000 sestertii for their crimes. Several modern historians have used the written work of Frontinus as a literary source to develop their own comprehensive studies of the aquae of ancient Rome.[7]

---

[6] *Strategems and Aqueducts,* by Frontinus, translated by C.E. Bennet and M.B. McElwain, Loeb Classical Library, Harvard, 1925.

[7] The best of these studies is the work of Thomas Ashby, *The Aqueduct of Ancient Rome,* Oxford University Press, England, 1931.

In medieval times, the popes who ruled over Rome restored, renovated, and renamed many of the aqueducts. Today, Rome is still served by four of these systems, some of them entirely reconstructed over the ancient channels but using the same water sources. The Italian Acqua Vergine is the ancient Roman Aqua Virgo, and it still supplies water to the famous Fountain of Trevi. It was restored by Pope Pius V in 1570. The Acqua Felice was built in 1585 to replace the Roman Aqua Alexandrina. The Aqua Traiana was restored in 1611 and renamed the Acqua Paola, after Pope Paul V. The great Aqua Marcia was reconstructed in 1870 and named the Acqua Pia or Marcia-Pia, after Pope Pius IX.[8] It still delivers excellent quality, cold drinking water to the modern citizens of Rome.

It is interesting to note that in the first century A.D., when the population of Rome was about one million people, the daily water supply provided by all the aquae is estimated to have been 428.5 gallons (1800 liters) per person. In the Rome of 1897, with a population of about half a million people, the supply of water dwindled to 180 gallons (760 liters) per head.[9] This comparison is not given here as a criticism of 19th century Roman sanitary standards, but rather it is meant to be high praise and a belated compliment to the abilities of ancient Roman engineers.

---

[8] *Roman Life,* by Mary Johnston, Scott, Foresman and Co., Chicago, 1957, page 336.
[9] *The Ruins and Excavations of Ancient Rome,* by R. Lanciani, reprint by Bell Publishing Co., New York, 1979, page 55.

Chapter 15

The Forum Romanum

Some of the tourists visiting Rome today are disappointed by the ruins of the Forum Romanum Magnum, the Great Forum of the ancient city. This early civic center is not very impressive, and the small area it occupies suggests that the space was less than majestic. However, judging from the buildings and monuments of the Forum illustrated on ancient coins, it was a magnificent setting for some of the major events in world history. The last great Roman historian, Ammianus Marcellinus, A.D. 300-395, wrote that the emperor Constantius II, 337-361, even though he was accustomed to the splendors of Constantinople and other fabulous Asiatic cities, gazed with amazement at the wondrous urban scene presented by the imperial fora when he visited the city for the first time.[1]

The Romans considered their Forum to be the *navel,* or the center, of the world and this focal point of Roman life was very compact in size for several reasons. The Forum area was surrounded by hills, and this restricted its physical enlargement. Also, the Roman historian Suetonius, A.D. 69-150, tells us that the emperor Augustus, who rebuilt the Forum, kept it small because he did not want to expropriate land from the citizens of Rome unless it was absolutely necessary.[2] The Roman architect Vitruvius, describing the planning of the ideal Forum, said that it should be very compact and "proportionate to the number of inhabitants, . . . so that it not look like a desert waste for lack of population."[3] The Forum probably was a congested space full of buildings and monuments, however, it was frequently rebuilt in later imperial times, and many older structures were removed to make room for the new ones.

The Forum Romanum was founded on the swampy ground in the valley between the Palatine and the Capitoline hills. This was a strategic, central location for a market and meeting place that would be accessible to all the tribes occupying the surrounding villages. The early Etruscan monarchs of Rome drained the Forum area with a ditch, which later became the Cloacina Maxima, one of the largest sewers of the city. The Forum eventually developed into the political and religious center of Rome, with temples, government centers, courts, shops, and national monuments built around the edges of the meeting area. In later times, the buildings of the Forum became inadequate for the growing population, and Julius Caesar as well as the emperors Augustus, Vespasian, Nerva, and Trajan built subsidiary fora nearby for new commercial, cultural, and religious establishments. However, the ancient, central Forum Romanum always retained its position as the principal public space of the empire and the location for all the major national events.

The Forum was a trapezoidal shape, approximately 500 feet (152 m) long, with a width varying from 150 feet (46 m) to 115 feet (34.5 m) at its narrowest point. In ancient days, before arenas and amphitheaters were built, gladiatorial exhibitions were often held in the Forum. On special occasions, wooden stages and platforms with seating were built in the central open area. The surrounding buildings were raised up on high foundations to avoid the periodic floods of the Tiber

---

[1] *The Historical Work of Ammianus Marcellinus,* translated by J.C. Rolfe, Loeb Classical Library, Cambridge, 1937, Book XVI, 10,13.
[2] *The Twelve Caesars Augustus,* 56, by Suetonius, translated by Robert Graves, Penguin Classics, London, 1967, page 82.
[3] *De Architectura,* by Vitruvius, translated by M.H. Morgan, Dover Publications, New York, 1960, Book V, Chpt. I, page 131.

River, but also to provide viewing platforms for the spectacles. Some buildings, such as the basilicas, had second floors which were used as spectator galleries. Also, the Forum was designed to provide a setting for the many religious ceremonies, triumphal processions and parades, as well as political events such as voting by the citizens. It even functioned as an outdoor museum, where strange curiosities and animals were displayed. Suetonius related that Augustus exhibited an African serpent, almost 90 feet (27 m) long, in the Forum area.[4]

The ancient Forum was the terminal point of the Sacra Via, the "sacred way" or main road of Rome, and it contained some of the most important national buildings and monuments. Many of these are depicted on coins, and the overall appearance of the Forum Romanum can be reconstructed from these examples of the engravers' art.[5] The principal monuments of the Forum, as they existed in 10 B.C., are described and shown on the map below. This date for the map was chosen because it marks the transition of the Forum from a Republican tribal, ceremonial square

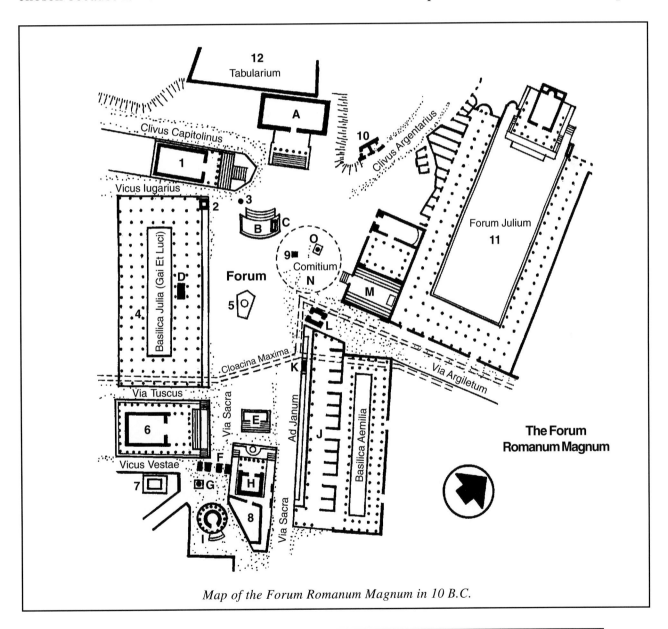

Map of the Forum Romanum Magnum in 10 B.C.

4 *The Twelve Caesars*, as above, Augustus 43, page 76.
5 These coins are also described in *The Monuments of Ancient Rome as Coin Types,* by Philip V. Hill, Seaby Publications, London, 1989.

into an Imperial civic center. By 10 B.C., the great rejuvenation and rebuilding of the Forum by Augustus had just been completed, and the area had reached one of its finest stages of development.[6] As Suetonius said in his work, Augustus could boast on his deathbed that "I found Rome built of bricks; I leave her clothed in marble." (*The Twelve Caesars, Augustus,* 28).

The buildings and monuments given a letter designation on the map are described on the coins illustrated in this chapter. Those with a number are not pictured, except for number 7, but are described. The map attempts to show the actual location and relationship of these monuments in the Forum, but in some cases the site is problematic, and only an informed guess can be offered.

A tourist visiting the Forum Romanum in 10 B.C. might begin his tour in the west end, just below the Capitoline Hill, at the earliest historical monuments. Lacking a printed tour guide, it is possible he might consult some of the coins in his purse for illustrations of the monuments and buildings he was about to see.

A. The Temple of Concordia. This temple was erected in 367 B.C., according to legend, to commemorate the healing of a bitter political dispute between the plebian and the patrician families of Rome. The temple is located at the foot of the Capitoline Hill in front of the Tabularium. The structure was restored in 121 B.C. by L. Opimius, and Pliny the Elder told us that it became a

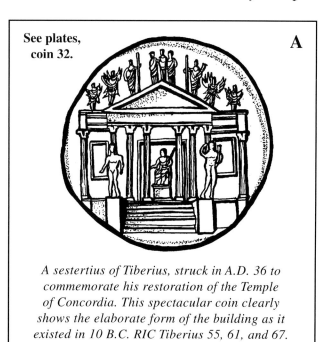

See plates, coin 32.

A

A sestertius of Tiberius, struck in A.D. 36 to commemorate his restoration of the Temple of Concordia. This spectacular coin clearly shows the elaborate form of the building as it existed in 10 B.C. RIC Tiberius 55, 61, and 67.

museum for many sculptures, paintings, and souvenirs which had historical associations. For example, Augustus deposited there a fabled sardonyx gem set in a golden horn, and a sculpture of four elephants carved out of obsidian.[7] The platform and the pediment of the temple was decorated with the statues of several deities, such as Hercules and Mercury on the podium, and Jupiter, Juno, Minerva, and winged Victories on the roof.

1. The Temple of Saturn. This temple was founded in 498 B.C., and was one of the oldest and most venerated monuments in Republican Rome. The Aerarium, the state treasury, was kept here in several underground strong rooms. The temple was also the setting for a licentious and very popular festival, the Saturnalia, celebrated yearly on December 17. On that festival, even the slaves could make merry and, in a reversal of roles, their masters served them meals. The structure was rebuilt and embellished by Munatius Plancus, a friend of Augustus, in 42 B.C.

2. The Lacus Servilius or the Fountain of Servilius is of ancient origin, and probably was built around a spring or pond in the early Forum. It acquired some notoriety during the civil wars in 82 B.C., when the dictator Sulla used the fountain to display the severed heads of the Romans he had proscribed and executed. Agrippa rebuilt and ornamented the fountain during the reconstruction of the Forum undertaken by Augustus.

3. The Milliarium Aureum, the golden milepost, was a gilded bronze column which marked the spot in the Forum from which all the milestone markers, placed along the highways radiating

---

[6] In the *Res Gestae Divi Augusti,* 20, the emperor said that he restored 82 temples in Rome in 28 B.C.
[7] *Natural History,* by Pliny, translated by D.E. Eichholz, Loeb Classical Library, Cambridge, 1962, Books XXXVI, ii, 4 and XXXVII, lxvii, 197.

out from Rome, were measured. It was erected by Augustus in 29 B.C. to commemorate his improvements to the Roman road system, such as repaving the Flaminian Road. It was located in the Forum between the Temple of Saturn and the Rostra.

B. The Rostra. This was the platform from which important orations were given to the Roman people. The name, location, and appearance of this dais is disputed by many scholars. It is shown here in the location favoured by most archaeologists, in front of the Temple of Concordia and at the edge of the Comitium. The Rostra was decorated with the rams or "beaks" of enemy ships captured in the battle of Antium in 338 B.C. The Latin word for these rams is rostra, which became the name for the platform itself. Historians believe that Julius Caesar rebuilt and relocated an old rostra, originally located east of the Comitium, to this position, and it is possible that Augustus completed this work. This assumption gave rise to other suggested locations and names for this rostra, such as the "New Rostra" or "Rostra Augusta," and even the "Rostra Julia." Taking the path of least resistance through this complicated debate, archaeologists say that there were two or even three rostra in the Forum, and that the old one, called the Rostra Vetera, was rebuilt in front of the Temple of Concordia, but it retained the round shape and adornments of the old one. Also, Augustus built a new dais for Julius Caesar in front of the Temple of Divus Julius at the opposite end of the Forum (**E** on the map). However, there may have been another, smaller rostra in the Forum for less important events, because a coin of Augustus, struck by C. Sulpicius Platorinus in 13 B.C. (RIC Augustus 406), shows Augustus and Agrippa seated on a small unidentified platform adorned with ships' prows. The coin shown here, illustrating the Rostra, shows the curved form of the older structure and the rams set in archways of the foundations as described by ancient writers.

C. The Equestrian Statue of Octavian was erected in the Forum around 40 B.C. to commemorate the imperator's military victories. According to the Roman historian and senator C. Velleius Paterculus, 19 B.C.-A.D. 30, the statue was erected on the Rostra.[8] On the map, it is shown on this dais, despite the fact that this location is hotly disputed by some historians. The coin illustrating this statue also shows a prow and ram of a ship in the exergue, which probably alludes to some naval

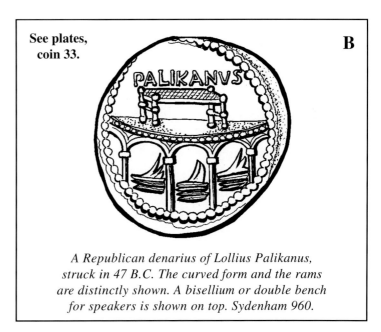

See plates, coin 33. **B**

A Republican denarius of Lollius Palikanus, struck in 47 B.C. The curved form and the rams are distinctly shown. A bisellium or double bench for speakers is shown on top. Sydenham 960.

C

A denarius of Octavian, struck around 40 B.C., showing the Equestrian Statue of Octavian. The SC in the exergue indicates that the statue was erected by order of the senate. Sydenham 1319.

---

8 *De Divinatione*, by Cicero, Book I.

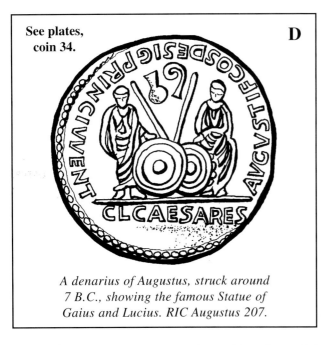

See plates, coin 34.

D

A denarius of Augustus, struck around 7 B.C., showing the famous Statue of Gaius and Lucius. RIC Augustus 207.

victory, but perhaps indicates that the statue was indeed erected on the Rostra.

D. The Statue of Gaius and Lucius Caesars may have been located in the portico of the Basilica Julia. Augustus wanted to rededicate this basilica to Lucius and Gaius, his adopted heirs, but this event may not have occurred, even though the intention is mentioned in the emperor's posthumous biography, the *Res Gestae Divi Augusti*. Some historians claim that the statue may have been placed in the portico of the Basilica Aemilia, which perhaps was then called the Portico Gaii et Lucii. At any rate, the statue on the coin shown here is believed to be a copy of the original placed in the Forum area.

4. The Basilica Julia. This large structure was begun by Julius Caesar about 54 B.C., and dedicated while still under construction in 46. It was rebuilt and enlarged by Augustus after a fire, and reopened in 12 B.C., perhaps renamed as the Basilica of Gaius and Lucius. (See **D** above) The building incorporated a large atrium, which often served as a court of law, and had a large second storey for spectators.

5. The Lacus Curtius was an extension of a spring which began at the Palatine Hill. It originally formed a large pond in the swampy ground of the Forum, and later was contained in a masonry fountain, built by the Etruscans, which became the major water source in the area.

E. The Rostra Julia, which also may have been called the New Rostra or the Rostra Augusta, was supposedly decorated by Augustus with the rams taken from ships captured at the battle of Actium, 31 B.C., in his war against Antony and Cleopatra. Some historians state that the Rostra Julia was actually the large staircase and porch of the temple itself. From the ruins found in the Forum, however, some archaeologists believe that it was a freestanding structure in front of the temple, as shown on the map. It is illustrated on a sestertius of Hadrian, and the Rostra is clearly identified by the three rams projecting from the base. The Temple of the Deified Julius is shown in the background, but the picture on this coin does not resolve the issue of whether the Rostra is attached to the temple or freestanding.

6. The Temple of Castor and Pollux, better known to the Romans as the Aedes Castoris or the Temple of Castor, was built in 482 B.C. in honor of the Dioscuri who, in legend, appeared nearby, at the Lacus Juturnae or the Spring of Juturna (**7** on the map), to announce the Roman victory at Lake Regillus in 496. It was rebuilt in 119 B.C. by Metellus Dalmaticus with the money from the booty of the Dalmatian War. The temple was set on a very lofty substructure, lifting it well above the other buildings in the Forum. This prominence made it

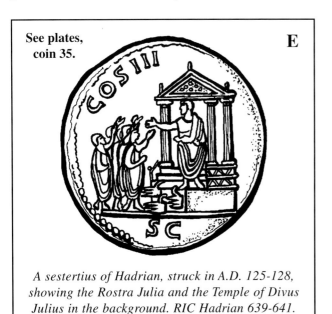

See plates, coin 35.

E

A sestertius of Hadrian, struck in A.D. 125-128, showing the Rostra Julia and the Temple of Divus Julius in the background. RIC Hadrian 639-641.

into a rallying point, and the scene of many political events such as the riotous battle between the followers of Sulla and Marius in 88 B.C.

F. The Arcus Augusti, the triple Parthian Arch of Augustus built around 20 B.C., was squeezed into a narrow space of the Via Sacra between the Temple of Divi Julius and the Temple of Castor. This arch commemorated the diplomatic treaty with the Parthians that restored the Roman military standards lost by Crassus in 63, Decidius Saxa in 40, and Mark Antony in 36 B.C. The triple arch replaced a single arched structure dedicated to Octavian in 29 B.C. which was erected for his victory over Antony and Cleopatra at Actium. This lost "Actian Arch" can be seen on denarii of Octavian (RIC 267). The coin illustrated here shows the three openings in the Parthian Arch to be of equal size, but the ruins in the Forum indicate that the monu-ment had a wider central arch.

G. The Puteal of Scribonius or **Libo** was an altar shaped like a wellhead, possibly erected on a spot where lightning had struck the earth. Ancient historians specifically describe it as being located in the Comitium, and that it was used by businessmen who swore oaths upon it when concluding a deal.[9] In 1950, archaeologists identified the remains of a puteal discovered behind the Arcus Augusti, close to the Temple of Vesta. They claim that this was the Puteal of Scribonius, but the discrepancy between this location and the one described by the ancient writers remains unresolved. However, the denarius of Scribonius Libo shown here gives a clear picture of the appearance of this unusual type of sacred altar.

7. The Lacus Juturnae was a pond or fountain, which was built around a spring flowing from the Palatine Hill. It is legendary because it was at this fountain that the Dioscuri were seen watering their horses and announcing that the Romans had won the battle of Lake Regilius.[10] The ancient pond was drained and replaced by a well or puteal. A Republican coin portrays the Dioscuri watering their horses at this puteal, which is shown as a formal type of basin fountain.

---

9 *Roman History,* by C. Velleius Paterculus, translated by F.W. Shipley, Loeb Classical Library, Cambridge, 1924, Book II, lxi, 4.
10 *Plutarch's Lives*, Coriolanus, 3.

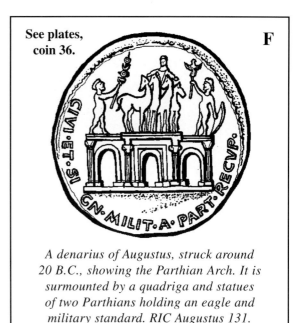

See plates, coin 36.

F

A denarius of Augustus, struck around 20 B.C., showing the Parthian Arch. It is surmounted by a quadriga and statues of two Parthians holding an eagle and military standard. RIC Augustus 131.

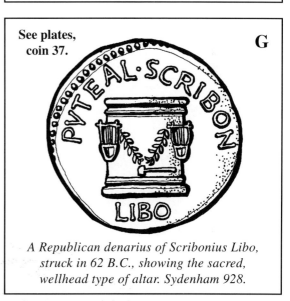

See plates, coin 37.

G

A Republican denarius of Scribonius Libo, struck in 62 B.C., showing the sacred, wellhead type of altar. Sydenham 928.

7

A Republican denarius struck by A. Postumius Albinus in 119-91 B.C., showing the Dioscuri and their horses at the Fountain of Juturna. Sydenham 612.

See plates, coin 38.

H

A Republican denarius struck by Octavian around 28 B.C. It shows the Temple of Divus Julius as tetrastyle. The inscription DIVO IVI appears on the pediment. Sydenham 1337.

See plates, coin 39.

I

A Republican denarius struck by Q. Cassius around 57 B.C., showing the fourth Temple of Vesta in the Forum. Sydenham 917.

H. The Temple of Divus Julius. A temple to the deified Julius Caesar was proposed by the triumvirs Antony, Octavian, and Lepidus in 42 B.C., but construction only began under Octavian's reign in 31 B.C. It was erected on the actual site of Caesar's cremation pyre in the Forum. The temple was a small but imposing shrine, elevated above the Forum and connected with the Rostra Julia, making it an important focal point for political activities. The coin indicates that it was a tetrastyle temple, however, the archaeologists concluded from the remains of six columns found in the portico that it was actually hexastyle. Two columns on the coin were omitted through artistic license in order to show the cult statue of Julius Caesar inside the shrine.

I. The Temple or Shrine of Vesta dates back to the very beginning of Rome's history. Originally, the structure was built to contain the communal fire, but later a powerful religious cult developed around the goddess Vesta, the ancient deity of fire, hearth, and of family life. The Temple of Vesta, located in the Forum in 10 B.C., was probably the fourth temple built on this site. The early temple was built of wood and stone to reflect the primeval character of the cult, but Augustus rebuilt it in marble around 29 B.C. after it was damaged in a flood. This temple was a round structure, called a "tholos" in Greek, with a conical roof in imitation of the rough thatch huts built by the ancient Latin tribes. This edifice contained the Palladium, one of the most sacred penates or household gods of the Roman people, and several other relics of the early

Roman culture and religion. The coin illustrated here shows the fourth Temple of Vesta in a highly stylized form, but the circular shape can be clearly seen.

8. The Regia was the ancient home of the Pontifex Maximus, the high priest of Rome. Originally, the site was thought to be the house of Numa Pompilius, the second Etruscan king of Rome, 715-673 B.C., who by legend was the founder of most of the religious institutions of Rome. The Pontifex was the governor of the Vestal Virgins, and his house is located across the street from the Temple of Vesta.

J. The Basilica Aemilia. This large, opulent building, on the northeast side of the Forum, was first built in 179 B.C. by M. Aemilius Lepidus, then restored in 78, 55, and 34 B.C., and rebuilt by Augustus in 14 B.C. It had a long atrium in the center and a second storey gallery. The colonnades were made up of red, black, and white marble columns from Africa and green ones from Asia.[11] The basilica was also used by merchants who occupied the small stalls along the portico, and these later became the offices of bankers, money lenders, and gold or silversmiths. The second storey of

---

11 *The Roman Forum,* by Michael Grant, Weidenfeld and Nicholson, London, 1970, page 137.

the basilica can be clearly seen on the coin illustrated. This gallery was used to view the spectacles and ceremonies taking place in the Forum, and ancient writers mentioned that spectators were charged a small amount for admission. Round shields, used as trophies of war, were hung on the columns of this basilica to commemorate Roman victories, and these can be seen on the coin.

K. The Shrine of Venus Cloacina was an unusual monument dedicated to Venus, the "Purifier" of the sewers. The Cloacina Maxima, the main sewer which drained the area, intersected the Forum near the Basilica Aemilia, and the shrine was located at this exact place. Pollution must have been as big a problem in ancient Rome as it is today. The sewers were combined sanitary waste and storm drains which emptied into the Tiber, but the river was also used by the Romans for drinking water, bathing, and for fishing. As religion was very closely integrated with everyday life, it was only natural for the Romans to seek the help of a deity to purify the sewers, a task presumably no mortal could do. The coin pictured here shows that the open-air shrine contained two statues of Venus the Purifier on a single marble base. A stylized representation of the portico of the Basilica Aemilia appears in the background at the left of the shrine to positively identify its location.

L. The Temple or Shrine of Janus. This famous temple is difficult to locate in the Forum area. Most recent reconstruction maps do not even attempt to show it, but it is so well documented in ancient writings and on coins that anyone writing

See plates, coin 40.

J

A Republican denarius struck by M. Aemilius Lepidus in 66 B.C., showing the two storey Basilica Aemilia. Sydenham 833.

See plates, coin 41.

K

A Republican denarius struck by L. Mussidius Longus in 42 B.C., showing the Shrine of Venus Cloacina. Sydenham 1093-1094.

about the Forum is obliged to make a guess. I have shown it on the map at the side of the Basilica Aemilia, a location strongly favoured by nineteenth century scholars. The Temple of Janus was a small building, and its tiny foundations were probably obliterated by later structures erected in the area. Some authors even claim that it was portable, and moved around the Forum. Ancient authors mention it several times, and place it at the entrance to the street called the Via Argiletum. Other writers describe the roadway in front of the Basilica Aemilia as leading up to the Temple of Janus, and call it the "Ad Janum," that is "to the Janum." This street was frequented by bankers, brokers, and money lenders, and the Roman authors Cicero and Horace describe the street called the "Ad Janum Medium" as being the bourse or exchange of Rome.[12] This name means "to the Janum in the middle," which implies that there were three temples to Janus in Rome, the one in the Forum being in the middle location and therefore named the Medium Janus.

Janus was an old, entirely Latin god, and was not borrowed from Greek mythology. Numa Pompilius is supposedly the king who introduced the Romans to this deity as a powerful war god, great-

---

12 *The Ruins and Excavations of Ancient Rome,* by R. Lanciani, reprint by Bell Publishing Co., New York, 1967, page 252.

er even than Jupiter. One of Janus' many surnames was Quirinus, which also was the ancient Latin name for a war god similar to Mars. However, the origins of Janus as a deity are obscure. An "Ianua" means a door or a gate, and Janus, the early god of war and peace, became associated with gates and doors. Also, the cult statue of Janus was double faced (bifrons) so he could look both ways, towards war or peace, past or future, and beginnings and endings. This double-faced statue suggested a surname for the god, "Geminus," from the celestial twins, Gemini. The association of Janus with beginnings and endings led the Romans to give the name January to the first month of the year in their calendar. The Temple of Janus had doors at both ends to accommodate this double headed concept. Furthermore, the doors of the temple were always closed in times of peace, and Augustus shut the doors three times in his reign, these being only the third, fourth, and fifth times they were closed in Roman history up to that time.[13] The temple shown on the coin here may have been the small Janus Geminus or Janus Quirinus, located somewhere in the Forum.

A sestertius struck by Nero around A.D. 65, showing the Temple of Janus Quirinus, or Geminus, with the doors closed to commemorate peace with the Parthians. RIC Nero 439.

M. The Curia. This was the house of the senate of Rome, and was one of the most important buildings in the Forum. The first Curia was supposedly built in the early Forum by Tullus Hostilius, the third Etruscan king of Rome, 673-642 B.C. The senate house was rebuilt several times, and may also have changed its location. A later building was repaired by Sulla in 80 B.C., and this Curia was being reconstructed in 44 B.C. by Julius Caesar, but the work ceased with his assassination. The project was completed in 29 B.C. by Augustus, who named it the Curia Julia. The building was located in the Comitium, and was closely associated with many of the activities taking place on the nearby Rostra. The coin here, illustrating the Curia, shows an imposing edifice, almost temple-like, raised up on a platform. This building was converted into a church in medieval times, and the basic structure survives intact to this day.

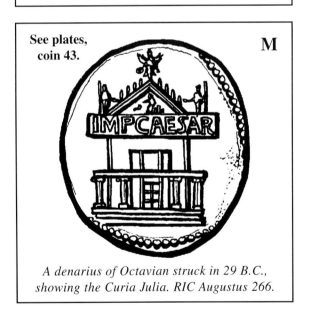

A denarius of Octavian struck in 29 B.C., showing the Curia Julia. RIC Augustus 266.

N. The Comitium was an open space in the Forum adjacent to the Curia which was used as the place of assembly for the citizens of Rome. Originally, the space was a circular area lowered a few steps below the pavement, and it was closely related to the old Rostra, which reflected this curved shape. The Comitium was used for elections and voting, and as a court of appeal. Later, commercial dealings were conducted there, and it became a rendezvous for businessmen who were negotiating contracts. Some scholars say that the Comitium was actually a space enclosed by fences, and archaeologists have found postholes in the pavement of the Forum, which indicate that certain

---

[13] *Res Gestae Divi Augusti*, 13.

areas could be temporarily fenced off with re-movable wooden barricades. The illustrated coin, showing the Comitium, depicts such a fence parti-tioning off the assembly area during a vote by the citizens.

O. The Rostrated Column of Duilius was erected in the Forum in 260 B.C., in honor of this consul's great naval victory over the Carthaginians in the First Punic War. Duilius was the first admiral to command a victorious Roman naval fleet. The column was made of marble, with the bronze rams of enemy ships protruding from the sides. A part of this column was discovered by archaeologists in the Comitium area, in the location shown on the map above. The emperor Augustus copied or restored this column to record his victory in the sea battle of Nauchlochus in 36 B.C., and he also raised several other rostrated columns in the Forum before 10 B.C., to commemorate his and Agrippa's victories at Actium. They are mentioned in ancient literature as having been moved by later emperors and re-erected on the Campus Martius.

9. The Lapis Niger or "black stone" dates from the late sixth century B.C. This was as-sumed to be part of an ancient monumental pave-ment over the tomb of Romulus, who by legend founded Rome in the 8th century B.C. This tomb may have been the most sacred national monu-ment in Rome, and the inscription, in old Latin letters, found on the stone is a warning that the area around the tomb was sacred and must not be desecrated. Scholars suggest that the tomb of Romulus and the Black Stone were originally located to one side of the Rostra Vetera, and remained there when the dais was later moved to a position in front of the Temple of Concor-dia.

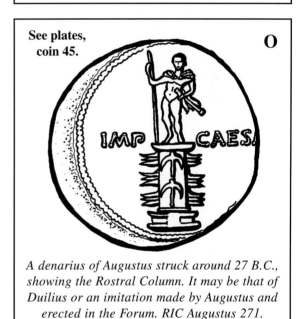

A Republican denarius struck by P. Licinius Nerva in 106 B.C., showing the Comitium and citizens voting. Sydenham 548.

A denarius of Augustus struck around 27 B.C., showing the Rostral Column. It may be that of Duilius or an imitation made by Augustus and erected in the Forum. RIC Augustus 271.

10. The Carcer Mamertinus or Tullianum, the Mamertine jail, was the state prison where the enemies of Rome were held, tortured, and executed. It was located in a cave within an ancient quarry at the foot of the Capitoline Hill close to the Temple of Concordia, and can still be seen today.

11. The Forum Julium was begun by Julius Caesar and dedicated by him in 45 B.C., although still under construction. It was completed by Augustus in around 28 B.C. This new forum was the first one built in an effort to relieve the congestion in the Forum Romanum.

12. The Tabularium was the records office and archives which held the state papers of the Roman people. It was a massive building, and most of the lower floors still exist. It was built on the cliff edge of the Capitoline Hill, facing the Forum, and formed a backdrop for the other historic buildings. The Tabularium was probably built by Q. Lutatius Catulus in his reconstruction of the

A reconstruction of the Forum Romanum Magnum, 10 B.C., looking toward the Capitoline Hill.

Forum after the fire of 83 B.C. Its main feature was the arcaded facade with statues of famous Romans placed in each archway.

Much of the ancient Forum cannot be reconstructed because a large part of it is covered over by a modern road. When it is removed sometime in the future, a clearer picture of the Forum, the greatest urban space and civic center in the history of the world, may be revealed.

Chapter 16

The Forum of Trajan

The Forum Romanum, the main civic center for the city of Rome and the entire Roman empire, became too small to fulfil its function by 50 B.C., and the rulers who reigned after this date enlarged it by constructing new fora in the areas nearby. Julius Caesar began to construct a new forum in 51 B.C., but was assassinated before it was finished. The Forum Julium was dedicated in 45 B.C. but the construction was completed by Augustus in 28 B.C. This forum contained the Temple of Venus Genetrix, the goddess from whom the Julian clan supposedly descended, and the temple was built by Caesar to commemorate his victory over Pompey at Pharsalus in 48 B.C. The Forum of Julius Caesar consisted of a sacred area enclosed by colonnades, with the Temple of Venus in the center at the northeast end. This plan became the prototype for all the other new fora built in Rome.

The second, new imperial forum was constructed by Augustus to supplement the areas of the Forum Romanum and the Forum Julium. This forum contained a magnificent temple to Mars Ultor, Mars the Avenger, which Augustus built in 41 B.C. after he had avenged the assassination of Julius

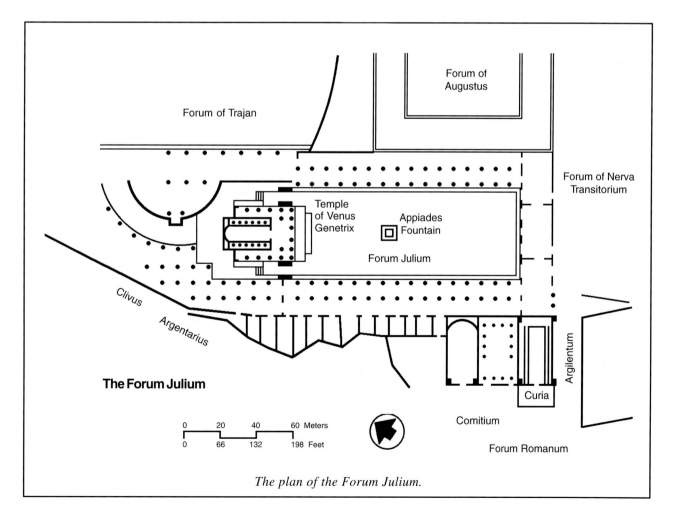

The plan of the Forum Julium.

108

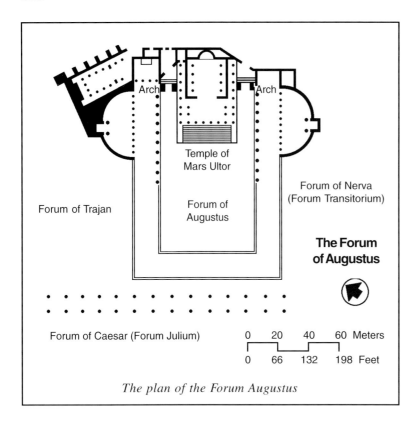

Arch

Arch

Temple of
Mars Ultor

Forum of Trajan

Forum of
Augustus

Forum of Nerva
(Forum Transitorium)

**The Forum
of Augustus**

Forum of Caesar (Forum Julium)

0   20   40   60 Meters

0   66   132   198 Feet

The plan of the Forum Augustus

Caesar. The temple was flanked by two hemicycle structures which contained niches for statues of victorious Roman generals and heroes. Remains of the octastyle Corinthian temple of Mars Ultor can be seen in Rome today.

The next new forum to be built was actually not a forum, but a very large temple with a forecourt or precinct. This was the Templum Pacis, the Temple of Peace, built by Vespasian in A.D. 71 to commemorate his victories in Judaea (*Suetonius, Vespasian 9*). It was labelled a forum only in the fourth century, when the open landscaped area was used for civic functions. The famous marble plan of Rome, called the *Forma Urbis Romae*, was placed on one of the walls of this Temple of Peace during a restoration undertaken in the reign of Septimius Severus, A.D. 193-211. The Forum of Peace was located adjacent to the Sacra Via at the northeast edge of the Forum Romanum, but was not connected to the nearby Forum of Augustus.

The fourth imperial forum was started by Domitian and completed by the emperor Nerva, 96-98. This forum connected the Templum Pacis with the Forum Augustum and the Forum Julium, and it enclosed the Argiletum, the main roadway between the two fora which led into the Forum Romanum. It was called the Forum Transitorium because it was a long narrow precinct, more like a wide street, with traffic flowing through it. The colonnaded area of the Forum Transitorium contained a temple to Minerva, and today this forum is often referred to as the Forum of Nerva.

The last and most magnificent forum was built by Trajan, from plans prepared by his architect, Apollodorus. This was constructed between A.D. 112-114, and it was an architectural and engineering masterpiece. Naturally, several parts of it were commemorated on coins. To make space for this large new forum, the engineers enlarged the valley to the east of the Capitoline Hill, and removed a part of the steep Quirinal Hill. This hill was probably 128 feet (39 m) high at that time. The enormous amount of earth removed in this operation was disposed of by simply spreading it as a thin layer over the large cemetery outside the walls of Rome. The open court area of the Forum Traiani was 383 feet (116 m) by 313 feet (95 m) wide, and the complex around it was made up of seven parts.[1] These consisted of a triumphal arch gateway which connected the open area to the Forum Augustum; the court, which contained an equestrian statue of Trajan; the Basilica Ulpia, with hemicycles at each end; the two libraries, called the Bibliotheca Ulpia and Traiani; a double colonnade with two flanking hemicycles; the Column of Trajan; and the Temple of Trajan. Adjacent to this complex was Trajan's new market, a fashionable three level shopping center which was cut into the Quirinal hillside. Substantial remains of this large market building can still be seen in Rome today.

[1] *The Ruins and Excavations of Ancient Rome*, by R. Lanciani, 1897, reprinted by Bell Publishing Co., New York, 1967, page 312.

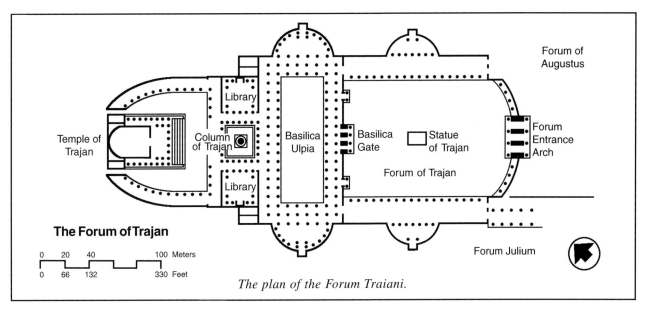

The Forum of Trajan

0   20   40   100 Meters
0   66   132   330 Feet

The plan of the Forum Traiani.

Hadrian completed the Forum of Trajan and built the temple, surrounded by porticoes at the north end of the complex, dedicated to Trajan and the empress Plotina. It was a Corinthian octastyle structure, and was noted for its colossal proportions. The columns were six feet (1.8 m) in diameter and the capitals alone were six feet (1.8 m) high. When finished, the Forum of Trajan was a marvellous sight that impressed Romans and foreigners alike. The Roman his-torian Ammianus Marcellinus (*Roman History,* xvi. 10) reported that the emperor Constantius II, visiting Rome, was very impressed by the Forum of Trajan. When he saw the equestrian statue of Trajan, he said to his hosts that he would make one like it for himself in Constantinople. A Persian prince in his entourage quipped that he must first provide a splendid stable like the Forum for his horse. This famous equestrian statue has disappeared, but can be seen on coins struck by Trajan in A.D. 112-114, RIC 291.

The triumphal arch of Trajan's Forum was an impressive feature that created a formal gateway to the very large court space inside. This arch is often identified as a building in numismatic reference books, but the form of the structure and the statuary on the top clearly indicate that it was a triumphal arch, probably commemorating Trajan's victories in Dacia. This elaborate arch gateway is shown on gold and silver coins struck by Trajan in A.D. 112-114. The legend FORVM TRAIAN on the coin identifies it as a part of the Forum complex. See RIC 255.

Complimenting this coin is another fine aureus,

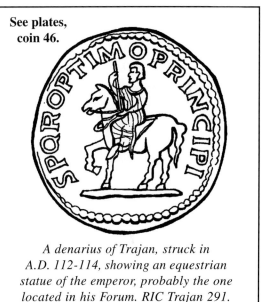

See plates, coin 46.

A denarius of Trajan, struck in A.D. 112-114, showing an equestrian statue of the emperor, probably the one located in his Forum. RIC Trajan 291.

See plates, coin 47.

An aureus of Trajan struck in A.D. 112-114 showing the triumphal arch gateway to the Forum of Trajan. RIC Trajan 255.

110

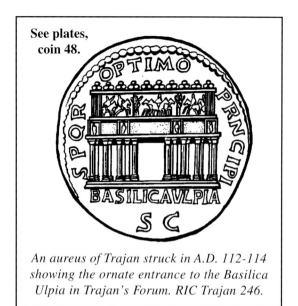

See plates, coin 48.

An aureus of Trajan struck in A.D. 112-114 showing the ornate entrance to the Basilica Ulpia in Trajan's Forum. RIC Trajan 246.

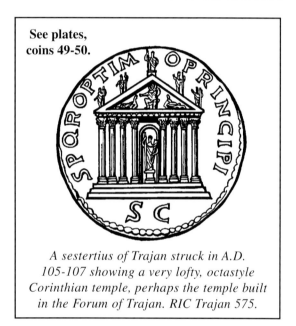

See plates, coins 49-50.

A sestertius of Trajan struck in A.D. 105-107 showing a very lofty, octastyle Corinthian temple, perhaps the temple built in the Forum of Trajan. RIC Trajan 575.

struck at about the same time, which shows the entrance to the Basilica Ulpia. See RIC 246. The basilica was a civic building used for official events and as a court of law. The structure was two storeys high, with a floor plan that measured 260 feet (80 m) long by 178 feet (54 m) wide. It was flanked by a colonnade with a double line of columns, 96 in all. Trajan's clan, originally from Spain, was called Ulpia, he being named Marcus Ulpius Traianus, and the basilica was given his family name. The building also contained two large hemicycle structures that contained statues or the busts of famous Romans in niches. The friezes over the doors of the basilica were engraved with the names of the legions that had fought in the two Dacian campaigns.

According to the *Augustan History*, the temple in the Forum, dedicated to Trajan and his wife Plotina, was built by Hadrian after Trajan's death.[2] The structure was monumental in size, and was surrounded by a precinct and two porticoes. The plan measured approximately 198 feet (60 m) long by 132 feet (40 m) wide, and the building was very lofty, perhaps with columns 60 feet (18 m) high. The temple sat directly behind the famous column erected to celebrate Trajan's victories over the Dacians, on the long axis of the symmetrical plan of the Forum. Unfortunately, Hadrian never commemorated this temple on any of his coins. However, an unusual, lofty, octastyle Corinthian temple does appear on the coins of Trajan struck in A.D. 105-107. See RIC 575. This temple is depicted on the coins as being very high and with very tall Corinthian capitals. Philip Hill, in his work, identified this temple as an edifice dedicated to the deity Honos, but this attribution was based solely on the fact that the central cult figure holds a scepter and a cornucopia.[3] Honos is shown with these same attributes on coinage of Galba, Vitellius, and Vespasian (RIC Galba 474, Vitellius 113, Vespasian 423). However, this is slender evidence for a conclusive identification of the temple, and another theory may be considered. Perhaps Trajan began his own temple in the Forum, intending to dedicate it to his wife Plotina, and he commemorated the temple on his coinage in 105-107 while it was still in the planning stages.[4] Pre-construction dedication was a common propaganda practice for large imperial building projects. The statue on the coin could be Plotina, or even the emperor himself, holding an imperial scepter and a cornucopia to indicate his generosity to the people. If this was so, then after Trajan died, Hadrian, as the act of a grateful succeeding emperor, completed the temple and dedicated it to his predecessor. Therefore, Hadrian did not commemorate this temple on his own coinage

2 *Lives of the Later Caesars, the Augustan History*, Hadrian 19.1, translated by Anthony Birley, Penguin Classics, London, 1976, page 78.
3 *The Monuments of Ancient Rome as Coin Types*, by Philip V. Hill, Seaby, London, 1989, page 9.
4 This theory is well explained in "Das Traiansforum in Rom", by Paul Zanker, in *Archaeologischer Anzeiger*, 1970, page 499.

because he did not actually build it.

Whether completed by Trajan or Hadrian, the Forum Traiani was a major group of structures that became a magnificent civic center. This complex of buildings fully reflected the grandeur of the Roman empire at its highest point in history, and such a large scale development of buildings would never again be attempted in Rome.

One monument in Trajan's Forum deserves special attention. The Column of Trajan, completed

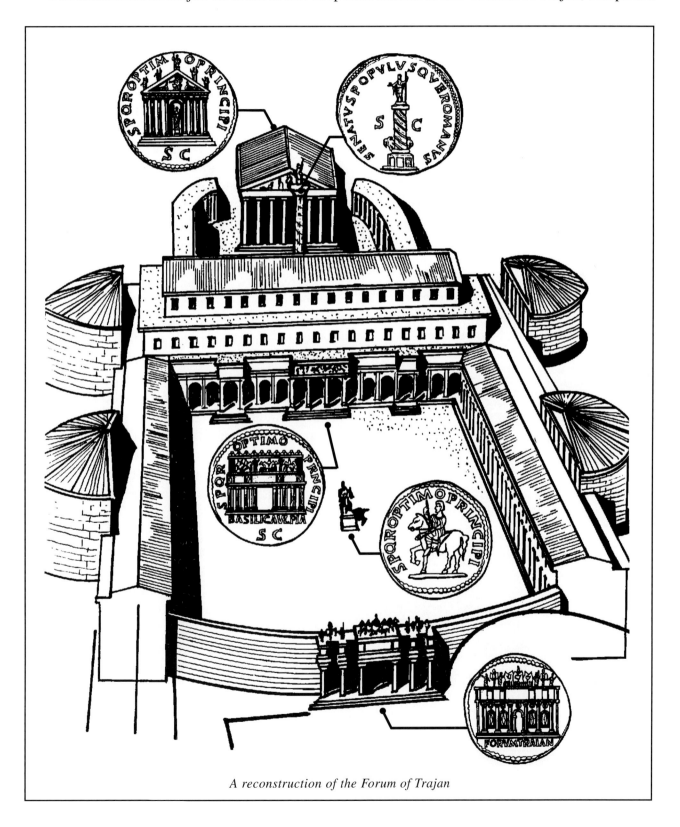

A reconstruction of the Forum of Trajan

around A.D. 113, is one of the greatest works of Roman art, and a unique, outstanding document of ancient military history. It has recently been restored and, still standing on its original site, can be examined and admired by thousands of tourists. The Column is over 12 feet (3.6 m) in diameter and about 128 feet (39 m) high. It was originally surmounted by a bronze statue of the emperor Trajan, the "Optimus Princeps," "the best first citizen" (ruler or prince), who reigned over the Roman empire at the height of its power, A.D. 98-117. This statue portrayed Trajan holding the imperial attributes, a scepter and a globe. In 1588, Pope Sixtus V replaced the statue of Trajan on top of the Column with one of Saint Peter.

It was believed that the ashes of Trajan himself were buried in a golden urn under the pedestal, but the monument was completed in A.D. 113, four years before Trajan's death, and as archaeologists could find no trace of an underground crypt, the burial cannot be confirmed. The myth about the buried ashes was derived from a statement made by the Roman historian Dio Cassius, A.D. 155-230, in his work *History of Rome,* Book LXIX. ii. 3, but this was written more than 100 years after the death of Trajan, and was based on a popular folk tale. The designer and master builder of the Column was Apollodorus of Damascus, Trajan's famous chief architect, artist, and engineer. He was also responsible for the design of the bridge over the Danube built in Dacia (modern Romania), the Forum, Baths, Basilica, and Ports of Trajan, as well as many other buildings. In his writings, Dio Cassius described the horrible fate that befell this talented architect. During the reign of Hadrian, A.D. 117-138, Apollodorus was asked to comment on the design of the proposed, large temple to Venus and Roma. The emperor was a self taught architect and had designed this vast building by himself. Tactlessly, Apollodorus judged the design in a very critical manner, using harsh words that ridiculed the emperor. In anger, Hadrian banished Apollodorus from Rome, and later supposedly had him executed.[5]

The Column was constructed of 34 solid blocks of Carrara, white marble. The pedestal and base were made from nine blocks, the

A reconstruction of the Column of Trajan.

---

[5] *Roman History*, by Dio Cassius, LXIX. iv.1.

column shaft from 23, and the top capital and statue base were made from an additional two blocks. The horizontal joints between the stones are accurately fitted, and are cleverly hidden in the sculptured reliefs. Some scholars believe that the scenes were carved in one piece after the entire Column was erected. Others contend that the drums were sculpted in groups on the ground, then raised up to make the shaft. The blocks were actually cut out as hollow drums, with an interior, circular staircase of 185 steps. Forty-three small windows give light to this interior. Similar to the joints, the windows are worked into the compositions of the sculpted scenes so as not to interfere with the major parts of the artwork. The carving is done as a helical or spiral band, making 23 turns, for an actual length of 656 feet (198 m) from the top to the bottom of the Column. The sculpted frieze records the two Dacian campaigns of Trajan, A.D. 101-3 and 104-6, culminating in the climax of a final scene at the top. The carvings consist of more than 2,500 figures in 155 scenes, and the emperor himself appears over fifty times.

The sculpture is of the highest artistic quality, skillfully executed and showing marvellous detail. It was originally gilded and painted in polychrome colours, some traces of which were recorded by historians as late as 1833. The scenes on the Column have been well illustrated in many documents on ancient art, sculpture, and military tactics, and the best photographs of the sculptural panels were made in 1942 by P. Romanelli and published in his book *La Colonna Traiana*. Remarkably, the sculptures are fluid, natural looking, and animated, capturing the actions of the soldiers in a realistic manner.

The detailed scenes on the Column have taught us more about the Roman army and its maneuvers on campaigns than any other existing historical document. Much of the equipment and many of the tactics of the army are fully illustrated, as would be proper for a monument dedicated to a famous soldier/emperor. Clearly and accurately shown are pontoon bridges set up across rivers, battle formations, soldiers' weapons, fortifications, and siege machines. The military equipment depicted on the Column includes a strange mechanism mounted on the wall of a Dacian fortified city which has puzzled scholars for many years. Many historians believe it to be a battering ram attached to the wall by the Roman besiegers. Others claim

The mysterious war machine depicted on the Column of Trajan.

that it is a type of "man trap" which dropped down to ensnare the attacking soldiers.[6] Some have even suggested that it is a signalling apparatus, like a railroad "wig-wag" semaphore, for relaying messages to other fortresses nearby.

In light of our recent knowledge of Roman military machines and of similar ancient devices, it

---

6 *Trajan's Army on Trajan's Column*, by Sir Ian Richmond, The British School at Rome, 1982, page 42.

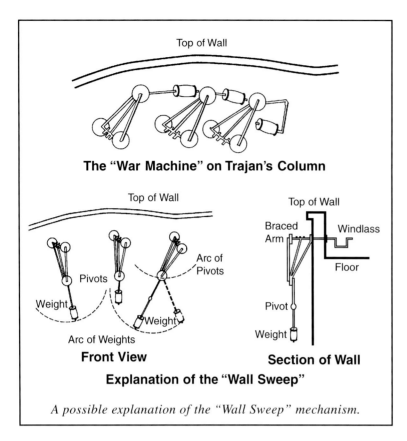

The "War Machine" on Trajan's Column

Front View

Section of Wall

Explanation of the "Wall Sweep"

A possible explanation of the "Wall Sweep" mechanism.

may be suggested that the machine was in fact a pendulum type of wall sweep, operated from within the fort by a windlass, which "swept" the wall in order to dislodge climbing soldiers or scaling ladders. Used in groups of three, as shown in the sculpture on the Column, the sweeps would cover a large area of wall, and exert enough force to upset heavy climbing structures and even siege towers that were erected against the wall.

Among his many talents, Apollodorus, the architect of the Column, was a military engineer who devised war machines and instruments of defense. Parts of his written work on making war mechanisms, titled *Poliorcetica,* exist today.[7] However, the wall sweep machine appears to be too sophisticated and complicated a device to find on a Dacian fortress. It looks almost modern in its details and construction. Perhaps Apollodorus included this machine in his sculpture as a way of advertising his own ingenious, futuristic inventions which had never been built or tested in battle.

The pedestal of the Column was uncovered during the reign of Pope Paul III, 1534-1549, who had the small medieval church of Saint Nicolao de Columna demolished to facilitate the excavation. The church had used the Column as its bell tower. The existence of this early church at the base of Trajan's Column was probably the reason that it had not been defaced by iconoclasts or demolished by stone robbers and lime burners during the dark ages in Rome. An inscription found over the door in the pedestal records that the Column was raised in the TRI. POT. XVII (17th Tribunitia Potestas) of Trajan, or the year A.D. 113. Another part of the inscription states: AD DECLARANDVM QVANTAE ALTITVDINIS MONS ET LOCVS TANT-(is) missing piece (operi)-BVS SIT EGESTVS, usually translated into English as "in order to show how high a mountain had been cleared away." This indicates that the Column was raised to show the height of that part of the Quirinal Hill which had to be removed to make way for Trajan's market building adjacent to the Forum. The Column was so spectacular that it became the model for later, similar monuments such as the Column of Marcus Aurelius located in the Piazza Colonna in Rome. The scenes on the Aurelian Column were made in a similar spiral form, sculpted sometime between A.D. 180-193, to commemorate the emperor's wars with the German tribes. Trajan's Column was also the prototype for the Vendome Column in Paris, built by Napoleon in 1806-10 to commemorate the campaigns of the Grand Army of France.

This spectacular and monumental Column to the victories of Trajan is something of a conundrum to scholars because it raises several perplexing questions. The function and actual construction of the Column and its frieze caused several disputes. Recently, Amanda Claridge, of the

---

[7] *Illustrated Encyclopedia of the Classical World,* by M. Avi Yonah and I. Shatzman, Harper and Row Publishers, New York, 1975, page 50.

British School at Rome, proposed that the Column had been erected as a plain shaft in Trajan's time, and later Hadrian had it carved with the sculptural panels when he re-dedicated the Column after Trajan's death.[8] Her arguments for this theory are forceful, but not convincing. The second nagging question about the Column is: Who was expected to see the small, intricate carvings at the top of the shaft more than 100 feet above the pavement? Even painted and gilded, the detail of the scenes would be unrecognizable at that height. Some historians claim that the Column was meant to be viewed from the upper floors and roof of the nearby basilica and the library buildings, but this explanation is inadequate. The answer may simply be that the scenes depicted on the Column were not meant for mortal eyes.[9] As the archaeologist and author Mortimer Wheeler says about Trajan's Column, "It is history scribed around the presence of one great man—the apotheosis of the individual."[10] Also, Pliny the Elder clearly states that the Romans set statues of famous Romans on columns to elevate them above all mortals.[11] Following this line of reasoning, the Column may be seen as an instrument used in the process of the deification of the emperor, and that the scenes portrayed were a record of his great achievements for the other gods to admire and judge.

This great monument to Trajan is depicted on all the denominations of coins struck in Rome. The engravings on the coins show much detail, including the spiral band, the statue on top, the windows, and the pedestal with its doors. In many cases, eagles are also shown adorning the base of the Column, and these can still be seen today. The legend on most of the coin reverses is some form of SENATVS POPVLVSQVE ROMANVS. SC., which means "The Senate and the People of Rome (erected this column). By the Authority of the Senate." Another common, abbreviated legend is SPQR OPTIMO PRIN-CIPI SC, which is usually translated as "The Senate and the People of Rome (erected this column) for The Best of Rulers. By the Authority of the Senate." The Column of Trajan appears on the following coins: aurei, RIC Trajan 235, 292; denarii, RIC 238, 239, 292, 307, 313, 356; sestertii, RIC 579, 580, 600-602, 677-80, 683; dupondii, RIC 603; and Asses, RIC 60.

Other than the architect Apollodorus, we know nothing about the talented artists who actually carved the magnificent sculptures on the Column of

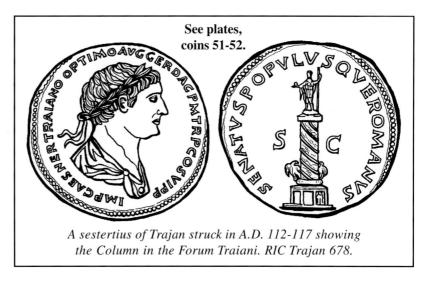

See plates, coins 51-52.

A sestertius of Trajan struck in A.D. 112-117 showing the Column in the Forum Traiani. RIC Trajan 678.

Trajan. Were they foreign slaves or freedmen? Where did they get training in their craft? Did they sculpt other monuments in Rome? Unfortunately, as far as history is concerned, they remain forever anonymous. However, one of the artists surreptitiously carved his Greek name, *Orestes*, into the marble on one of the higher panels of the Column.[12] Orestes must have realized that he was creating an exceptional and ageless work of art, and undoubtedly he wanted his name to be associated with this masterpiece for as long as it existed.[13]

---

[8] "Hadrian's Column of Trajan," by Amanda Claridge, in the *Journal of Roman Archaeology*, Vol. 6, 1993, page 5.

[9] *Visual Narratives, Storytelling in Etruscan and Roman Art,* by Richard Brilliant, Cornell University Press, Ithaca, 1984, page 101.

[10] *Roman Art and Architecture*, by Mortimer Wheeler, Praeger World of Art Series, Praeger Publishers, New York, 1969, page 178.

[11] *Natural History*, by Pliny, Book XXXIV 12, 27, translated by D.E. Eichholz, Harvard University Press, Cambridge, 1962.

[12] *Roman Art and Architecture*, as above, page 9.

[13] One of the best books on the Column of Trajan, complete with the earliest photographs made by Cichorius from casts of the reliefs, is *Trajan's Column,* by Frank Lepper and Sheppard Frere, Allan Sutton Publisher, Gloucester, UK, 1988.

Chapter 17

The Circus Maximus

The Circus Maximus in Rome was a famous hippodrome, and one of the largest architectural monuments of ancient times. If historians ever decide to record the architectural marvels of the Roman empire in a catalog similar to the Hellenistic "Seven Wonders of the World", the Circus Maximus would occupy first place on the list. Today, only the bare site of this enormous structure remains as an open park in the center of Rome. The stones of the stadium's arches, walls, and seats, which would have reached a length of 40 miles (64 km) if placed end to end, were used to build the many churches, palaces, and fortifications of medieval Rome.

The Circus Maximus is believed to have been the oldest stadium in Rome, dating to perhaps 600 B.C., but according to the Roman historian Livy, the permanent starting gates for the chariot races were constructed only in 329 B.C. By tradition, the Circus was established by the fifth Etruscan king of Rome, Tarquinius Priscus, 616-579 B.C., who also laid the foundations for the Capitol and built the famous main sewer of Rome, the Cloaca Maxima. The Circus was located in the shallow valley between the Palatine and the Aventine hills, a natural amphitheater which could accommodate a large number of people. In ancient days an oval racecourse was marked out in the valley, and spectators sat on the edges of the hills. Over the years, wooden seats and then stone benches and arcades were added, to make it into one of the largest and finest architectural monuments in the city. By the first century A.D., the Circus had reached its fullest stage of development. It was over 2,000 feet (600 m) long by 495 feet (150 m) wide, and had a 700 foot (212 m) long, low barrier dividing strip, called a "spina" or spine, running down the center. On this spine were several statues, monuments, columns of Victory, and shrines to the goddesses Consus, Cybele, and Pollentia. These were minor grain deities who also favored or patronized sporting events. At the ends of the spina were a group of three round pillars, used as the turning posts or goals. These were called the *metae* by Romans because they resembled the conical, lower grindstone, a "meta" in Latin, of a flour mill. The metae were 17 feet (5 m) high, and were gilded to reflect the sunlight and to increase their visibility. The glare of the reflected light also excited or scared the horses at the turns. This group of three conical posts, the metae, became the principal graphic symbol used in art work to represent the Circus.

One end of the arena was curved in a full arc, and functioned as the turning radius of the racecourse. The other end was slightly curved, and contained the starting gates, called *carceres*, literally prisons, because they resembled jail cells. The slight curve at the starting gates was meant to compensate for the difference in length of the racetrack between the inside and the outside post positions on the turns. The fully curved end had a triumphal gate through which the winner of the race left the stadium. A smaller triumphal gate was also located at the starting gate end, and through this portal triumphal processions entered the arena. Also at the starting gates were two towers, one on each side of the stadium, with porticoes for musicians. The arena itself was a sand field, and the English word arena actually comes from the Latin for sand, *harena*. The sand was placed on the course to protect the feet of the unshod horses, and to soak up the blood of slaughtered animals and gladiators.

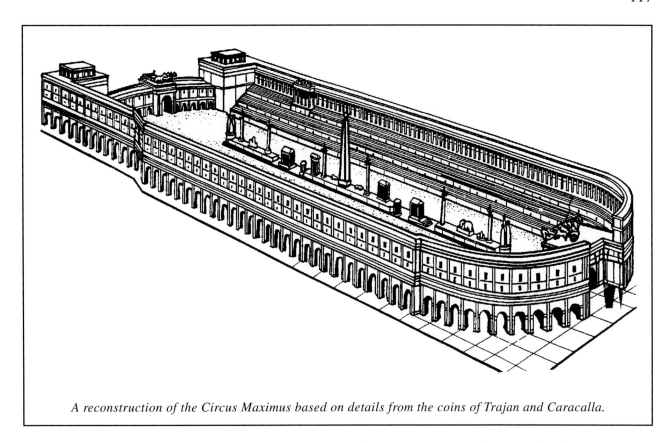

A reconstruction of the Circus Maximus based on details from the coins of Trajan and Caracalla.

At the beginning of the reign of Augustus, the Circus was reported to seat 60,000 spectators. Over the years many emperors enlarged the stadium, and by the time of Constantius II, A.D. 337-361, it could seat more than 200,000. To satisfy the hunger of such large numbers of sports fans, the lower arcades of the stadium were filled with food shops, bars, and taverns selling wine, sausages, chick peas, spiced lentils, and other delicacies that would be equivalent to our own modern ball-park beer, soda pop, hotdogs, peanuts, and popcorn.

A chariot race, called a *missus* in Latin, consisted of seven laps of the course. The laps were marked or recorded for the spectators by seven dolphins and seven eggs mounted on platforms on the spina. The dolphin was the symbol of Neptune, and the egg of the Dioscuri, the two Roman divinities who protected horses. One dolphin and one egg were removed from the display racks to indicate the end of a lap. Usually only eight chariots competed, but after the reign of Domitian, A.D. 96, as many as 12 could be entered in a race. The types of chariots used were *bigas* with two horses, *trigas* of three horses, or *quadrigas* with four horses, and later a spectacular six-horse vehicle was introduced into the Circus. Speed in the race was never the main objective. The real pleasure of the races for the Roman spectator was the danger of the turns, where many accidents occurred. A crashed chariot was called a "shipwreck", and it caused great excitement among the spectators. Just to finish a race in one piece was a victory for the charioteers.

The Latin word *circus* means a ring, and today the word has come to mean performances given in a ring-shaped or circular arena. The Circus Maximus was primarily a racecourse, but many other events took place there. The *Ludi Circeneses,* or public circus games, were held in this stadium. These consisted of several different contests, such as gladiatorial combats, foot races, wrestling, and boxing matches. Special events were also held, such as the performances of the *desultores,* men who rode two horses at a gallop and jumped back and forth from one to the other. Also performed in the Circus was a spectacle called a *venatio*, a hunt in which men stalked or fought against wild animals. On certain occasions, massive hunts were held in which exotic animals such as bears, hippopotami, lions, panthers, and elephants were hunted down and slaughtered. Augustus even created a lake in the Circus Maximus, and imported Egyptian crocodiles to be attacked from boats. This event was a great delight to the bloodthirsty spectators, especially when the crocodiles caught the hunters.

Over the centuries, many emperors renovated the Circus and added arcades, triumphal arches, trophies, and statues. Augustus placed the 78 foot (23.5 m) high obelisk of Rameses II, 1292-1225 B.C., in the center of the spina. This stone "needle" was brought to Rome from Heliopolis, Egypt, in 10 B.C., and was moved by Pope Sixtus V in 1589 to the Piazza del Popolo, where it stands today. The obelisk was so impressive that having one in the center of the spina became mandatory for all future circuses, and these distinctive monuments, along with the metae, were often used on coins as symbols to identify a building as a circus. Tiberius and Nero placed statues on the Circus structure, and the Flavian emperors added triumphal arches to the entrances of the arena. Later emperors continued to embellish the Circus as part of their public works program. In A.D. 357 Constantius II erected a second, taller obelisk, 108 feet (32.7 m) high, in the Circus Maximus. This was a monument made in Thebes for the Egyptian pharaohs Thothmeses II and IV in 1492 B.C. After the fall of Rome, it was broken into three pieces, and lay buried in the Circus area for centuries. It was discovered in 1590 and re-erected in the Lateran Square, where it stands today.

The Circus Maximus was the first and largest, but not the only hippodrome in Rome. In 221 B.C. the censor C. Flaminius built a second circus for public use. This was called the Circus Flaminius, and it was located in the southern part of the Campus Martius. It was 989 feet (300 m) long by 400 feet (120 m) wide, only one-half the size of the Circus Maximus. Its general location is known, but except for some isolated fragments of walls it has disappeared. The third circus built in Rome was started by Caligula and completed by Nero, A.D. 54-68. It was located on the site where St. Peter's Cathedral now stands, but we know little about it except that it was the smallest circus in the city. This stadium was supposedly the setting for the martyrdom of the Christians who were blamed for the Neronian fire that destroyed a large part of Rome in A.D. 64. Also, it is believed that Saint Peter was crucified in this arena. Naturally, this stadium also had the obligatory Egyptian obelisk erected on its spina. This monument was brought from Egypt by the emperor Caligula in a specially built, large ship which was later sunk by Claudius in the port of Ostia to support the lighthouse. The obelisk of Caligula's circus is 84 feet (25.5 m) high, and now stands in the nearby St. Peter's Square.

A fourth circus built in Rome was the Circus of Domitian. This stadium is believed not to have specialized in chariot races because it lacked a spina and permanent starting gates. It was built in A.D. 86 for the Capitoline Games, and historians estimate that it could seat 30,000 spectators. Domitian's stadium was approximately 1,400 feet (424 m) long by 400 feet (121 m) wide, and its stone walls now serve as the foundation for the buildings around the Piazza Navona, which preserves the arena's oval outline and shape. The obelisk presently in the Piazza Navona was not originally erected in Domitian's Circus. This Egyptian needle stood in the private circus of Domitian at his Alban villa, was later relocated to the Circus of Maxentius in A.D. 309, and was moved to the modern Piazza Navona in 1649.

The fifth circus in Rome was the Circus Varianus near the Amphitheatrum Castrense, a theater used by the Praetorian Guards, whose permanent camp was located nearby. This new stadium was built sometime in A.D. 219-22 on the large land holdings and gardens of the Varian clan, the family of the emperor Elagabalus (Heliogabalus). Excavations of this area in 1570 uncovered an obelisk broken into three parts. At first this was believed to be an Egyptian needle placed on the spina of the stadium, but it is now known to be a Roman imitation obelisk made in the time of Hadrian to memorialize his companion Antinous (Antinoos), who drowned in the Nile. This obelisk had been erected at a monument or cenotaph, which had been built earlier, near the location of the Circus

Varianus. Hadrian's obelisk was re-erected in the garden on the Pincian Hill, where it can be seen today. The foundations of the Circus of Varianus completely disappeared into the later city walls erected by Aurelian, and under an extension of the Acqua Felice aqueduct built in 1585. The size of this Circus was determined to have been about 1,865 feet (565 m) long and 412 feet (125 m) wide.[1]

There were three more circuses devoted to chariot racing located just outside Rome. About five miles away from the city, on the Via Portuensis, stood the private circus of the Arval brothers. Three miles away from Rome on the Appian Way was the Circus of Maxentius, built about A.D. 309, which seated 23,000 people. The remains of this stadium are well preserved and can be seen today. It was 1,730 feet (524 m) long by 360 feet (109 m) wide, and contained the obelisk from Domitian's villa in Albano, which is now located in the Piazza Navona. The most distant circus was 12 miles (19 km) away from the walls of Rome, in the ancient town of Bovillae. This stadium was quite small, and reportedly held only 8,000 spectators. By the 4th century A.D., chariot racing and other games could be performed in eight circuses, five of these inside the boundaries of the city. The expression *panem et circenses*, literally "bread and circuses," was first coined by the Roman satirist Juvenal, A.D. 60-127, who said that "having conquered the world, the Romans now cared

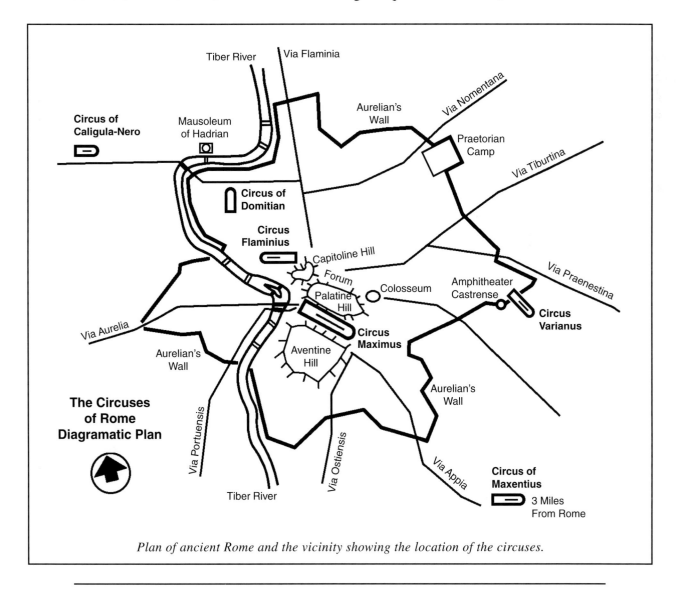

Plan of ancient Rome and the vicinity showing the location of the circuses.

[1] *A Pictorial Dictionary of Ancient Rome,* Vol I, by E. Nash, London, 1961, page 241.

120

for nothing except the free dole of bread and free games at the Circus." Juvenal spoke the truth; it is reported that the Circus Maximus, by itself, was open for games and events 240 days of the year.[2]

The structure of the Circus Maximus suffered from the many natural and man-made disasters that occurred in Rome. It was largely destroyed by fire in 31 B.C. and restored by Augustus. Another fire on the Aventine Hill in A.D. 36 caused great damage to the seating, and this was repaired by Tiberius. The great fire of Nero in A.D. 64 consumed a major area of the stadium on the Palatine Hill side, and this—along with later fire damage in A.D. 80—was finally repaired by Domitian. A minor catastrophe occurred when some of the structure's arches collapsed in the reign of Trajan, and he undertook a major restoration which was completed in A.D. 103. Trajan commemorated the opening of his reconstructed Circus Maximus by striking one of the most magnificent Roman architectural coin types. Using an oblique type of graphics composition, the coin, RIC 571, gives an overall view of the Circus, showing the enclosure, seating, and the spina complete with the obelisk erected by Augustus.

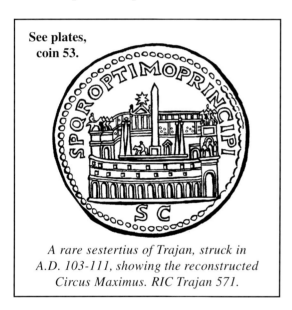

See plates, coin 53.

A rare sestertius of Trajan, struck in A.D. 103-111, showing the reconstructed Circus Maximus. RIC Trajan 571.

See plates, coin 54.

A very rare sestertius of Hadrian struck after DCCCLXXIIII, 874 years from the founding of Rome—A.D. 121, commemorating the "Natalis Urbis" first held in the Circus. RIC Hadrian 609. The same reverse appears on a rare aureus, RIC 144.

Under the emperor Hadrian, A.D. 117-138, the Circus was extensively repaired, and perhaps embellished with more statues and shrines. Also, this emperor introduced some of the exotic games and races which he had witnessed in his travels all over the Roman empire. Later, Hadrian inaugurated a new, formal celebration of the anniversary of the founding of Rome, to be held in the Circus Maximus each year. An older festival perhaps named the *Parilia* had been observed up to that date, but was replaced by Hadrian's more elaborate and important ceremony, which was possibly called the *Natalis Urbis*, the "Birth of the City." To announce and document the institution of this new holiday, Hadrian struck some of the most remarkable coins in the entire Roman Imperial series, RIC 144, 609. These very rare aurei and sestertii are the only coins to record the date of an event by inscribing the year in Roman numerals. The legend on the reverses reads ANN DCCCLXXIIII NAT VRB P CIRC CON. The translation of this legend is still in dispute because of the uncertain meaning of the letter "P" in the inscription, but most authorities believe it is the abbreviation for *Primum*, the Latin word "first."[3] Accepting this interpretation, the full inscription would be read as, ANNO 874 NATALIS VRBIS PRIMVM CIRCENSES CONSTITVTI—that is—"In the 874th year, for the anniversary of the city (of Rome) for the first time, games were held in the Circus." The coin

---

[2] *Rome of the Caesars,* by Leonardo B. Dal Maso, Bonechi, Rome 1979, page 84.
[3] See *Coins of the Roman Empire in the British Museum,* Vol II, by Harold Mattingly, London, 1966, page cxxxii.

shows a reclining male figure, thought to be the Genius of the Circus, holding a wheel and with one of the metae—which some numismatists iden-tify as three obelisks—behind him.

During the reign of Antoninus Pius, A.D. 138-161, a section of the wooden seats in the Circus collapsed, and these were replaced by stone ar-cades and benches. The emperor Septimius Sev-erus, A.D. 193-211, may have also continued the renovation of the Circus or introduced new games and festivals into the arena. He certainly held games in the other circuses of Rome because he struck an impressive aureus which showed an oblique graphical overview of the stadium built by the emperor Domitian, A.D. 81-96. The small size of the coin did not permit much of the architectural detail to be engraved, but the form of the structure, with one curved end, and the contestants wrestling, boxing, and running in the arena clearly identify it as a circus. These athletic events are believed to be the anniversary games held by Severus and his son, Caracalla, in 206 B.C.[4]

Caracalla, the son of Septimius Severus, en-larged the seating capacity and embellished the Circus in A.D. 213. This was a major renovation, and Caracalla commemorated his work by striking some exceedingly rare aurei and sestertii, dated A.D. 212-213 (COS IIII), which showed the entire Circus with the spina, metae, and an obelisk in the center, RIC 211B. Caracalla's engravers obvious-ly copied this design from the earlier reverse of Trajan's Circus sestertius of A.D.103-111. The form of the buildings and many of the architect-ural details are almost the same as those shown on the coins of Trajan, but are less skillfully engraved.

The Circus was used for ceremonial games and exhibitions as well as for chariot races, and many special bronze medals, called *contorniates* by modern numismatists, were struck to be given as prizes to contestants or as gifts to the spectators. These contorniates were large, coin-like medallions with raised rims and incised circular grooves around their circumferences. They were engraved in the highest artistic style of the times and by the best craftsmen. Most of these Circus contorniates were made sometime in the 4th and 5th century A.D., and several of these medals depict the Circus building almost exactly as shown on the earlier sestertii of Trajan and Caracalla. However, many of them show chariot racing scenes or other important events related to the Circus and the history of Rome.

The most magnificent example of a contorniate

See plates, coin 55.

A very rare aureus of Septimius Severus struck in A.D. 202-210 (COS III) showing the Stadium of Domitian and the anniversary games taking place in the arena. RIC Septimius Severus 260.

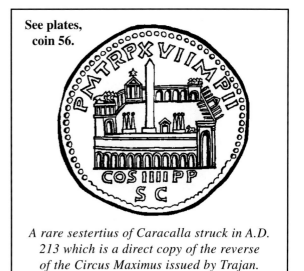

See plates, coin 56.

A rare sestertius of Caracalla struck in A.D. 213 which is a direct copy of the reverse of the Circus Maximus issued by Trajan. RIC Caracalla 500. He also struck an aureus with a similar reverse, RIC 211B.

---

[4] For further information on this coin and the games it commemorates, see the article by Ben Damsky, "The Stadium Aureus of Septimius Severus", *American Journal of Numismatics* 2 (1990), pages 77-105.

122

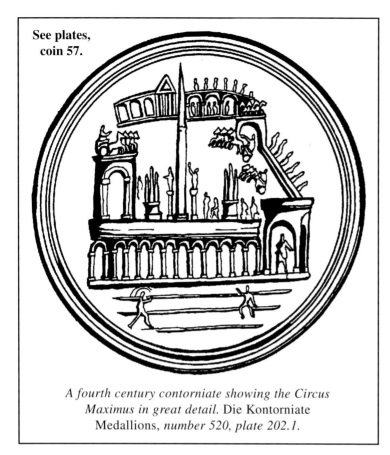

See plates, coin 57.

A fourth century contorniate showing the Circus Maximus in great detail. Die Kontorniate Medallions, *number 520, plate 202.1.*

See plates, coin 58.

A contorniate medallion struck in the 4th-5th century A.D. for the deified emperor Trajan. It shows a spectacular chariot race with four chariots, one a shipwreck, in the Circus Maximus. Cohen, Contorniates, Vol. VIII, no. 255.

portraying the Circus is one struck in the late 4th century A.D. It shows the stadium in great detail, including the arched front, the triumphal arches at each end, the spina complete with metae and obelisk, and a chariot race taking place in the arena. A modified one-point, aerial perspective is used to render the composition. Two athletes perform in the foreground with the view of the Circus as a background. The obverse of this medallion depicts a diademed emperor on horseback hunting down a lion, perhaps in celebration of a great venatio that may have taken place in the Circus at that time.

Another outstanding example of a contorniate showing the Circus Maximus is dedicated to DIVO NERVAE TRAIANO, the deified Trajan, but was struck long after his reign, probably in the 4th century. This medal depicts a racing scene in the Circus with four quadrigas, one of which is wrecked and with the horses falling to the ground. Also prominently shown is the central spina, complete with the obelisk, statues, and the metae. The composition is done with great panache, using a typical Roman engraver's technique of placing rear chariots above the buildings in the front to make a perspective. This medal displays a great action scene, and may have been a part of the prizes awarded to the victor of the race.

Many other types of contorniates, used as prizes or gifts distributed in the Circus, depict a chariot race similar to the scene shown on the medallion above, but without the wrecked chariot and fallen horses. Two examples of this reverse are a contorniate of Divus Trajan, Cohen 253, and a medal which portrays the head of Alexander the Great on the obverse,

Cohen 45. These Alexander the Great medallions were presumably fabricated at the same time as the contorniates dedicated to Divus Trajan, because the reverses appear to be struck from similar dies.

A remarkable example of a medallion showing the variety of contests performed in the Circus Maximus is a contorniate dedicated to Gordian III. This medal depicts the emperor in a six-horse chariot, being crowned by Victory while watching several events, including a chariot race, a gladiatorial combat, a foot race, boxing and wrestling matches, and the winning contestants parading around the arena carrying victory palm branches. The obelisk and metae on the spina clearly identify the scene as taking place in the Circus. See Cohen 282.

A bronze medallion struck for Gordian III, A.D. 238-244, showing a whole catalog of games and events which took place in the Circus Maximus. Cohen, Contorniates, 282. Also illustrated in Roman Medallions, page 165.

Other elaborate and dramatic spectacles or exhibitions were performed in the Circus on special holidays. These events, such as the *Pompa Circensis* (Circus Procession), took the form of a parade which opened the public games. This procession was similar to a triumph, and it included mounted and marching soldiers, scenic floats, musicians, athletes, and priests. Also, triumphs for the emperors and generals normally followed a route which entered the Circus Maximus, perhaps circled the spina, and then proceeded to the Forum Romanum and the Capitoline Hill for the climax. A famous performance which probably took place regularly in the Circus Maximus was the *Ludus Trojae*, the Game or Spectacle of Troy. In this performance, young noblemen on horseback executed intricate cavalry maneuvers similar to those performed by the legendary Ascanius and his friends as described in the *Aeneid*, Virgil's national epic poem of the Romans.[5] This elaborate ceremony may have been a part of the "rites of passage" to mark the coming-of-age for the young Roman knights.

Besides games and athletic contests, the Circus Maximus was the theater stage for the re-enactment of the great historical events in Roman history. These would be similar to our modern day "pageants" put on during national holidays. An illustration of such a Roman pageant occurs on a marvellous contorniate of Constantius II, A.D. 337-361. See Cohen 175. This emperor glorified the Circus Maximus by raising the second and tallest obelisk on the spina. The medallion shows the famous "Rape of the Sabine Women," a momentous foundation legend of early Rome that related how the wifeless soldiers of Romulus, the founder of Rome, obtained their mates. The soldiers invited the nearby Sabine tribes to attend a festival in Rome, and during the feast, they treacherously seized and carried off the wives and daughters of their neighbors. This event supposedly took place in the very fields occupied by the early Circus Maximus. The medallion shows a central metae, the symbol of the Circus, surrounded

---

5 *Roman Life,* by Mary Johnston, Scott, Foresman and Co., Chicago, 1957, page 281.

124

A contorniate of Constantius II struck during his reign to commemorate the legendary rape of the Sabine women, which supposedly took place in the area of the Circus Maximus. Cohen, Contorniates, 175.

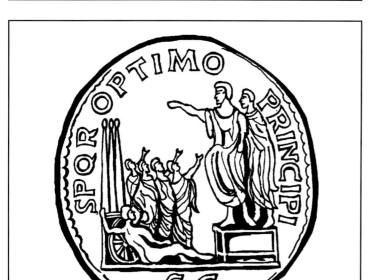

A sestertius of Trajan struck in A.D. 103-111 showing Trajan in the Circus Maximus addressing the citizens of Rome. The Genius of the Circus, with the wheel and metae in the foreground, symbols of the great hippodrome. RIC Trajan 553.

by four soldiers seizing six Sabine women, who plead for mercy with outstretched arms. The legend is simple and clearly evocative, SABINAE. This contorniate may illustrate an annual pageant in the Circus of the famous rape scene, with a cast of thousands of actors or the citizens of Rome re-enacting the event.

The emperor Trajan appears to have celebrated many official, political, or religious events in the Circus during A.D. 103-111. He commemorated these occasions by striking a sestertius which shows him on a platform in the Circus, addressing four Roman citizens who are imploring him or receiving gifts with their hands raised. The Genius of the Circus is shown in the foreground, with the metae and a chariot wheel behind. These events may have involved the official forgiving of debts, declarations of holidays, deification of preceeding emperors, relieving of taxes, or the giving of donativa to the people.

From all these coins and medals we may conclude that the Circus Maximus was more than a sports stadium. It was often the setting or stage for many of the political, religious, and festive events which regulated the daily life of the Roman people. As such, it must have functioned as the major, national focal point of the city, and it served for 1,000 years as a binding chord tying together their past history with the daily lives of the people of Rome.

Chapter 18

The Colosseum

"While stands the Colosseum, Rome shall stand,
When falls the Colosseum, Rome shall fall,
And when Rome falls — the World."

This famous aphorism was first written in Latin sometime before A.D. 730 by a scholarly British monk, the Venerable Bede.[1] He had never seen the Colosseum, but learned about it from pilgrims returning to England. A thousand years later, the poet Lord Byron translated these lines into English, and used them in his poem "Childe Harold." The proverb became famous and was incorporated into the great literature of the Western world. To historians, this poetic saying signified that the Colosseum was a symbol of the greatness of Rome, and that the amphitheater was directly related to its history and fate.

The Colosseum is ranked as one of the best known ancient monumental buildings of all time: everyone recognizes it by name. It appears on Roman coins of the emperors Titus, A.D. 79-81, and Severus Alexander, A.D. 222-235, and on medallions of Gordian III, A.D. 238-244. There is also a cast of a coin of the emperor Domitian, A.D. 81-96, in the British Museum, which has a reverse showing the Colosseum in a similar style to the coin of Titus, but its authenticity is questioned by most numismatists.[2] All these coins are exceedingly rare and are seldom seen outside of museums. The stadium we call the Colosseum was known to ancient Romans as the Flavian Amphitheater. The construction of the building was begun by the emperor Vespasian in A.D. 72 as a part of his plan to reconstruct the central part of Rome, which had burned down before his accession. The site chosen for the new amphitheater was the *stagnum,* or artificial lake created by the emperor Nero, 54-68, as part of his sumptuous palace called the "Golden House." This pool lay between the Caelian and Esquiline Hills in ancient Rome. The site was chosen for practical purposes, the lake's depression became the excavation for the stadium, and for political purposes in that land, appropriated by Nero for his personal use, was returned to the public. The Colosseum was given its popular name sometime in the 8th century, either for its enormous size or from a gigantic statue of Nero, called the Colossus, which was located nearby.

The Colosseum was a marvel of Roman architecture and engineering. It had an elliptical plan 620 feet (188 m) by 513 feet (155 m), and was 157 feet (47.5 m) high. The stadium had 80 archway entrances. It could hold between 45,000 to 50,000 spectators, and these statistics are comparable to the modern day "Astrodome" stadium in Houston, Texas, which is a circular building 710 feet (215 m) in diameter and accommodates 40,000 people. The core structure of the amphitheater was built of brick and concrete, and the exterior of travertine stones held together without mortar, using only metal clamps. The interior was faced with expensive marble and wood. A basement and sub-basement provided spaces for storage rooms, quarters for gladiators and guards, armories, animal cages, stage machinery, and elevators to raise animals up to the arena floor. The Colosseum also

1 *The Colosseum,* by Peter Quennell, Newsweek Book Division, New York, 1971, page 88.
2 *The Monuments of Ancient Rome As Coin Types,* by Philip V. Hill, Seaby Publications, London, England, 1989, page 40.

126

had a moveable canvas roof, called a *velarium* in Latin, which could be unrolled on suspended cables to shade and protect the spectators. Masts mounted on the top of the edifice held the pulleys and ropes used to manipulate the roof. Manpower for moving the awning was provided by squads of sailors recruited from the imperial navy.

Archaeologists discovered that the structure had been divided into four quadrants for easy and rapid construction, and that four different contractors, each building his own quadrant, were employed in the work.[3] This is clearly indicated by the noticeable variations of workmanship and the poorly coordinated construction joints at the quadrants' edges.

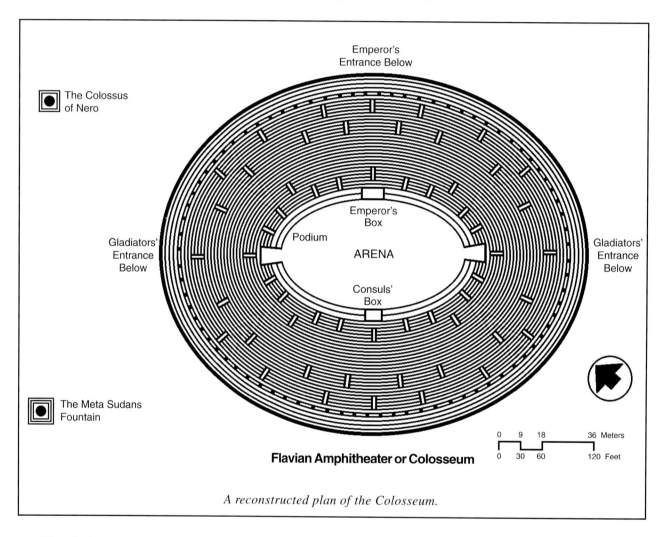

A reconstructed plan of the Colosseum.

The Colosseum's facade was designed by using columns, according to their order, as suggested by the Roman architect Vitruvius.[4] His instructions dictated the placement of the heavy Roman adaption of the Greek Doric columns, called Tuscan, on the building's ground floor, the lighter Ionic columns on the second floor, and the decorative Roman Corinthian columns, used as pilasters, on the upper floors. Large arches were constructed to support the floors and tiers of seats, and a statue was placed in each exterior arch of the facade. Vespasian died in A.D. 79, and his son Titus dedicated the unfinished stadium in the year 80. Games lasting 100 days were held to celebrate the opening of the building. During this event, 5,000 animals were reported to have been slaughtered

---

[3] *The Mute Stones Speak,* by Paul MacKendrick, St. Martin's Press, New York, 1960, page 231.
[4] *De Architectura, The Ten Books on Architecture,* by Vitruvius, translated by M.H. Morgan, Dover Books, New York, 1960, page 102.

A reconstruction drawing of the Colosseum as it may have appeared in the first century A.D.

along with a large number of gladiators.[5] A very rare and famous sestertius was struck under Titus to commemorate the dedication of the amphitheater. See RIC 110. All the details of the structure are correctly shown on the coin, including the statues in the arches and the interior of the stadium full of spectators. The master artist who engraved these dies combined two types of three-dimensional graphics techniques, one-point perspective and isometric, in order to depict the total exterior of the building as well as most of the interior.

Neighboring structures, such as the Meta Sudans fountain on the left, and a temple or the porch of Nero's Golden House on the right, are also shown around the amphitheater to accurately locate the site in the city.

The Colosseum was finally completed during the reign of the emperor Domitian, A.D. 81-96, the

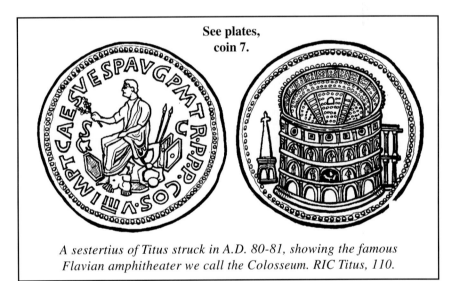

See plates, coin 7.

A sestertius of Titus struck in A.D. 80-81, showing the famous Flavian amphitheater we call the Colosseum. RIC Titus, 110.

A dupondius of Titus struck in A.D. 80-81, showing the Meta Sudans fountain that was located alongside the Colosseum. RIC Titus, 115.

5 "The Colosseum: World's Bloodiest Acre," by J. Bryan III, in *Secrets of the Past,* Berkley/Reader's Digest Books, New York, 1979, page 200.

second son of Vespasian. Domitian paid for many spectacles and gladiatorial combats held during the Colosseum's final dedication in an attempt to exceed the number of events given by his brother Titus. Although doubted by most modern historians, the amphitheater was believed to have been the setting for the martyrdom of thousands of Christians persecuted by the Roman emperors from 110 to 312. However, brutal and bloody spectacles were normal performances in the Colosseum, and the emperor Septimius Severus showed only a faint glimmer of human compassion when he banned women gladiators from combat in the amphitheater in A.D. 200.

The Colosseum was constantly renovated and improved during the second and third centuries A.D. In 217, during the reign of Macrinus, the stadium was struck by lightning and the wooden interior was destroyed by fire. Rebuilding began under Elagabalus in 218, and the stadium was re-opened while still incomplete by Severus Alexander in 223. This emperor struck a series of impressive coins in bronze, gold, and perhaps silver to celebrate the re-dedication of the Colosseum.

A sestertius of Severus Alexander, struck after A.D. 223, showing the Colosseum. The reverse shows the Colosseum with two gladiators fighting in the arena. Severus Alexander is shown with two other figures, probably priests, sacrificing at the left before the Meta Sudans. At the right is a temple facade or perhaps the portico of the "Golden House" palace. RIC Severus Alexander, 410.

An aureus, struck by Severus Alexander in A.D. 223, showing the Colosseum. From the Nelson Bunker Hunt Collection. Illustration drawn from the Sotheby's auction catalog photograph.

See RIC 410. These coins depict the building in exactly the same way and graphic style as did the famous sestertius of Titus. This observation leads to an interesting speculation. The artists who engraved the dies must have closely examined the sestertius struck by Titus in order to duplicate the design so perfectly. Were the sestertii of Titus still in circulation in Rome 150 years after the date they were struck, or did the imperial mint have an archive or a museum of all the coins ever made in the Roman empire so that they could be studied by mint engravers?

Similar bronze Asses were also struck by Severus Alexander showing the same scene, RIC 411. A very rare gold aureus of this emperor, struck in A.D. 223, again shows the Colosseum. This coin was unknown in all major references, but was found in the famous Nelson Bunker Hunt Collection when it was auctioned by Sotheby's in New York on December 4, 1990. On this aureus, the amphitheater is shown with a colonnade or portico which appears to go around behind the building, and this may be a representation of a nearby temple. A denarius of this type exists, and it closely resembles the aureus, but it is considered by most numismatists to be spurious. (RIC Severus Alexander 33)

The emperor Gordian III, A.D. 238-244, completed the extensive restoration of the Colosseum started by Elagabalus and Severus Alexander, and struck some impressive, rare bronze medallions to record this momentous event. These are large, spectacular coins that show marvellous detail, including an elephant and rider fighting a bull in the arena while the emperor watches from his royal box. See Cohen 165.

In A.D. 248 Philip I, who succeeded Gordian III, celebrated the one thousandth anniversary of the founding of Rome with a great festival and the *Ludi Saeculares*, the "Secular Games." These ceremonies featured

A rare bronze medallion of Gordian III struck in A.D. 241-244. The obverse shows the emperor in armor. The reverse depicts the Colosseum with an elephant and rider fighting a bull in the arena. A statue of Fortuna (some say Hercules or Apollo) is shown on the left and a temple on the right. BMC Vol. VI, page 54, and Cohen 165 and 166.

gladiatorial combats and the slaughter of thousands of rare and exotic animals, many of which had been collected by Gordian III to celebrate his triumph over Persia. The various animals can be seen on the reverses of a series of antoniniani struck by Philip I during that year of the millennium of Rome (RIC Philip I, 12-23). In A.D. 250, as if to avenge the cruel killing of all the animals and gladiators, lightning struck the Colosseum, destroying the interior with fire. The emperor Trajan Decius restored the burnt-out stadium in his reign, A.D. 249-251. Finally, in 405, the emperor Honorius abolished all gladiatorial spectacles in the amphitheater, and the stadium fell into disrepair. The Colosseum was once again restored by Theodoric the Great in 523, and in that year the last recorded games were held in the arena.

As time passed, the abandoned stadium began to decay. The structure was damaged by several minor earthquakes recorded in 422, 442, 470, 508, 847, 1255, 1349, and 1703. In medieval and Renaissance times the Colosseum was converted into an impregnable fortress by the feuding aristocratic Roman families. An intense earthquake in 1349 toppled a large portion of the western wall into a hill-sized heap in front of the building. In 1362 Pope Urban V auctioned off this large pile of fallen rubble to building contractors, and the stones were used to construct many of the buildings in Rome, including the Vatican.[6] The beautiful marble wall facings and statues were burnt to make lime for mortar and stucco. The joints in the exterior stonework were cut into by miners to remove the scarce metal clamps that held the structure together, and the thousands of holes made in the joints can be seen today. Now, only a large, imperfect remnant of the original amphitheater remains. In 1744, the Colosseum was dedicated as a shrine to the Christian martyrs who supposedly died in the arena, and the systematic destruction of the building ceased. Some restoration and buttressing or reinforcing of the crumbling structure began in 1815, and continued in a random fashion until 1933, when the Italian dictator Mussolini cleared the area, repaired the building, and cut a new highway, the Via dei Fori Imperiali, around the edifice. This made the Colosseum into a national monument and freed it from the surrounding decrepit buildings, but it also brought tourist buses and automobiles, which produced road vibrations and exhaust fumes. These proved to be just as effective in damaging the building as any of the previous natural

6 *The Ruins and Excavations of Ancient Rome,* by Rodolfo Lanciani, Bell Publishing Co., New York, 1967, reprint of the 1897 edition, page 374.

disasters. In the near future, Mussolini's highway will be removed by the Italian government because the traffic continues to threaten the amphitheater, and it covers a large, important part of the ancient Roman Forum. Hopefully this action will preserve the remains of the Colosseum for at least another millennium.

Chapter 19

The Praetorian Fortress

The only way to describe the Roman "praetorian guards" in modern terms is to say that they were like the presidential bodyguards provided by the United States Treasury Department, the Military Police (MP's), the Central Intelligence Agency (CIA), the Federal Bureau of Investigation (FBI), and the "Green Berets" special service forces all rolled into one. These combined functions made them into a very powerful political and military force that greatly influenced Roman history. The praetorians had their origins in the early Roman Republic, when military leaders surrounded themselves with their trusted friends, who acted as counsellors and protectors. These escorts were not part of the regular army, but formed a retinue for the leader perhaps patterned after Alexander the Great's personal "companions." Later, Roman generals employed bodyguards taken from the regular military forces. This custom was started by Gaius Marius, the great reformer of the Roman army who died in 86 B.C. Sallust, the Roman historian, 86-34 B.C., said that Marius used a personal bodyguard of cavalry made up of the bravest soldiers available.[1] These guards became known as the "cohortes praetoriae" because the generals in those days held the rank of praetor, the highest elected official of the state. The position of consul later superseded the praetor in the Roman political hierarchy.

The early duties of the praetorian guards were to prevent or put down mutinies in the army, as well as to protect their commander. Mark Antony, 82-30 B.C., employed an exceptionally large praetorian guard of 6,000 men. These were organized into twelve cohorts of 500 soldiers each, and Antony issued a Legionary denarius to honor and pay these special units, Syd. 1212. The legend on the coin is COHORTIVM PRAETORIARVM, referring to the praetorian cohorts.

After the defeat of Antony at the battle of Actium in 31 B.C., Octavian established his own praetorian guard, made up of nine co-

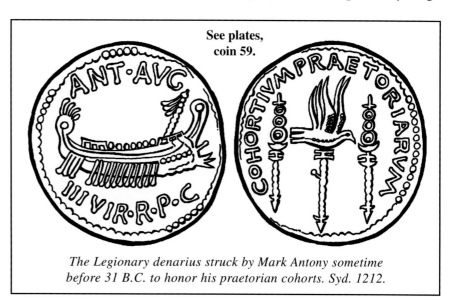

See plates, coin 59.

The Legionary denarius struck by Mark Antony sometime before 31 B.C. to honor his praetorian cohorts. Syd. 1212.

horts of 500 men plus a separate cavalry unit of 90 horsemen. Octavian was prudent enough to limit the influence and power of the guards by not having more than three of their cohorts stationed in Rome, and these were never housed together in any permanent camp or base.[2] The other six cohorts

---

[1] *Bellum Jugurthinumm* 98.1, by Sallust, translated by J.C. Rolfe, Loeb Classical Library, Cambridge, 1921.
[2] *The Twelve Caesars, Augustus 49*, by Suetonius, translated by M. Graves, Allen Lane, London, 1979, page 77.

132

were billeted in the towns around Rome. In deference to the traditional Roman Republican hatred of armed forces operating inside Rome, the praetorians did not wear their uniforms in the city, and performed their bodyguard duties wearing the toga, but with armor and weapons concealed underneath.[3]

From the earliest days, specialized forces called the "speculatores" were formed within the praetorian organization. Soldiers with this same special title had served in the Republican legions long before Antony's and Octavian's time. Ten were appointed to each legion, and they served as mounted messengers, scouts, and spies. In Mark Antony's army, the speculatores were used as intelligence gatherers or inquisitors, and they became numerous enough to form their own cohorts. These speculatores were attached directly to the commander, and were frequently given more sinister duties. They often functioned as undercover agents, guards and torturers of prisoners or hostages, assassins, and the executioners of suspected traitors and political prisoners. Later, under the emperor Trajan, these vile duties were taken over by a group of secret policemen called the "frumentarii." Frumentum is the Latin word for corn or grain, and the title frumentarii was originally given to the secret messengers who worked for the administrators of the national corn supply. The speculatores must have performed a vital function because Antony honored them separately from the praetorians when he struck Legionary denarii with the insignia and name of the speculatores cohorts. The legend on the coin is COHORTIS SPECVLATORVM, and it shows their special ensigns or military standards. See Syd. 1214.

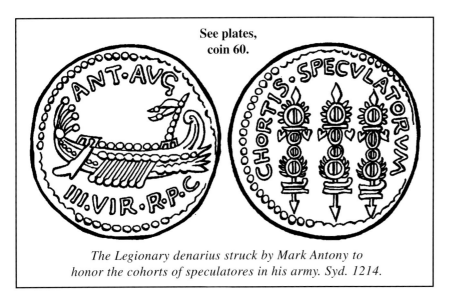

See plates, coin 60.

The Legionary denarius struck by Mark Antony to honor the cohorts of speculatores in his army. Syd. 1214.

Naturally, Roman military leaders made many enemies, both at home and abroad, and they were in constant fear of assassination. Beginning in late Republican times, paranoid commanders of the legions often had more than a single group of bodyguards. Sometimes an inner force of special guards was used to watch over the other units of regular bodyguards, who might become unreliable. The outstanding Roman politician and general Quintus Sertorius, who died in 72 B.C., was the first commander to use Spaniards as his personal, inner guards, and the employment of non-Italians for this important task continued into late imperial times. The imperators believed that foreigners were taller and therefore stronger than Romans, but they also thought that bodyguards who did not speak Latin could not be tainted by politics, and would be more difficult to seduce into betraying their master. Julius Caesar, who was murdered in 44 B.C., had a large personal bodyguard made up of Spaniards, but unwisely disbanded it just before his assassination. Octavian, Julius Caesar's nephew, maintained a Spanish bodyguard as a supplement to his regular praetorian guards, but after Actium, in 31 B.C., he replaced it with a force of Germans because of their traditional and proven fidelity to their masters. The personal bodyguards of Octavian were called the "corporus custodes." They were slaves or freed slaves attached directly to the ruler, and were never part of the regular army. Augustus' praetorians, on the other hand, were Roman citizens, and they made up a formal

---

[3] *The Army of the Caesars,* by Michael Grant, M. Evans and Co. Inc., New York, 1974, page 89.

military guard separate from the German inner circle of protectors. The Germans were stationed inside the imperial palaces, and accompanied the emperor or his relatives wherever they went. The praetorians had wider political duties, and formed the second line of bodyguards for the emperor, his family, and other high ranking officers during their travels and in battle. They also were used to control the large, unruly mobs in Rome, and to put down any insurrections, military or civilian. This important function eventually made them indispensable to the emperors.

During the reign of Augustus, a tribune of senatorial rank commanded each praetorian cohort and reported directly to the imperator. As the praetorians' duties increased, Augustus appointed a prefect as senior officer over the tribunes. These prefects were not senators, but knights who would be more loyal to Augustus than to the senate. Normally, two praetorian prefects were appointed as colleagues in case one became sick or disloyal, but in several instances only one prefect was appointed as commander of the guards. In addition, there was another military body in the city of Rome called the "cohortes urbanae," who functioned as the policemen of the capital. This police force consisted of three cohorts of 1,000 men each, but this number was later raised to 1,500. They often collaborated with the praetorian guard and were a part of the regular army. The city police received double the pay of the ordinary legionaries. The praetorian guards were an elite group, and were paid more than three times the salaries of the regular soldiers plus substantial bonuses.

Under Tiberius, A.D. 14-37, the nine cohorts of praetorians were gathered together in Rome and concentrated into a force of 4,500 men governed by the prefect, Sejanus. To house them, a fort-ified barracks or camp was constructed in A.D. 23 in the northwest area of Rome. This large force of soldiers and the permanent fortress gave the praetorian prefect enhanced powers that often rivalled those of the emperor himself. For example, Nero's praetorian prefects, Burrus and Tigellinus, played a large part in ruling the empire while the emperor indulged himself in the performing arts. The praetorian prefects eventually became so influential that the emperor Vespasian appointed his son and co-emperor Titus to the position, in order to maintain political control over the office. The emperors eventually had to contend with the increasing power and demands of the praetorians either by force or by bribes. Caligula increased the praetorian cohorts to twelve from the nine established by Augustus. Later, Vitellius discharged the entire praetorian guard and recruited a new one of sixteen cohorts. These cohorts were made up of 1,000 soldiers instead of the normal 500, making the force more than twice the normal size. Vespasian cut the praetorians back down to nine cohorts of 500 soldiers, but then Domitian enlarged the guard to 10 cohorts, and this number was maintained until they were finally disbanded 200 years later. Septimius Severus dissolved the troublesome praetorians and recruited a new force from his more trustworthy barbarian tribes, but he doubled the number of soldiers in the 10 new cohorts from 500 to 1,000. At all times in their later history, the praetorians were a substantial group of vocif-erous, murderous, rapacious, and politically active soldiers.

The camp constructed for the praetorians by Tiberius was located on the Viminal Hill, between the Via Tiburtina and the Via Nomentana, just outside the ancient walls that had been supposedly built by the Etruscan king Servius Tullius. It was a fortified city within a city and it dominated Rome. The camp was a rectangular area, 1,465 feet (444 m) wide by 1,265 feet (383 m) deep, planned as a typical Roman army camp, with two main roads, the Via Principalis and the Via Praetoria, intersecting and dividing the area into four quarters. In later times, the western main gate was approached through a triumphal arch apparently dedicated to Gordian III and his empress, Tranquillina.[4] The camp contained its own temples, baths, fountains, hospital, barracks, stables, storehouses, and a prison. The headquarters building, called the Principa, and the commander's villa, called the Praetorium, were located at the intersection of the two main roads. The walls,

---

[4] *The Ruins and Excavations of Ancient Rome,* by R. Lanciani, reprint by Bell Publishing Co., New York, 1967, page 440.

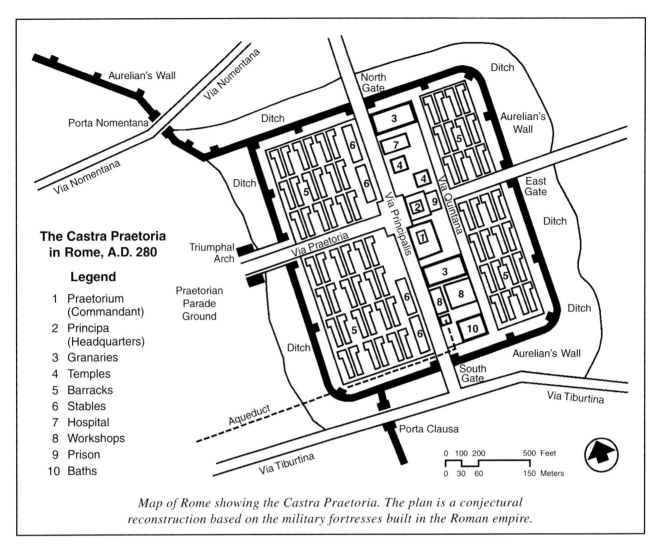

Map of Rome showing the Castra Praetoria. The plan is a conjectural reconstruction based on the military fortresses built in the Roman empire.

almost 16 feet (4.8 m) high, had battlements and towers, and a protective ditch surrounded these ramparts. In A.D. 272, Aurelian built a new wall around Rome, incorporated the walls of the Castra Praetoria into his defensive system, and added another 10 feet (3 m) to their height. The Aurelian wall was completed in A.D. 279 by the emperor Probus to fully protect Rome from barbarian invasions. Some of the remains of the praetorian fortress walls can still be seen in parts of modern Rome.

The Castra Praetoria appears on only a few ancient Roman coins. The best examples are the aurei and denarii struck by Claudius in A.D. 41-42. See RIC 6, 7. These coins show a soldier on guard, holding a spear, inside the camp and standing next to a military standard. The camp walls, gates, and battlements are recorded in great detail by the technique of showing the rear walls above the front facade of the fortress. The legend on the coin, IMPER RECEPT, means the "imperator was received or recognized." Some other coins, struck at the same time as these coins, carry the legend PRAETOR RECEPT, translating as the "praetorians receive or recognize the emperor." These

See plates, coin 61.

A denarius of Claudius, struck in A.D. 41, showing the Castra Praetoria. RIC Claudius, 6. The aureus is similar, RIC 7.

show Claudius clasping hands with a praetorian soldier, who holds a military standard, RIC Claudius 10 and 11.

A second coin type which may show the praetorian camp was struck many years later under the Tetrarchy, that is, the joint rule in A.D. 286 of the two emperors, Diocletian and Maximianus, and the two Caesars, Galerius Constantius I and Galerius. This coin is an argenteus, a silver coin of the weight and fineness of the denarii struck by Nero, introduced by Diocletian to replace the very debased silver coins of the preceding regimes. These are fairly rare coins, although they appear frequently in sale catalogs. The coins show the four tetrarchs sacrificing at a tripod before the main gate of a turreted fortress. We know of several types of this coin with slightly different designs and struck by each of the four rulers. The fortress may be shown with four, six, or eight towers, and its shape closely resembles the Castra Praetoria in Rome. The legends on these coins are usually some form of PROVIDENTIA AVGG, VICTORIA SARMAT, or VIRTVS MILITVM, translated as the "Providence of the two Augusti" (from the two "G"s in AVGG), "Victory over the Sarmatians," and the "Valor of the Military" respectively. The Tetrarchy fortress coins were struck at mints at Treveri in Gaul, Rome and Ticinum in Italy, Siscia in Yugoslavia, Heraclea, Cyzicus, Antiocha, Nicomedia in Turkey, and Alexandria in Egypt. Because this coin type appears to have been struck all over the empire, the building shown in the background is usually identified as an unknown frontier fortress or a turreted enclosure of a military camp. However, some numismatists insist that it represents the Castra Praetoria in Rome, and commemorates the acceptance of the Tetrarchy by the praetorian guard.[5] Perhaps corroborating this theory is the fact that the famous Sisak, Yugoslavia, hoard of argentei, buried in A.D. 296 and found in 1953, contained 529 coins of the Tetrarchy showing this fortress, and 344 of these coins were struck in Rome.[6]

See plates, coin 62.

An argenteus of Constantius I as Caesar under Diocletian, 293-305, struck at Rome in A.D. 294, perhaps showing the Castra Praetoria with six turrets. The legend VICTORIA SARMAT celebrates a victory over the Sarmatians. RIC Vol. VI, page 352, no. 18.

The Castra Praetoria developed into a military citadel in Rome, and it became the fortified "seat of power" for the guards, enabling them to interfere in the political affairs of the nation. After Tiberius retired to the island of Capri and gave the praetorian prefect, Sejanus, power to rule in his name, the praetorians became a governing force and virtually ruled the empire. They soon became emperor-makers and, unfortunately, they were the perfect historical example of that famous maxim—"Power corrupts—Absolute power corrupts absolutely." From that time onward, the atrocious acts of the praetorian guards flowed through the pages of Roman history like a river of blood.

Macro, the prefect who followed Sejanus, assisted in the murder of Tiberius and helped Caligula become the emperor. The praetorians hailed Caligula as the new emperor, but praetorian tribunes ambushed and murdered Caligula, his wife, and baby daughter in A.D. 41. Then the praetorians intimidated the senate and declared Caligula's uncle Claudius the emperor. Claudius paid them a substantial bonus for this service, thereby setting the dangerous precedent of bribing

[5] *The Monuments of Ancient Rome as Coin Types,* by Philip V. Hill, Seaby, London, 1989, page 99.
[6] *The Sisak Hoard of Argentei of the Early Tetrarchy,* by A. Jelocnik, Ljubljana, Yugoslavia, 1961.

the guards whenever new emperors were acclaimed. In 68 the praetorians treacherously abandoned Nero, and he committed suicide rather than be killed by his mutinous soldiers. Galba was betrayed and publicly murdered in the Forum by the praetorians in 68. Domitian was proclaimed emperor in the praetorian camp in 81, and he then mobilized the guards as an elite, special service military force for his wars in Moesia. The emperor even made the praetorian prefect the supreme commander of the army, but in 96, this same ungrateful prefect was instrumental in the murder of Domitian.

Hadrian's succession to Trajan in 117 was facilitated by the praetorian prefect against the wishes of the senate. In 161, the joint emperors Marcus Aurelius and Lucius Verus went humbly to the Castra Praetoria to have their accession sanctioned, and then paid the guardsmen an enormous bonus (donitiva) of 5,000 denarii each. In 192, the praetorian prefect arranged for a professional athlete to strangle Commodus. The praetorians proclaimed Pertinax emperor in 193, then immediately invaded the palace and murdered him for not delivering the bribes he promised. Afterwards, the praetorians sold off the Roman empire by holding an auction between Flavius Sulpicianus and Didius Julianus. Julianus won with a bid of 6,250 denarii for each guardsman, but he was soon deserted by the praetorians and survived for only 66 days. In 212, Caracalla murdered his brother and co-emperor Geta, then placated the offended and disgruntled praetorians by paying them a bonus of 2,500 denarii each. The praetorian prefect, Marcus Oppellus Macrinus, ordered that Caracalla be murdered in Mesopotamia in 217, and had himself declared emperor.

The praetorians were bribed in 222 by Julia Maesa and her daughter Julia Mamaea to murder Elagabalus and declare Severus Alexander emperor. In 238 the praetorians invaded the imperial palace and cruelly tortured to death the two elderly senators, Balbinus and Pupienus, who had been appointed emperors by the senate. The praetorian prefect Philip I had his master, Gordian III, murdered and himself declared emperor by his guardsmen in A.D. 244. Later, the praetorian guard supported the emperor Maxentius, 306-312, and fought against the invading army of Constantine I. When Maxentius was defeated, Constantine abolished the praetorian guard, destroyed their base, demolished the western wall of the fortress, and returned the land of the camp to the Roman people. Finally, in the year A.D. 312, a horrible, 300-year-old nightmare came to an end.

PART IV

ROMAN TEMPLES
ON COINS

Chapter 20

The Capitolium

The paramount temple in Rome was the "Capitolium," the temple on the Capitoline Hill dedicated to the sacred triad of Roman divinities: Jupiter, his daughter Minerva, and his sister and consort Juno. The Capitoline Hill was the ancient citadel in the center of Rome. This acropolis contained two knolls; the southern was called the Arx, and the northern one the Capitol. The lower area, almost a valley between the two prominences, was called the Asylum. The Capitol dominated the nearby Forum Romanum, and was accessible to it by monumental stairways. The three deities of the Capitolium were each served by several other temples in Rome, but the temple on the Capitol was the national religious shrine and the most sacred of them all.

The sanctuary in the Capitolium was divided into three cellae. The central one contained the statue of a seated Jupiter, and the two side chambers housed statues of Minerva on his right and Juno on his left. The original temple was an Etruscan structure started during the reign of the Etruscan kings of Rome. It is recorded that Tarquinius Priscus, 616-579 B.C., had vowed to build a temple to the Etruscan cult of Tinia, Uni, and Menrva on the Capitoline Hill. These three divinities were the equivalent of the Roman Jupiter or Jove, Juno, and Minerva. Apparently,

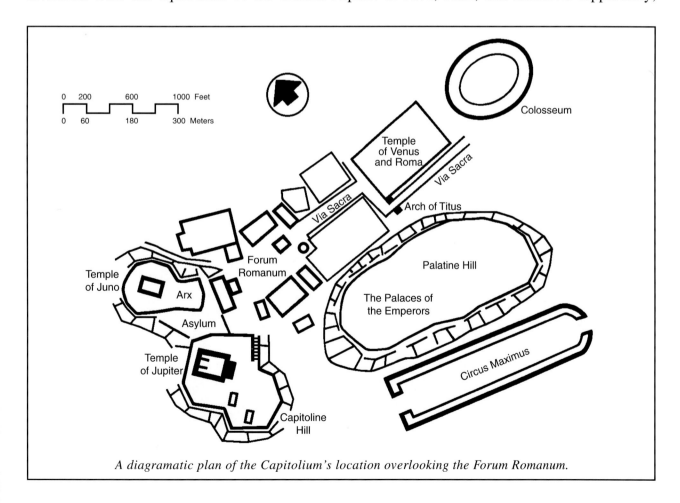

A diagramatic plan of the Capitolium's location overlooking the Forum Romanum.

Tarquinius Priscus only laid the foundations for his temple, and the construction of the superstructure was started and carried almost to completion by Tarquinius Superbus, the last king of Rome.[1] The Romans completed the construction of the temple in the first year of the Republic, 509 B.C., and the structure was consecrated by the consul Marcus Horatius Pulvillus.[2]

The early temple was designed as a typical Etruscan religious building, almost square in plan, made of wood but with stone columns. The front consisted of eight columns which formed a portico or porch. Three doors led into the three separate chambers for the deities, and a famous Etruscan sculptor named Vulca was brought from Veii to make the terracotta statues that adorned the temple's roof line. This temple was probably tetrastyle—that is, with four columns across the front—as were most Etruscan temples. Also, typically Etruscan, the facade was the most important part of the building, and the rear and sides were very plain and unadorned. The three cellae or chambers contained the statues of the deities, with the largest cella in the center dedicated to the main deity, Tinia or Jupiter. This temple was named the temple of Jupiter Capitolinus—that is, Jupiter of the Capitol.

The earliest coins to display the Etruscan/Roman temple on the Capitolium were struck by the moneyer M. Volteius M. F. in 78 B.C., Syd. 774. These coins show the temple with four columns

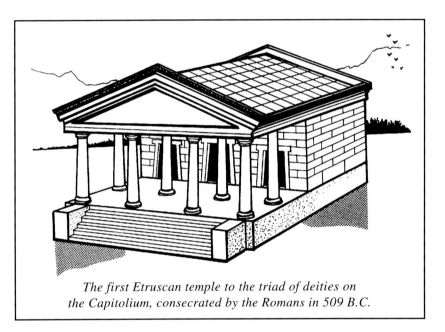

The first Etruscan temple to the triad of deities on the Capitolium, consecrated by the Romans in 509 B.C.

and the doors to the three separate sanctuaries for the triad of deities. The engraver of this coin concentrated on illustrating the three separate and important doors to the cellae of the deities, and he also tried to describe the very elaborate sculptures on the roof edge, but the coin flan was too small and he could only represent these with abstract, curved forms. However, archaeologists have discovered Etruscan roof ornaments which closely resemble the curled forms shown on the coin, and they may have been the original roof decorations. The thunderbolt shown in the pediment indicates that this is the temple to Jupiter Optimus Maximus, Jupiter the Best

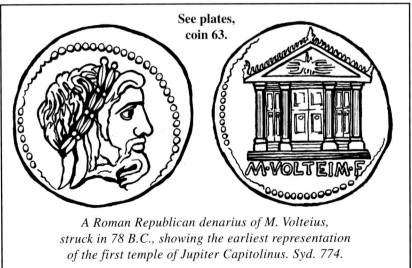

See plates, coin 63.

A Roman Republican denarius of M. Volteius, struck in 78 B.C., showing the earliest representation of the first temple of Jupiter Capitolinus. Syd. 774.

[1] *The History,* by Tacitus, Book 3, 71, gives a detailed account. *The Complete Works of Tacitus,* edited by Moses Hadas, Random House, New York, 1942, page 582.

[2] *Plutarch's Lives,* Poplicola, translated by Dryden, revised by A.H. Clough, Little Brown and Co., Boston, 188, Volume I, page 216.

and Greatest god. The column capitals are simplified on the coin, but probably represent the Tuscan order, which was adopted from the Greek Doric style and used by the Etruscans on their temples. The obverse of the coin portrays a bearded head of the god Jupiter.

After some early renovations by the Romans, the temple size was fixed at 185 feet (56 m) wide and 200 feet (60 m) long. The columns were supposedly 57 feet (17.3 m) high and 6 feet (1.8 m) in diameter.[3] The building was set on a very high podium, and approached from the Forum Romanum, below the hill, by a ceremonial stairway. It is recorded in ancient literature that at the climax of their triumphal processions, Julius Caesar and the emperor Claudius ascended these stairs to the Capitolium on their knees.

The temple of the Capitoline Jupiter was the center of religious and political life in Rome. The senate held its first meeting of the year in this temple, and it was the scene for the ending of all triumphs celebrated in Rome, when the victorious leaders placed their golden crowns of laurel leaves on the statue of Jupiter. In 83 B.C., the temple was destroyed by a fire set by an unknown malcontent, and the rebuilding was immediately started by the dictator

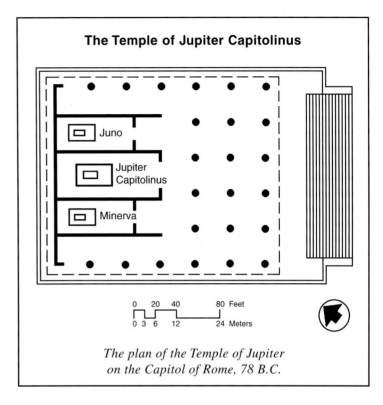

The plan of the Temple of Jupiter on the Capitol of Rome, 78 B.C.

Sulla, who proposed to use some of the marble columns taken from the plundered Temple of the Olympian Jupiter in Athens. This plan was never carried out, probably for political and cultural reasons.

According to the Roman historian Tacitus, *History, 3. 72*, the reconstructed temple was substantially completed in 78 B.C. by the consul Lutatius Catulus. At that time, it appears that this second temple to Jupiter was rebuilt as a hexastyle structure, with six columns across the front, and these columns may have been of the Corinthian order, the latest Roman architectural fashion of the day. Eighteen columns were erected to make a front porch, and single lines of three columns were placed on the sides to make the colonnades.

Roman Republican coins depicted this second temple on the Capitolium, and illustrated the latest renovations with accurate details. These denarii were struck by the moneyer Petillius Capitolinus in 37 B.C. Judging from his name, Capitolinus, the family of this moneyer must have had some hereditary, ceremonial position connected to the temple. Petillius struck two coins that depicted the facade and the statues embellishing the second temple structure. The first coin, Syd. 1149, shows a hexastyle temple with what is described in reference books as garlands between the three central columns. These ornaments are engraved as a series of pellets, and one should remember that ancient coin engravers often used such pellets to represent statues in small, restricted areas of the design. Careful examination of unworn specimens of these coins reveals that the garlands are indeed representations of the statues of the three deities of the triad. The statues on

---

[3] *The Ruins and Excavations of Ancient Rome,* by R. Lanciani, Bell Publishing Co., New York, page 296.

142

See plates, coin 64.

A Roman Republican denarius of Petillius Capitolinus, struck in 37 B.C., showing the second temple of Jupiter Capitolinus. Syd. 1149.

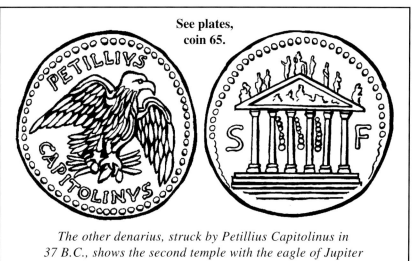

See plates, coin 65.

The other denarius, struck by Petillius Capitolinus in 37 B.C., shows the second temple with the eagle of Jupiter on the obverse, and the temple with statues of the deities between the columns shown by a series of dots. Syd. 1150-52.

the roof edge and in the pediment are also very crudely rendered and cannot be positively identified. The column capitals are shown as basic shapes, but by their size they probably represent the Corinthian order. The obverse of the coin portrays a very fine, classical head of Jupiter.

The second coin type struck by Petillius, Syd. 1150, shows a splendid eagle—the principal symbol of Jupiter Capitolinus—on the obverse, and a facade of the Capitolium on the reverse. On this facade, the three statues between the columns are also rendered by a series of pellets, but they clearly do not look like garlands. However, the artist was not skilled enough to illustrate the sculptures on the roof and pediment, and the columns on the facade are engraved without any detail in the capitals.

Julius Caesar had completed the adornment of the second temple in 46 B.C., probably adding statues to the roof edge. This second temple became the national temple of the Roman nation, and as it was considered to be sacred, the original size, appearance, and details were maintained whenever it was restored. Later, in 9 B.C., Augustus renovated and embellished the edifice as part of his civic improvement plans for Rome, perhaps adding marble facings to the facade. We may recall that, in his last testament or biography, called the *Res Gestae Divi Augusti* or the Accomplishments of the Deified Augustus, the emperor said that he built and renovated many structures and temples in Rome. Also, Suetonius, in his biography *The Twelve Caesars,* said that Augustus found Rome a city built of bricks, and he left it as a city clothed in marble.[4]

With the death of the emperor Nero in A.D. 68, Rome fell into a disastrous civil war, and three emperors, Galba, Otho, and Vitellius, tried to reign during those tumultuous years. In the year 69 B.C., a "Civil War" series of coins were struck without the portrait or title of any ruler. These coins were meant to appeal to the patriotism of the people, and to encourage them to support any new leader who would come forward to stabilize the empire. One of these coins, believed to have been struck in Gaul, shows the second Capitoline Temple on the reverse, as it existed in A.D. 69, RIC (Civil Wars) Gaul, 42. Inside the temple on this coin is a statue of a seated Jupiter holding

---

4 *The Twelve Caesars,* by Suetonius, translated by Michael Graves, Penguin Books, London, 1979, Augustus 28, page 63.

a scepter and a thunderbolt. The legend on the coin, IO. MAX. CAPITOLINVS, gives the abbreviated Latin name and title "Jove Maximus Capitolinus." The temple is shown with only two Corinthian columns because the engraver did not have enough space on the coin, and omitted the other four columns in order to show the important statue inside the temple. Exactly the same reverse was struck by the emperor Vitellius in 69, for a similar propaganda purpose, RIC Vitellius 31 or 56. As Corinthian columns are clearly shown on both these coins, it may be concluded that they were installed in the temple before the major reconstruction undertaken by Vespasian, perhaps in 78 B.C., or by Augustus.

Vitellius also struck a bronze As showing the same scene, but with the legend IO MAX CAPITO, SC, RIC Vitellius 127. This coin displayed four columns instead of six, but still showed the large statue of Jupiter in the center.

Towards the end of the civil war, supporters of Vespasian barricaded themselves in the temple of Jupiter Capitolinus, and the soldiers of Vitellius burned it down to dislodge them. When Vespasian defeated his opponents and became the emperor, he rebuilt the temple, retaining the original size and the same style Corinthian columns of the second structure. He also added many new statues to adorn the pediment and roof line.

Vespasian commemorated this new building, the third Capitoline Temple, by striking rare sestertii in A.D. 71 and 76 showing the front facade of the new temple, adorned with Corinthian columns and many new statues. The best representation of the temple, in all its glory, is seen on the later coins of Vespasian struck in A.D. 76. These sestertii were large enough to permit the artist to accurately show the temple complete with six columns and extensive statuary, and from coins, RIC Vespasian 577, we can see what the temple looked like at its peak. The statues in the pediment area clearly represent Jupiter seated in the center, with Minerva and Juno at his

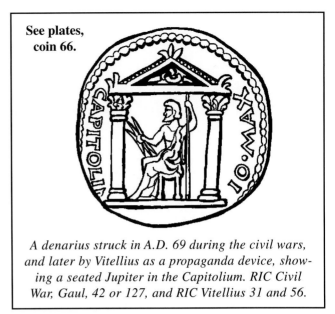

See plates, coin 66.

A denarius struck in A.D. 69 during the civil wars, and later by Vitellius as a propaganda device, showing a seated Jupiter in the Capitolium. RIC Civil War, Gaul, 42 or 127, and RIC Vitellius 31 and 56.

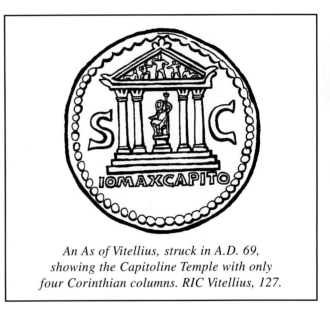

An As of Vitellius, struck in A.D. 69, showing the Capitoline Temple with only four Corinthian columns. RIC Vitellius, 127.

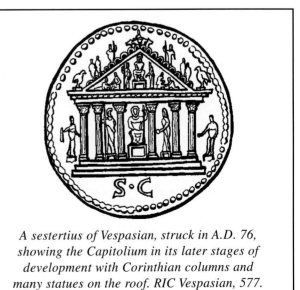

A sestertius of Vespasian, struck in A.D. 76, showing the Capitolium in its later stages of development with Corinthian columns and many statues on the roof. RIC Vespasian, 577.

A reconstruction of the Temple of Jupiter on the Capitoline Hill
showing the building as it appeared in the first century A.D.

sides. Vespasian also struck earlier coins in A.D. 71 showing the temple, but as it was undergoing reconstruction at that time, the coins may only present the design concept or the preliminary proposal for the building. This coin is a sestertius, RIC Vespasian 452.

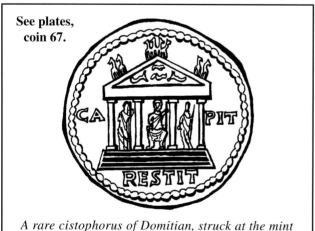

See plates, coin 67.

A rare cistophorus of Domitian, struck at the mint in Ephesus, Asia, in A.D. 82, showing the fourth Capitolium with bigas on the roof line. Two columns on the facade are omitted so that the three statues of the deities can be clearly shown. RIC Domitian, 222.

From the detail on these coins, it is possible to reconstruct the Capitolium as it may have looked in the first century A.D. By this time, much of the Etruscan detail had disappeared, and a truly Hellenistic/Roman style of temple had emerged.

In A.D. 80, only a few years after Vespasian reconstructed the temple, it was struck by lightning and burned to the ground. Titus, oldest son of Vespasian and now emperor, immediately began to rebuild the temple, but he died before it was completed. Titus' brother, Domitian, finished the work in A.D. 82, and re-dedicated the new structure as the fourth temple on the site. The emperor embellished the facade of the renovated temple with more statues, and he appears to have added two bigas to the roof edge. These may actually have been placed on the temple by earlier Roman consuls, but they appear clearly for the first time on Domitian's coins. The bigas can be seen on the cistophorus coins of Domitian struck in Asia to commemorate his civic works and building programs, RIC Domitian 222. The legend CAPIT RESTIT means the Capitolium is restored.

The Temple of Jupiter Optimus/Maximus/Capitolinus retained its status as the main Roman religious edifice up until the end of the late empire. Even during the early Christian era, it was respected as a national shrine and left untouched by religious fanatics. It was plundered and partially destroyed in A.D. 455 by the Vandals, led by Genseric, who stripped the gilt bronze tiles from the roof. Later, citizens of Rome used the ruins of the temple as a quarry, and burned the marble facings and the statues to make lime. Some of the fine marble columns and capitals were re-used by sculptors to carve statues for the Christian churches that were built nearby. The remains of the temple were finally razed to the ground and disappeared from recorded history. A palace was built over the site in medieval times, and when this was excavated in 1880, a part of the stone foundation wall of the Capitoline temple and some pieces of the columns were uncovered. These can be seen on the site in Rome today, but they are only fragments, and do not convey even a tiny hint of the grandeur of the great temple that was the national sanctuary of the greatest power in the ancient Western world.

Chapter 21

The Temple of Jupiter Ultor or Victor

Jupiter, or Jove, was the king of the gods in the Roman pantheon and, naturally, had many temples dedicated to his worship in Rome. In addition to the great national religious shrine, the temple of Jupiter Capitolinus, there were several temples, large and small, provided in the city for this supreme deity, in all his manifestations. Jupiter Tonans—that is, Jupiter the Thunderer—was revered by Augustus, who narrowly escaped being struck by a lightning bolt during the Cantabrian campaign in 26 B.C. (*Suetonius, Augustus 29*). The emperor built a temple to Jupiter Tonans in 22 B.C., on a site at the entrance to the Capitoline Hill. This small temple is shown on coins of Augustus as a hexastyle, Corinthian structure, but no remains of it have ever been found. See RIC 27.

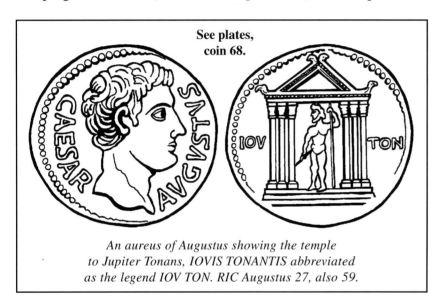

See plates, coin 68.

An aureus of Augustus showing the temple to Jupiter Tonans, IOVIS TONANTIS abbreviated as the legend IOV TON. RIC Augustus 27, also 59.

Other temples to Jupiter in Rome were equally important. A temple to Jupiter Custos, the Custodian or Guardian, was built by Domitian on the site of the house of the gatekeeper on the Capitoline Hill, where Domitian took refuge from the rampaging soldiers of Vitellius in A.D. 68. A temple to Jupiter Stator, the Jupiter that stays the retreat of soldiers in battle, was dedicated by Q. Caecillius Metellus after his triumph in 146 B.C. This temple was built entirely of marble, somewhere inside the Porticus Metelli near the Circus Flaminius (*Vitruvius, Book III, Chap. 2, 5*). Another temple to Jupiter Stator was built in Rome on the Sacra Via at the foot of the Palatine Hill, next to the Arch of Titus. Unfortunately, none of these temples appeared on coins.

The famous temple for Jove Ultor, Jove the Avenger, built in Rome, is the source of much debate among historians, and this dispute illustrates how a building recorded on ancient coinage can sometimes confuse rather than clarify an identification. There are several theories about the location and construction of this grand edifice for Jupiter Ultor, but all of these lack conclusive evidence and must be considered as conjectural. To understand the controversy enveloping this temple, it may be best to give the most plausible theory, and then compare it to all the opposing hypotheses. A magnificent architectural reverse of a large temple complex appears on a sestertius of Severus Alexander, with the legend IOVI VLTORI, of Jove the Avenger. See RIC 412. Some historians (Nash, Platner, and Ashby) claim, but with some reservations, that this is the renowned temple of Jupiter Ultor that was located on the northeast corner of the Palatine Hill. It supposedly sat on a terrace, 363 feet (110 m) wide by 495 feet (150 m) long, which was approached from the Clivus Palatinus, the modern Via di S. Bonaventura, through a monumental gate structure of five

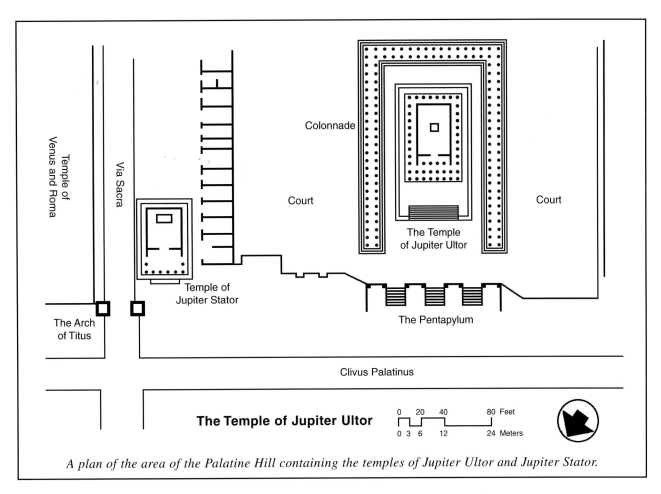

A plan of the area of the Palatine Hill containing the temples of Jupiter Ultor and Jupiter Stator.

openings which was called the Pentapylum. This gateway is mentioned in several ancient documents. The modern church of St. Sebastiano apparently sits on a part of the ruins of the ancient temple structure. The small temple of Jupiter Stator, the Jupiter who prevents panic in soldiers during battle, was located close by, adjacent to the Arch of Titus, at the foot of the Palatine Hill.

The principal theory about the temple of Jupiter Ultor claims that the artificial platform, making up the site for this temple, was originally built by Domitian as a garden during the construction of his palace on the Palatine Hill. It is recorded that a temple to Sol Invictus, a Syrian deity, was later located there by the emperor Elagabalus, A.D. 218-222. A literary reference to this temple in the *Historia Augusta* reports that there existed a "temple of Elagabalus called Sol by some and Jupiter by others" (*Lives of the Later Caesars*, Elagabalus xvii.8). Elagabalus, a cruel degenerate, was so hated by the people that his successor, Severus Alexander, re-dedicated this temple of Sol to the main Roman deity Jove Ultor—that is, Jupiter the Avenger. This act of re-dedication may be commemorated on the sestertii struck by Severus Alexander in A.D. 224 (RIC 412). These coins show the temple as a magnificent Corinthian hexastyle structure, with two flanking porticoes and the Pentapylum

A sestertius of Severus Alexander showing the magnificent temple complex for Jupiter Ultor on the Palatine Hill. RIC Severus Alexander, 412.

148

gate in front of the temple complex. A statue of a seated Jupiter holding a scepter is shown in the center of the facade, and several priests, who appear to be on top of the Pentapylum, stand in the courtyard in front of the temple. This reverse is considered to be the most impressive architectural type ever struck by third century Roman minters.

The opposing theories, all of which question the identification of this building, are academically sound and must be seriously considered. A nineteenth century historian (Lanciani) identifies this platform terrace built by Domitian on the Palatine Hill as being the "Horti Adonaea," or the Gardens of Adonis. This identification is based on a fragment of the *Forma Urbis Romae*, the Severan marble plan of Rome, found in the Forum of Peace, which labels this area as the "Horti Adonaea". The map shows many trees and plants sacred to the gods growing in this garden, but no temple structures. Another hypothesis claims that this coin of Severus Alexander actually shows the older temple of Jupiter Victor, which several historians suggest was also located on the Palatine Hill. This temple to Jupiter Victor was vowed by Q. Fabius Maximus Rullianus during the battle of Sentinum in 295 B.C. Supposedly, this ancient temple is depicted on a small, rare bronze As or medallion of Elagabalus (Gnecchi, Vol III, pg. 41, plate 152, N 11). It is also proposed that this

See plates, coin 6.

A rare As or sestertius of Trajan showing the temple to Jupiter Victor or Ultor on the Palatine Hill. RIC Trajan, 577.

same original temple of Jupiter Victor is shown on the bronze coins of Trajan struck in A.D. 107. These coins illustrate a temple complex very similar to the one shown as being dedicated to Jupiter Ultor, and they include the prominent flanking porticoes. However, it is an octastyle structure, not hexastyle, and has no Pentapylum gate in the foreground. See RIC Trajan 577.

Philip V. Hill provides the strongest support for this theory by suggesting that the many numismatic and literary references take precedence over any other evidence, and that these records place the temple of Jupiter Victor on this terraced site on the Palatine.[1] Hill also sets out the history of this temple, by noting that the ancient temple vowed by

Fabius Maximus Rullianus in 259 B.C. was probably destroyed by the great fire in Rome, A.D. 80, and rebuilt by Domitian on the Palatine terrace constructed by his architect, Rabirius, as a part of a new palace. Apparently, the emperor Trajan embellished or renovated it in A.D. 106, and this restoration was commemorated on his coinage shown above. Presumably, the Pentapylum gate is not shown on Trajan's coinage because he did not restore it in his rebuilding of the temple.

In 221, Elagabalus re-dedicated the temple to his patron deity, Sol Invictus, and in 224, Severus Alexander returned it to the service of the great Jupiter. Hill notes the similarity of the two temples seen on the coins of Severus Alexander and Trajan, and explains the omission of two columns on the sestertius of Severus Alexander, and the Pentapylum gateway on the coins of Trajan, as simply artistic necessity resulting from the small area of the coins' surfaces. However, Hill does not attempt to explain the legend of IOVI VLTORI instead of IOVI VICTORI appearing on the coins of Severus Alexander.

Hill's scholarship is impeccable, but it should be noted that, in the official tourist guide books for the Palatine, a different site and group of ruins is labelled as the temple to Jupiter Victor, or

[1] *The Monuments of Ancient Rome as Coin Types,* by Philip V. Hill, Seabys, London, 1989, page 33.

perhaps of Apollo. This site is located on the north part of the hill, close to the House of Livia, and this is the original location for a temple to Jupiter Victor that is mentioned in some other historical documents.

Adding my own thoughts regarding the legend of IOVI VLTORI instead of IOVI VICTORI on the later coins, it may be proposed that if Elagabalus converted the original temple of Jupiter Victor on the Palatine to his own personal deity, Sol Invictus, then perhaps Severus Alexander rededicated the same temple, not to the original Jupiter Victor, but to Jupiter the Ultor—that is, "the Avenger"—to proclaim that the king of the Roman gods took vengeance on the Syrian god Sol, and on Elagabalus for his horrible and evil excesses.

Chapter 22

The Temple of Divus Augustus

No positively identified ruins of the temple of Divus Augustus have ever been found in Rome. It is difficult to even locate the site of this temple, because the literary sources mention that there were two temples dedicated to the deified emperor Augustus. The earliest one was located on the Palatine Hill near the emperor's official residence. This temple was built by his widow, Livia, just after his death in A.D. 14. Pliny the Elder (*Natural History, XII.94*) states that it was destroyed by fire, but it must have been reconstructed immediately because it is mentioned again by Suetonius in *Augustus, 5.* No ancient description of this first temple survives. The construction of the second temple dedicated to Divus Augustus was commenced by Tiberius and Livia, and completed by Caligula in A.D. 37. Tacitus, the Roman historian, tells us about this edifice in his *Annals, 6.45.* It is often referred to in Roman documents as the "templum novum," the new temple, as opposed to the first temple, which may have been called the old temple.

It is surprising that the location of this structure was not well recorded in ancient literature because Augustus was certainly the most highly respected of all the Roman emperors. The only literary clue we have to the actual site of the temple is in the description of Caligula's grandiose scheme to erect a high level pedestrian bridge from the Palatine Hill imperial palace to the

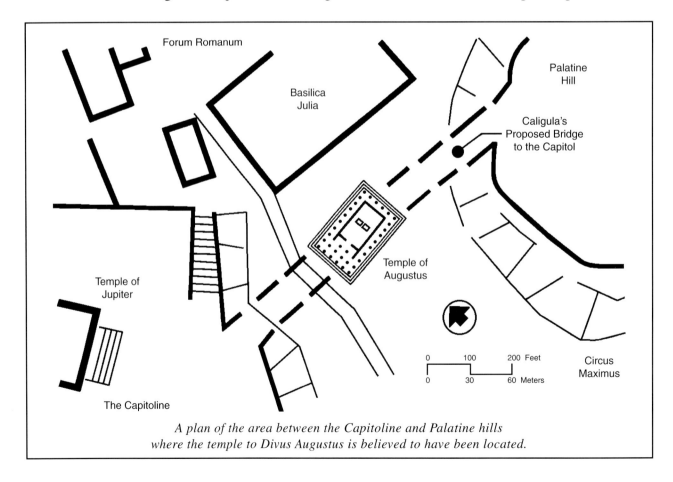

A plan of the area between the Capitoline and Palatine hills
where the temple to Divus Augustus is believed to have been located.

Capitoline Hill, so that the emperor could share the home of his patron god, Jupiter. This scheme is documented by Suetonius in *Caligula, 22, 37*. Caligula proposed to use the temple of Divus Augustus as the middle support for this bridge, so it must have been located in the valley between the two hills, and somewhere behind the Basilica Julia of the Forum Romanum. Archaeologists have discovered some ruins in this area, but they had been built over several times and cannot be identified as a temple. However, from the outline of these remains, it has been determined that the structure was approximately 140 feet (42 m) wide by 200 feet (60 m) long. It must have been at least 60 feet (18 m) high if it was considered as a support for Caligula's bridge over the valley.

When Caligula completed the temple to Augustus in A.D. 37, he struck some spectacular commemorative sestertii showing the dedication ceremony with the temple as the backdrop scenery. See RIC 37. Caligula repeated this coin type with only slight compositional variations in A.D. 39 to 40, and the temple is shown with very clear details. It was a hexastyle facade of Ionic columns, and at the apex of the pediment there was a quadriga, probably driven by Augustus. The quadriga is flanked by two Victories bearing wreaths. The acroteria on the left roof edge was a statue of Romulus, and at the right edge, a group of statues portrayed Aeneas carrying his fa-

ther, Anchises, and leading his son, Ascanius, away from the destruction of Troy. Ascanius was considered to be the founding ancestor of the Julian clan. In the center of the pediment, a statue of Augustus was displayed flanked by two figures, one holding a spear and the other a globe. The legend in the field, DIVO AVG, identified the temple as dedicated to the deified Augustus. Caligula is seen with two priests, sacrificing a bull on an altar in front of the garlanded temple.

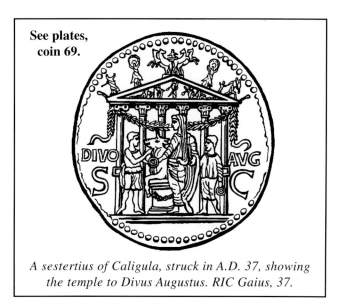

See plates, coin 69.

A sestertius of Caligula, struck in A.D. 37, showing the temple to Divus Augustus. RIC Gaius, 37.

This temple may have been damaged in Caligula's attempt to use it as a bridge support, or it may have been ruined by the great fire in the Forum Romanum in A.D. 69. It was renovated and perhaps completely rebuilt by Domitian during his reign in A.D. 81-96. This restoration may have been commemorated on an undated denarius of Domitian showing a Corinthian octastyle temple, RIC Domitian 208, but historians cannot prove this conclusively. The coin lacks any identifying inscription other than IMP CAESAR on the entablature, and the cult statue shown inside the temple cannot be identified by its attributes. However, historians do not recognize this edifice as being one of the many recorded temples erected by Domitian, and by the process of elimination, conclude that it could only be the temple of Augustus that the emperor is known to have restored. The temple is shown on this coin as octastyle and

A denarius of Domitian showing an unidentified octastyle Corinthian temple which may represent his restoration of the temple to Divus Augustus. RIC Domitian 208.

with Corinthian columns, compared to Caligula's coin which shows a temple that is Ionic hexa-style. This change may indicate that Caligula's harebrained bridge scheme or the fire in the Forum completely destroyed the temple, and it was totally rebuilt by Domitian's architect, Rabirius, in a more contemporary, fashionable style.

The temple of Divus Augustus was restored once again by Antoninus Pius, almost one hundred years later in A.D. 158. This act is commemorated on many coins struck by this emperor. These coins show a Corinthian octastyle temple, and this may be confirmation that the temple shown on the coin of Domitian is indeed the temple of Augustus. The legends on these coins vary, but the earliest inscription is AED DIVI AVG REST COS IIII, meaning the Temple of Augustus was restored in the emperor's fourth Consulship, RIC Antoninus Pius 755. Later coins of A.D. 159 show variations of this inscription, such as TEMPLVM DIV AVG REST COS IIII (RIC 998).

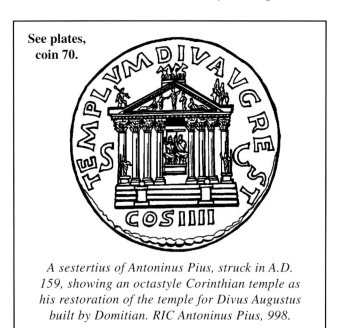

See plates, coin 70.

A sestertius of Antoninus Pius, struck in A.D. 159, showing an octastyle Corinthian temple as his restoration of the temple for Divus Augustus built by Domitian. RIC Antoninus Pius, 998.

These inscriptions positively identify the structure as the restored temple to Divus Augustus. The temple also appears on denarii, dupondii, and Asses of this emperor, RIC 284, 1017, and 1024 respectively. All these coins show the temple with two cult images seated on a high dais inside the temple. These probably represent Augustus and Livia, seated side-by-side as equal part-ners, just as they were in real life. A quadriga is seen at the apex of the roof, and the acroteriae at the roof edges are clearly Romulus on the right and Aeneas, carrying Anchises and leading Ascanius, on the left. The pediment contains sculptures which are not easily recognized, but the statue in the middle may be of Augustus. These coins are the only physical evidence we have for the existence of the temple of Divus Augustus, but they are conclusive because of the inscription, and therefore serve as a record of this exceptional edifice dedicated to the founding ruler of the Roman empire.

Chapter 23

The Temple of Venus and Roma

The temple of Venus and Roma was the largest and most magnificent temple in ancient Rome. As a double temple dedicated to two separate deities, Venus and Roma, it was the most unusual type of religious building ever constructed by the normally conservative and tradition-bound Romans. This temple was conceived by the emperor Hadrian, A.D. 117-138, started in 121, and completed sometime around 140-144 during the reign of Antoninus Pius. With the consecration of the unfinished building in 136 or 137, Hadrian also created a new religious cult to reaffirm the primacy of Rome, represented by Roma, and the power of the Roman people, represented by Venus.

This new cult was a part of the emperor's efforts to renew the concept of an "Eternal Rome," exalting the origins and strength of the city and of the Roman nation. He had already started this process by transforming the traditional birthday festival of Rome's founding, the "Parilia," into a great national ceremony perhaps called the "Romaia" or the "Natali Urbis." This important anniversary was held yearly in the Circus Maximus. The date of the establishment of this new holiday, designed to instill greater pride in the Roman nation, is given on his coins struck in A.D. 121, see RIC Hadrian, 144 and 609. The coupling of the national divinity Roma with Venus was theologically acceptable because Venus had been venerated in Rome since the early third century B.C. as the protector of the Julian dynasty, and through them, the Roman people. Venus had also become the patroness of the triumphatores, the victorious generals or emperors awarded a triumph, and many Roman military victories were attributed directly to her.[1]

Hadrian was one of the most interesting and talented of the second century Roman emperors, and he ruled over the empire during its apex of power. A multifaceted personality, the emperor was a competent general, a good administrator, a scholar, a lover of the arts, and an admirer of all things Greek. Hadrian was also an active architectural designer, to the extent that he is sometimes known as the "architect-emperor" compared to his predecessor, Trajan, who was called the "soldier-emperor." As the emperor, Hadrian designed many of his own buildings, and his masterpieces included his own mausoleum, now called the Castello Sant' Angelo in Rome, his famous villa complex at Tivoli, the Pantheon, and of course, the enormous temple of Venus and Roma. In his designs, Hadrian experimented with different construction methods using concrete, and he was fascinated by the newly developed domes and intersecting vaults that could easily enclose spaces wider than 100 feet (30 m). Hadrian's roof dome for the Pantheon, 142 feet (43 m) in diameter, is larger than the dome of St. Peter's in the Vatican, which is only 140.3 feet (42.5 m) in diameter. However, St. Peter's dome was constructed with some difficulty by the great Renaissance architect Michelangelo in 1546-64, more than 1,400 years later than the Pantheon.[2]

Hadrian began exploring the potential of using domes for structures while he was just a young man. Trajan was one of his guardians, and Hadrian was educated and tutored by the many scholars and advisors attached to the imperial court. Among these accomplished men was Trajan's personal architect, Apollodorus of Damascus, who may have taught Hadrian all about the design

[1] *Hadrian and the City of Rome,* by Mary Taliaferro Boatwright, Princeton University Press, Princeton, 1987, page 131.
[2] *The Companion Guide to Rome*, by Georgina Masson, Prentice Hall Inc., New Jersey, 1980, page 98.

of buildings, military siege machines, and fortifications. As he matured, Hadrian began to create his own building designs using newly conceived structures made up of domes and vaults. He must have had several disputes with Apollodorus about these architectural concepts, because it was mentioned that when young Hadrian offered his opinion on a building design to Trajan, Apollodorus harshly chided him as an amateur and told him to "go away and draw your pumpkins (squashes)," alluding to Hadrian's favorite domes.[3]

When he became the emperor, Hadrian supposedly took a terrible revenge on Apollodorus for his insulting remarks. Hadrian had personally designed the vast temple of Venus and Roma, and asked Apollodorus to make comments on the proposal. Apollodorus tactlessly criticized the building and ridiculed the emperor. He said that the temple was too squat and that the statues inside were too large for the spaces provided. The architect also said that the area under the platform of the temple should have been excavated, and made into storage chambers for the scenery and machines used in the Colosseum, which was located close by. In his anger, Hadrian supposedly banished the architect from Rome, and later had him executed.[4]

This story is enigmatic because modern archaeologists, who excavated the temple in the early nineteenth century, found it to be a very lofty structure, sited on an artificial platform over 25 feet high, and the area under it was excavated and had been made into storage chambers. Perhaps Hadrian took Apollodorus' advice after all, or the Roman historians may have simply concocted this dreadful story to explain Apollodorus' sudden disappearance from Roman society.

The Temple of Venus and Roma was a perfect demonstration of the traditional Greek influence on Roman architecture. The temple has often been described by art historians as a Greek composition set within a Roman civic space. The structure was decastyle—that is, it had 10 columns across the front. It also had 20 columns forming a colonnade along the sides. A decastyle structure was the largest size of temple ever attempted by ancient architects. The temple was "pseudodipteral," meaning that instead of two rows of columns (dipteral) in the colonnades along the sides, it had only one row, but with space left for a future second row. This enormous temple had two interior cellae, back to back, containing the statues of the two deities. It is believed that the western cella, facing the Forum Romanum, contained the statue of Roma, and the eastern cella, facing the Colosseum, held the statue of Venus. The cellae themselves had ornate vaulted roofs with columns, and parts of them still remain and can be seen in Rome. The plan of the temple was 175 feet (53 m) wide by 350 feet (106 m) long, and these numbers give a ratio of 1 to 2 for the width of the plan to the length. This 1:2 ratio is called the "golden mean," a mathematical formula recommended by Hellenistic architects to make a perfectly proportioned plan layout.

An artificial temple platform was constructed to create an open court area or precinct, 337 feet (102 m) wide by 541 feet (164 m) long. It had been built to level the area and raise the site of the building above the surrounding hillside streets.[5] This was the largest temple precinct and open court area in all of Rome. The precinct was enclosed on two sides by porticoes made up of many fine, grey granite columns. The raised platform was located flanking the Summa Via Sacra, a road leading to the Forum, and adjacent to the Arch of Titus, which it touched with its southwest corner. This famous victory arch had been completed by the emperor Domitian in A.D. 81.

The temple of Venus and Roma was the only decastyle temple in Rome, and it was designed to exceed the size and scale of such enormous Greek structures as the octastyle temples of Artemis at Ephesus and of Hera at Samos. In fact, it probably was a copy of the largest Greek temple in

---

[3] The story is quoted, without sources, in *Roman Architecture,* by Frank Sear, Cornell University Press, New York, 1982, page 183.

[4] *Roman History,* by Dio Cassius, translated by W.E. Cary, Loeb Classical Library, Cambridge, 1924, Book LXIX, iv. 4.

[5] *The Architecture of Greece and Rome,* by W.J. Andersen, Batsford, London, 1907, page 212.

the world, the decastyle, dipteral temple of Apollo at Didyma, near Miletus, constructed in the fourth century B.C. However, the granite or porphyry columns of the temple of Venus and Roma were of the Roman Corinthian style, and not of the Ionic order used in Greek temples. These columns were over 6 feet (1.8 m) in diameter at the base and 60 feet (18 m) high. Including the height of the gable roof, the temple of Venus and Roma was at least 110 feet (33 m) high. The side walls were made very thick to carry the heavy roof structure, and niches were carved into these walls for statues of divinities. Unfortunately, Hadrian's temple was destroyed by fire in A.D. 307, and was rebuilt and altered by the emperor Maxentius, 306-312. It is the remains of Maxentius' temple that were excavated, beginning in 1810, and are visible in Rome today. In the Middle Ages a church, now called the Santa Maria Nova or the Santa Francesca Romana, was built on part of the site near the Forum, possibly using some of the stones and columns from the ruins of the original temple.

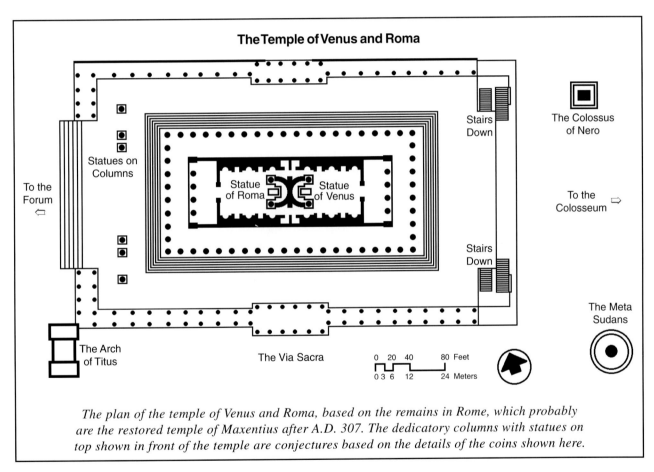

The plan of the temple of Venus and Roma, based on the remains in Rome, which probably are the restored temple of Maxentius after A.D. 307. The dedicatory columns with statues on top shown in front of the temple are conjectures based on the details of the coins shown here.

Hadrian built his great temple on the site of Nero's "Domus Aurea," the Golden House, on the hill above the east end of the Forum and overlooking the Colosseum area. Vespasian, A.D. 69-79, had destroyed most of Nero's palace and returned the land to public use. He built the Colosseum in the bed of the decorative lake attached to the palace, but he left part of the grand porch of the building intact. This contained the enormous bronze statue of Nero called the "Colossus Neronis," which later gave the name Colosseum to the amphitheater built by the Flavians. The Colossus may have originally portrayed Nero dressed as Apollo, but Vespasian supposedly replaced the statue's head with that of his own son, Titus. Hadrian demolished the remnants of the porch and relocated the Colossus statue closer to the Colosseum, in order to clear the site for his temple. To move this heavy, 110 foot (33 m) high statue, Hadrian commissioned an architect named Decrianus, who encased the statue in a crate made of heavy timbers, and used 24 elephants to lift and drag it, in an upright position, to its new location closer to the Colosseum.[6]

The temple of Venus and Roma was shown on numerous Roman sestertii struck by Hadrian and Antoninus Pius. It also appears on Asses of Hadrian, see BMC, III, 1345, and on sestertii of the deified Faustina I struck by Antoninus Pius, see *Roman Imperial Coins in the Hunter Coin Cabinet*, II, no. 147. It does not appear on any of the silver or gold currency, probably because only the large flans of the bronze coins enabled the artists to depict the true size and details of this enormous temple. These temple coins were struck with several major reverse types, usually classified by their different legends, and with many minor variations in the designs, especially in the number of steps shown in the podium or in the statues shown on the temple.

The main type of temple coin struck by the emperor Hadrian exhibits the letters S and C, for SENATVS CONSVLTO, each side of the temple, and the abbreviation SPQR, for SENATVS POPVLVSQVE ROMANVS, in the exergue. These legends indicated that the senate sanctioned the issuance of the coin, SC, and that the new cult and temple was dedicated to the senate and all the Roman people, SPQR. When Hadrian became emperor, he publicly declared that he would administer the state as if it belonged entirely to the Roman people, and not to himself, and these legends confirmed his intention.[7] This coin type shows the temple with 10 Corinthian columns, and with five steps in the podium, RIC Hadrian 783. Some reference books suggest that the figures in the pediment are Jupiter in the center, with Juno and Minerva on each side. Two other minor deities or perhaps Victories recline in the angles of the pediment. On the roof ridge there is a quadriga, probably containing the emperor, and at the roof edges are two Victories, facing and holding open wreaths. This coin, struck in A.D. 134-138, may depict the architectural concept or "blueprint" of the temple as an unfinished, unadorned basic building, just before its consecration in A.D. 136-137.

The main type of the temple of Venus and Roma reverse, with the SC, SPQR legends and the podium of five steps, struck by Hadrian A.D. 134-138. RIC Hadrian 783.

The second major type of this temple coin struck by Hadrian is a sestertius showing the legend of SPQR with EX SC in the exergue, RIC 784. These legends convey the same message as the coin described above, however, the temple on this coin appears with statues on the bases of four columns, two at each side of the building. Because the temple is engraved as only a two-dimensional, front elevation or facade, and as no perspective technique was used by the coin artist, these statues may actually have been located in the court in front of the building. Also, on the right and left of the temple there is a freestanding column with a statue on top of a Corinthian capital. These have been interpreted as being victory columns, with

[6] *Lives of the Later Caesars,* called the *Augustan History,* Hadrian, 19.12, translated by Anthony Birley, Penguin Classics, London, 1976, page 78.

[7] *Lives of the Later Caesars,* as above, Hadrian 8.4, page 65.

a statue of Victoria holding a wreath and palm branch. The podium of the temple on this coin usually has four or five steps. As this coin was also struck in the time period of 134-138, the reverse may represent the building in its still uncompleted state in A.D. 138, but embellished with the four statues and two victory columns placed in front of the temple, on the Forum side, as shown on the reconstructed plan drawn above.

The third type of coin struck by Hadrian has the usual legend SPQR, SC, a podium of three steps, and the two freestanding victory columns with statues on top, but only two statues on the columns, on each side of the temple. This minor variation may be the same coin as type two above, but with an engraver's error or shortcut in leaving out two of the statues on the columns. The legend of SPQR, SC, however, also makes it a minor variety of the first reverse type. This coin is not mentioned in RIC or BMC but can be found in another specialized, comprehensive reference book for imperial sestertii, *Los Sestertios del Imperio Romano, Vol. II*, by Juan R. Cayon (cited as Cayon), numbers 716 and 717.

The fourth type of coin struck by Hadrian shows a temple on a podium of four steps, two statues on the end columns of the building, no freestanding victory columns, and the legend of SC and EX SC in the exergue. However, the columns are spaced out so that there is an opening in the center of the temple, and a large dot or pellet appears in this space. The dot is usually an engraver's abbreviation or symbol to represent a statue, and the use of a dot instead of a figure is a common occurrence on Roman coins where the area allocated to contain the statue is too small. This coin is not in RIC or BMC, but is illustrated in Cayon as no. 283.

The fifth architectural reverse type struck by Hadrian is a coin similar to the fourth, with the legend SC and EX SC, except that the coin artist has managed to engrave a proper statue in the open space between the central col-

The second main type of coin struck by Hadrian in A.D. 134-138, but perhaps closer to 138. It shows the four statues on the columns, the two freestanding victory columns with statues, and the legend SPQR, EX SC. RIC Hadrian, 784.

The third type of coin struck by Hadrian in A.D. 134-138, a minor variation showing the temple with only two statues on the edge columns and the legend SPQR, SC. Cayon, 716 and 717.

The fourth coin type struck by Hadrian in A.D. 134-138 shows two statues on the end columns and a space with a dot, representing a statue, in the center of the temple. The legend is SC and EX SC. Cayon, 283.

158

The fifth coin type, struck in A.D. 134-138, complete with the four end statues and the image of Roma in the center, but no commemorative, freestanding victory columns. The legend is SC, EX SC. Cayon, 283a.

A reconstruction of the Temple of Venus and Roma at the time of its consecration in A.D. 136-137, based on the details from the coins above and information from the excavation reports of 1827-29.

umns of the temple. Also, because the artist was very skillful, he showed the four statues on the end columns at the edges of the temple. The statue in the temple on this coin is believed to represent a statue of a seated Roma, wearing a helmet. This is an important variation in this series of temple coins, but unfortunately, it is not in RIC or BMC. It can be seen in Cayon, number 283a.

This lengthy and perhaps tedious listing of all the variations of these coins may seem irrelevant to the objectives of this book, but they are important because they show how coinage was used to chronologically document the concept, construction, dedication, and renovation stages of the architecture in the Roman world. All these coins were struck in the five years from 134 to 138, the end of Hadrian's reign, and their different designs provide for an accurate record of the progressive development of the temple.

The fact that there are five main types, and several minor variations of each, also indicates that numerous quantities of these bronzes were struck in that five-year period. The development of the building as it neared completion may be illustrated by the engraving of the temple with the different numbers of statues, and the commemorative victory columns in front of the facade. The most complete version of the composition, including all the statues, must certainly have been struck in the last year, A.D. 138. The intermediate versions of the coin may show what the temple actually looked like when it was consecrated by the emperor in 136-137.

The statues of Roma and Venus that were placed inside the twin cellae of the temple must have been impressive works of art. Apollodorus criticized them as being too large for the space they occupied, so they must have been gigantic. Presumably, Hadrian had them sculpted by his best artists, and they probably became as famous as the temple itself. To commemorate these statues and perhaps the consecration of the temple, Hadrian struck aurei and denarii in A.D. 134 to 138, the same period in which he issued the temple sestertii, which showed separately these statues of Roma and Venus. The coins depicting the statue of Roma carry the legend ROMA ETERNA,

Rome the Eternal, RIC Hadrian, 263a. This is exactly the same legend used later by Antoninus Pius on his temple coins struck to record the completion of the edifice. The coins portraying the statue of Venus, struck by Hadrian, carry the legend VENERI FELICIS, Venus the Fortunate, RIC 281. Again, this legend is the same as the one used on the later temple coins of Antoninus Pius.

From date stamps on the bricks found in the excavations, we know that the Temple of Venus and Roma was completed during the reign of Antoninus Pius, probably sometime around 140-144. Scholars are still debating the actual year that it was finished. However, Antoninus Pius struck a large series of sestertii commemorating the temple and its cult during those five years.

These coins consist of two major types, which can be categorized by the legend ROMAE AETERNAE on one type, and VENERI FELICI on the other. An interesting and puzzling fact is that all these temple coins do not show the statues on the end columns, nor the freestanding victory Corinthian columns with statues on top as shown on the coins struck earlier by Hadrian. This may indicate that the artists were now very familiar with these elements and, because they were located in the court area in front of the building, they chose not to depict them as if they were a part of the temple itself. There is also a possibility that these statues and commemorative victory columns, honoring Hadrian's ancestors and accomplishments, were removed or relocated to another part of Rome during Antoninus Pius' reign.

The main coin type, and most common in this series, displays the ROMAE AETERNAE SC legend, the temple on a podium of three steps, and sometimes a dot or

An aureus of Hadrian struck in 134-138 showing the statue of Roma, which was placed in the Temple of Venus and Roma. She sits on a curule chair and holds a Victory in her hand. RIC Hadrian, 263a.

The aureus or denarius of Hadrian struck in 134-138 showing the statue of Venus in the temple. She sits on an ornate throne and holds a Cupid in her hand. RIC Hadrian, 281.

The main type of temple coin struck by Antoninus Pius in A.D. 140-144. Sometimes, a dot in the central space represented the statue of Roma inside the temple. RIC, 622b, Cayon, 317.

160

An important variety of the main type of coin showing the statue of Roma inside the temple. RIC, 623, and Cayon, 353.

The main type of the VENERI FELICI legend coins struck by Antoninus Pius in A.D. 140-144. No attempt has been made to show the statue, or even a dot between the central columns, so as not to destroy the realistic appearance of the facade. RIC Antoninus Pius, 651a, Cayon, 497.

The main variation of the Venus coin showing a dot between the central columns to represent the statue of the deity inside the temple. The quadriga on the roof was misinterpreted and engraved as three human figures. RIC,652, Cayon 497.

pellet representing a statue in the central space between the columns. This coin is RIC Antoninus Pius 622b or Cayon 317.

A major variety of this coin, struck in the same years, shows the same legend and temple, but the artist accomplished the difficult task of engraving a statue of Roma in the central open space. Also, several minor variations of this coin type exist where the podium may have from three to seven steps, RIC 623.

The second group of coins, struck in 140-144 by Antoninus Pius, shows the same temple, but also pays homage to the goddess Venus by displaying the legend VENERI FELICI SC. These coins illustrate the temple on a podium of three steps, but with the columns equally placed on the facade, and with no central space for a dot or statue. See RIC 651a or Cayon 497. This coin may have been the first issue using the VENERI FELICI legend, and the artists chose to use an image of the temple that described the facade as it would be seen in reality by anyone approaching the temple. In that case, the statue of the deity Venus could not be seen inside the building on the coin. However, the quadriga on the roof ridge of these coins is incorrectly engraved to look like three human figures, a large central one standing and two side figures kneeling or leaning outwards.

The main variation on this Venus coin has the temple columns spaced out to create an empty space in the middle and sometimes a dot representing the statue of Venus, is engraved between the central columns. This temple usually sits on a podium of three steps. As a point of interest, the quadriga on the ridge of the roof on all of the VENERI FELICI coins appears as three human figures, although the two figures at the sides lean outwards at an angle, just like the outside two horses of the chariot on the ROMAE AETERNAE coins. This may have resulted from the coin engraver's misinterpretation of the roof sculptures, or his inability to engrave a quadriga and the tiny images representing horses.

The decastyle temple sestertius of the deified Faustina I struck by Antoninus Pius, and the temple coin on the As denomination struck by the same emperor, BMC 1345, are both of the ROMAE AETERNAE SC type, with a dot in the middle representing a statue, similar to RIC 622b described earlier.

Hadrian's new cult of Venus and Roma flourished and spread throughout the empire, promoting loyalty and solidarity to Rome. This may be proven by the coins struck by later emperors, which featured these deities, alone and together, or by the legends "Roma Aeterna" and "Veneri Felici." The emperors Septimius Severus and Severus Alexander used these devices frequently on their coinage. In later years, a cult of Roma, by herself, became more important and superseded the one dedicated to both Roma and Venus. The cult of Roma had the longest existence of all the cults of pagan Rome, surviving even into the early Christian era in the fifth century.

The emperor Probus, A.D. 276-282, struck an enormous series of antoniniani showing a hexastyle temple with the legend ROMAE AETER. This temple may be a representation of Hadrian's temple to Roma and Venus, with four central columns removed to show the statue of a seated Roma in the center. However, the columns are engraved as Ionic, not Corinthian columns. This perhaps means that the temple shown on Probus' coins was a new one, built later and dedicated only to the deity Roma, and constructed with the more traditional Ionic order of columns.

On the other hand, it may simply be an engraver's whimsy to represent some ancient temple he was not familiar with.

The twin Temple of Venus and Roma never appeared on later Roman coinage to the same extent and in such glory as it did on the coins of Hadrian and Antoninus Pius. In 391, the temple was closed by Valentinian II and the site was abandoned. The structure was so enormous and solid that it survived the ravages of stone thieves for another two cen-

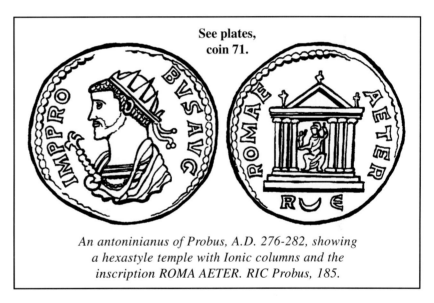

See plates, coin 71.

An antoninianus of Probus, A.D. 276-282, showing a hexastyle temple with Ionic columns and the inscription ROMA AETER. RIC Probus, 185.

turies. Pope Honorius I, 625-640, removed the gilt-bronze roof tiles from the temple and installed them on the roof of St. Peter's. Later, the ruins of the structure became a stone quarry for medieval builders, and the magnificent temple of Venus and Roma disappeared into that dark limbo of history that eventually absorbed all the great pagan relics of Rome.

162

Chapter 24

The Hadrianeum and the Temple of Matidia

The emperor Hadrian, A.D. 117-138, was known to be a patron and benefactor of Roman art and architecture. He donated many fine temples and civic buildings to the capital cities all over the empire. Also, the emperor was a practicing architect, responsible for the design of several famous buildings in Rome. One important group of these buildings can be used to illustrate the many projects associated with the emperor, which ranged from the restorations of older buildings, to renovations of newer structures, to the erecting of brand new monuments. This complex of edifices was located on the Via Flaminia in the Campus Martius, the field of Mars, a large open area in the north of Rome originally used by the army as a training field and a parade ground. The Campus was later developed with many civic buildings that were built as large porticoes or colonnaded structures enclosing open areas. Such a courtyard building was called a "Porticus" by the Romans. The colonnades provided covered, shaded corridors for the Romans to promenade through during the hot Roman summers, and several of the portico structures had their floors marked out to indicate the distance a person had to walk to cover a Roman mile. Also, some of these colonnades had water pipes installed to spray the walls and columns and keep the pedestrians cool.

One of the first porticoed buildings constructed on the Campus Martius was the Villa Publica. Little is known about this "porticus," but a representation of it appears on a coin struck during the Roman Republic. This coin shows a two-story colonnaded building which probably was the portico structure surrounding the space referred to as the Villa Publica. See Syd. 901.

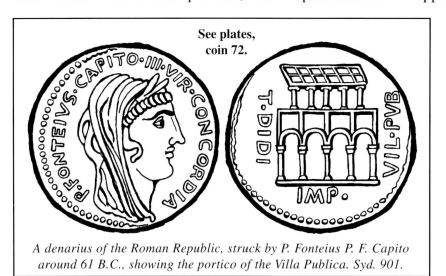

See plates, coin 72.

A denarius of the Roman Republic, struck by P. Fonteius P. F. Capito around 61 B.C., showing the portico of the Villa Publica. Syd. 901.

The Villa Publica, erected before 432 B.C., was probably located on the Via Flaminia, on the south borderline of the Campus Martius, near the cliffs of the Capitoline Hill. We know this because it was recorded in historical documents that the people of Rome assembled in the Villa Publica, at that location, for a census taken in 432 B.C. The Villa also served as a public ceremonial area in which to levy troops, receive foreign ambassadors, and to assemble the participants in the triumphal parades of victorious generals (Lanciani, page 472). Sulla soaked the Villa Publica with blood in 82 B.C. when he ordered that 8,000 prisoners of war be slaughtered in the open court area (*Lucan ii, 197*). T. Didius, the consul in 98 B.C., probably renovated the Villa Publica during his term, and the coin above was struck by P. Fonteius Capito in 61 B.C. to commemorate this restoration. This coin is the only known record of the building. The architectural design of the Villa Publica was so outstanding that it became the prototype of all the later porticoed structures erected in the Campus Martius.

One later building erected in the Campus Martius was called the "Porticus Argonautarum." It supposedly had illustrations of the voyage of the Argonauts painted on its colonnade walls. The actual appearance of this structure and its function was a matter of debate among historians, and it has been suggested that it served as the admiralty or naval headquarters of the Roman empire because a ruin located inside the colonnade was thought to be a temple to the sea god Neptune. This porticus was believed to have been constructed by Agrippa in 26 B.C., to commemorate the naval victories over Pompey Sextus at Mysae and Naulochos in 36 B.C., and the sea battle against Mark Antony at Actium in 31 B.C. The colonnaded structure enclosed an area 356 feet (108 m) by 324 feet (98 m), with a temple located in the middle. The porticus burned down in the great conflagration of A.D. 80, which devastated the entire Campus Martius, and the buildings of the Porticus Argonautarum were reconstructed by Hadrian in around 120, along with the Pantheon, also built by Agrippa, located nearby. At that time, the emperor also constructed a temple dedicated to his deified mother-in-law, Matidia, immediately behind the Argonautarum and north of the Pantheon. Hadrian owed a debt of gratitute to Matidia, the mother of his wife Sabina and daughter of Trajan's sister, Marciana, because she had played an important part in advancing Hadrian's political and imperial career.

The temple for the deified Matidia was unusual for a Roman edifice because it combined the normal form of temple with the colonnade type of porticus building found on the Campus Martius. The temple had two side, small shrines or aediculae, and also flanking, open-ended, two-story colonnades enclosing a court area that linked the temple to the Argonautarum. The two colon-

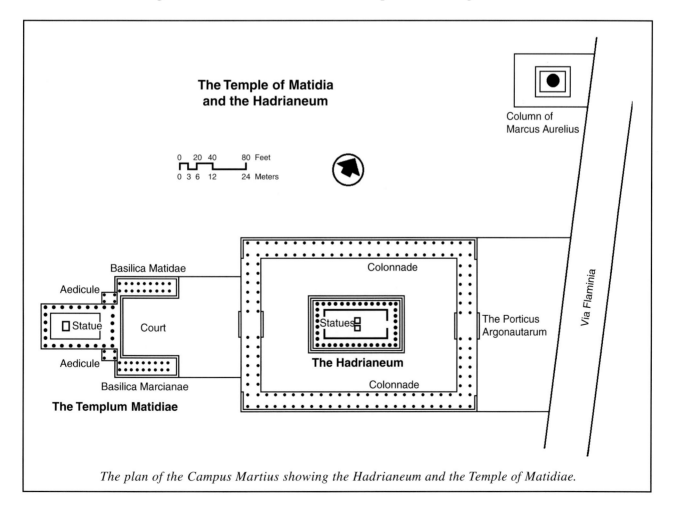

The plan of the Campus Martius showing the Hadrianeum and the Temple of Matidiae.

164

nades may actually be the structures referred to in the *Regionary Catalogue,* a fourth century list of buildings in Rome, as the Basilica Marcianae on the south side and the Basilica Matidaea on the north. Marciana, as the sister of Trajan and the mother of Matidia, had also been a great supporter of Hadrian's political ambitions.

The temple of Matidia, including its flanking basilicas, is shown on a rare medallion struck by Hadrian in A.D. 121. The legend, DIVAE MATIDIAE SOCRVI, appears in the exergue, be-

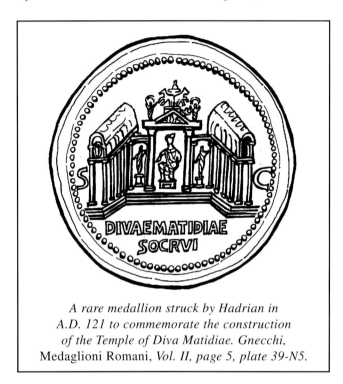

A rare medallion struck by Hadrian in A.D. 121 to commemorate the construction of the Temple of Diva Matidiae. Gnecchi, Medaglioni Romani, *Vol. II, page 5, plate 39-N5.*

low the buildings. *Socrus* is the Latin word for mother-in-law, and this beautiful medallion is a wonderful tribute to the mother of the emperor's wife. A drawing done by the famous artist Piranesi in 1756 shows the ruins of this temple in Rome with seven columns still standing.[1] Nothing remains of the building today, except for a stump of a column in the street called the Vicolo della Spada d'Orlando. Two other columns may be built into a house in the nearby piazza.

Hadrian's adopted son and successor Antoninus Pius, A.D. 138-161, was given the title Pius by the senate for his patient, judicious, and impartial rule, but also because he persistently recommended that Hadrian be deified, as had all the other great emperors. The senate had a grudge against Hadrian, because of his autocratic reign, and resisted

bestowing the usual posthumous honor of deification. Antoninus Pius finally convinced the senate to deify Hadrian, and he built a temple to Divus Hadrian in the middle of the Porticus Argonautarum. It was dedicated in 145 and probably completed in 151.

This grand temple, called the "Hadrianeum," is well illustrated on the sestertii of Antoninus Pius struck in 151. See RIC 873. These coins show an octastyle Corinthian temple with two statues displayed inside the cella. These are assumed to be the cult images of the emperor and his wife Sabina. Many numismatic reference books identify this coin as commemorating the restoration of the temple of Divus Augustus, but recently scholars have determined that the Hadrianeum is the temple illustrated.[2] Surprisingly, two palm trees are shown flanking the temple at the right and left side. The palm tree is normally an iconographic symbol for Judaea, but in Hadrian's battles against the Jews in the Second Jewish War of 132-135 the Roman army was humiliated. Judaea was conquered only with a great loss of Roman lives and prestige. This can be recognized in the fact that Hadrian, in his report to the senate at the end of the war, omitted the customary pronouncement in his salutation that "the emperor and the army are well."[3] However, the palm trees may represent trophies of the victory in Judaea and not the Jewish nation.

A substantial part of the Hadrianeum still exists and can be seen in Rome today. These remains consist of the cella wall and eleven columns of the northern side of the structure located in the Piazza di Pietra. In the excavations of this area during the 16th, 17th, and 19th centuries, sculptural

---

[1] *Pictorial Dictionary of Ancient Rome, Vol II,* by E. Nash, London, 1962, page 36.
[2] *Monuments of Ancient Rome as Coin Types,* by Philip V. Hill, Seabys, London, 1989, page 27.
[3] *Israel, A History of the Jewish People,* by Rufus Learsi, World Publishing Co., New York, 1949, page 192.

pedestals and decorative elements of the temple, showing personifications of the provinces and carvings of weapons or trophies, were discovered. These are presently on display in the museums of Rome and Naples. The legend in the exergue of the coin, PIETAS, alludes to the epithet and the personal quality and character of the emperor Antoninus Pius, and not to Hadrian.

This group of important but relatively unknown structures demonstrates Hadrian's connections and contributions to the architecture of Rome. These buildings represent one of his many restorations; the Argonautarum, one of his original building designs; the Temple of Diva Matidiae; and a great new temple, the Hadrianeum, dedicated to him by his successor.

A sestertius of Antoninus Pius showing the Hadrianeum. RIC, 873.

Chapter 25

The Temple of Divus Antoninus Pius and Diva Faustina

Along the Via Sacra, across from the temple of Divus Julius Caesar and overlooking the lower Forum, was the small but elegant temple of the deified Faustina Senior and her husband, the deified Antoninus Pius. When Faustina died in A.D. 141, the senate deified her and erected this temple in her honor. The temple was dedicated in 142 but, according to the dates on the coins, was probably completed in 150. A basic inscription of DIVAE. FAVSTINAE EX. S.C., meaning for the "Divine Faustina by Order of the Senate," was placed on the architrave over the entrance of the temple. When Antoninus Pius died in 161, the new emperor, his son Marcus Aurelius, re-dedicated the temple to both of his parents. This was done simply by carving another inscription on the upper part of the architrave beam above the inscription of Faustina. The inscription for Antoninus was carved with larger letters and stated DIVO. ANTONINVS. ET. The Latin conjunction ET, meaning "and," joined the two inscriptions into one sentence to say (for) The Divine Antoninus and the Divine Faustina, by Order of the Senate.

The temple cella, only about 57 feet (17 m) wide by 66 feet (20 m) long, was perhaps made this size to fit on the small ground site available for the building. The structure had a hexastyle facade of Corinthian columns with three freestanding columns at the sides. A large monumental set of stairs raised it above the street level. A fence or balustrade created a precinct in front of the stairs, and this contained the large altar placed before the temple. The columns were made of *cipollino,* a green and white marble veined like an onion, which had become very popular for temples in the

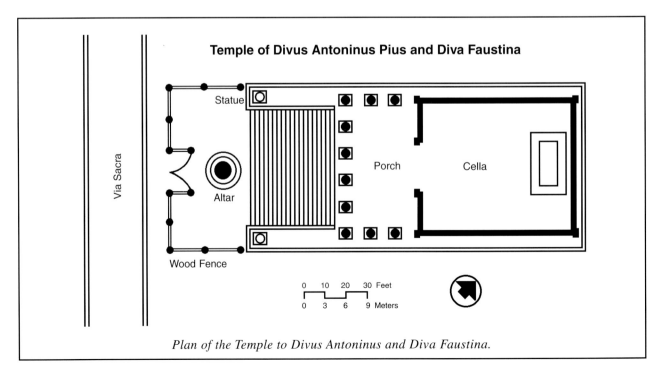

Plan of the Temple to Divus Antoninus and Diva Faustina.

reign of Hadrian. The pediment contained sculptures portraying Faustina surrounded by young girls, the famous *Puellae Faustinianae,* Faustina's girls. Antoninus had established a charity foundation, in the name of the empress, to look after the orphan girls of Rome. Faustina, in her lifetime, had always taken a great interest in these poor, unfortunate, and homeless youngsters. A quadriga surmounted the pediment, and Victories bearing wreaths above their heads were placed as acroteriae at the roof edges. A sculptured frieze on the entablature of the temple shows griffins, vases, candelabras, and garlands, all traditional Roman symbols of mourning. This frieze can still be seen on the site, and it is considered to be a fine example of the Roman sculptural art of the second century A.D.

The Temple of Antoninus and Faustina was preserved because a portion of the building was converted into a church in the eighth century by a devout woman named Miranda. This structure survives today as the church of "S. Lorenzo in Miranda", but the rest of the temple was destroyed in the Middle Ages, when the marble wall facing was stripped away to be used in the reconstruction of the church S. John in the Lateran, and the marble steps were removed to be used in the construction of Saint Peter's. However, the portion of the building that remains today is in excellent condition.

A reconstruction of the Temple of Divus Antoninus Pius and Diva Faustina.

This temple is well represented on the coinage struck by Antoninus Pius after A.D. 141. Aurei were issued with no legends but showing the hexastyle, Corinthian temple in great detail, RIC 406A. These fine, artistic gold coins appear to have been designed by the very best artists employed in the mint. The quadriga at the apex of the roof and the two Victories at the edges are clearly delineated. The Victories hold aloft wreaths, or as some numismatists interpret them, shields. The statuary in the pediment of the temple is less definite, but the central group looks like Faustina with her *puellae,* or young ladies, at her sides. The cult statue inside the cella is represented by a large pellet or dot engraved on the doorway.

Some denarii with accurate depictions of the temple also bear the legend AETERNITAS (BMC 383). Other denarii, struck with the legend AED DIVA FAVSTINAE (RIC 343), commemorate the dedication of the temple. Another similar denarius shows the legend DEDICATIO AEDIS (BMC 479). The temple is also well rendered on

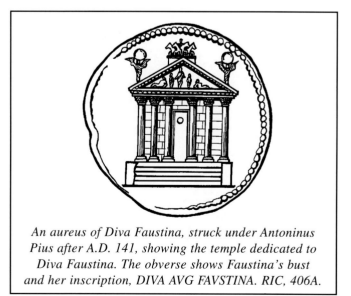

An aureus of Diva Faustina, struck under Antoninus Pius after A.D. 141, showing the temple dedicated to Diva Faustina. The obverse shows Faustina's bust and her inscription, DIVA AVG FAVSTINA. RIC, 406A.

168

A sestertius of Diva Faustina, struck by Antoninus Pius after A.D. 141, showing the Temple to Diva Faustina with the cult statue, fence, and altar. RIC, 1115.

The sestertius of Diva Faustina with the legend DEDICATIO AEDIS. RIC, 1137.

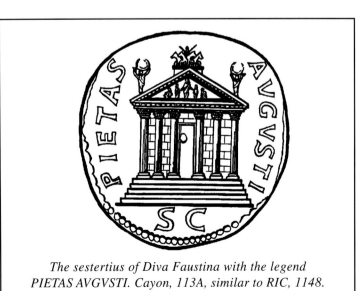

The sestertius of Diva Faustina with the legend PIETAS AVGVSTI. Cayon, 113A, similar to RIC, 1148.

several sestertii. These bear the legends AETERNITAS SC (RIC 1115), DEDICATIO AEDIS SC (RIC 1137), and some others appear with the legend PIETAS AVG (RIC 1148). The larger surface of the sestertius enabled the engravers to display more of the elements and details of the temple than can be seen on the aurei and denarii. The AETERNITAS reverse shows the edifice in all its glory, complete with the fence and altar in front, and two statues on plinths on the temple platform. These were probably mounted in front of the columns as shown on the plan above. A statue of a seated Faustina, which probably was the image inside the cella, is displayed in the center of the facade.

Other sestertii of Diva Faustina show the same temple, but with different details. The coin with the DEDICATIO AEDIS inscription shows the cult statue, but not the fence and the altar. The sestertius with the PIETAS AVG or AVGVSTI reverse shows the temple, but the statue is replaced with the pellet or dot. All these coins are scarce, but highly prized by collectors who specialize in architectural types.

Marcus Aurelius did not display nor commemorate this temple on his coinage when he re-dedicated it to his father after A.D. 161. Perhaps he neglected to do this because he had only added a short inscription to the temple, a minor renovation not worthy of a coin. Possibly, he was ashamed of the fact that he did not erect a great temple to the memory of his beloved father. However, history tells us that Marcus Aurelius was probably very busy, and had several more important events to commemorate on his coinage, as we shall see in the next chapter.

Chapter 26

The Shrine of Mercury

Religion played a very large part in the daily lives of the ancient Romans, and the city of Rome contained a multitude of temples and shrines. Most of these were consecrated to the traditional gods of the Roman pantheon, but as the city evolved into a cosmopolitan metropolis, some temples were dedicated to foreign deities such as Aesclepius from Greece, Isis or Serapis from Egypt, and Magna Mater from Syria. There were also several synagogues in Rome dating to as early as the second century B.C., and these probably became the first churches in Rome. Many of the religious edifices were founded at an early date, and their designs followed the strict classical formula of the column orders as set out by Hellenistic architects. In some rare cases, innovative designs were created by combining several architectural styles. This was usually done to create a temple or shrine that reflected the background mythology and the country of origin of the divinity. When we lack written descriptions for such unusual buildings, we can often turn to the ancient coins for illustrations of their appearance. Perhaps an example of this special type of architectural monument was the so-called temple of Mercury (Mercurius) established in early Rome.

According to the Roman historian Livy, the temple of Mercury in Rome was constructed in 495 B.C.[1] This temple was located on the north slope of the Aventine Hill, above and overlooking the Circus Maximus. Mercury was the patron deity of businessmen, and the foundation day of the temple, May 15, became the festival of the merchants in Rome. Mercurius was probably derived from the Greek god Hermes, but he may also have come to the Romans, in a derivative form, through the Etruscan religion. The Roman Mercury, as the messenger or herald of the gods, shared the same mythological background as the Greek Hermes and carried the same symbols: the caduceus, a herald's staff, and the winged hat and shoes. The cult of Mercury eventually became widespread in the Roman empire, especially among merchants, traders, and later—for some unknown reason—thieves. His name supposedly came from the Latin word "merx," meaning commodities and wares, or from the word "mercator," meaning a merchant or dealer, and the temple of Mercury later functioned as the headquarters and treasury of the powerful merchant's guild in Rome. It was still in existence in the fourth century A.D., but no trace of it has ever been found by modern archaeologists.

The so-called temple of Mercury is shown on only one Roman coin, a sestertius struck by Marcus Aurelius in A.D. 173, RIC 1074, but the coin is important for numismatic, historical, and architectural reasons. This coin shows an unusual temple facade, made up of a semicircular pediment held up by four columns which are sculpted in the shape of men. The statues shown in the pediment area are a tortoise, a cock with his head turned right, a ram with head turned right, the winged hat of Mercury called a "petasus," a caduceus or the herald's staff, and a purse. These are the ritual attributes always associated with Mercury. The sack type of a purse is often shown on sculptures of Mercury, and is sometimes used to represent "profit." The bigger the purse, the greater the profit. On the coin, a cult statue of Mercury, holding a caduceus, can be seen centrally

---

[1] *The Early History of Rome,* by Livy, Book 2, Chapter 21 and also 27, translated by A. De Selincourt, Penguin Classics, London, 1960, page 112.

A sestertius of Marcus Aurelius, struck in A.D. 176, showing the so-called temple of the god Mercury in Rome. RIC Marcus Aurelius, 1074.

located between the columns. The inscription on the coin is IMP VI COS III SC, and RELIG AVG, for RELIGIO AVGVSTI, in the exergue.

The statue columns shown on the coin have been interpreted in several ways. Some authors refer to these figures as "mummiform"—that is, resembling the Egyptian mummy-like statues used to represent the god Osiris. Others state that these columns are "telamones."[2] Telamones were the male form of "caryatids," those unusual Greek columns carved in the shape of women.

Vitruvius provided an explanation as to why human statues were used as columns in ancient temples. He said that in the war between the Greeks and Persians, the country of Caryae in Laconia sided with the Persian enemy. When the Greeks conquered Caryae, they enslaved all the people, including the aristocratic women. To further humiliate these ladies, they were forced to do menial work wearing their long robes, the traditional garb of respectable Greek matrons. To document this punishment, Greek architects designed temples with statues of these fully gowned ladies holding up the roof, to remind everyone about the shame of Caryae and the fate of the women after the triumph of the Greeks over the Persians.[3] These caryatides, named after the women from Caryae, can be seen in the porch of the Erechtheion, built in 421-410 B.C. on the acropolis of Athens.

Also, Vitruvius said that, after the defeat of the Persians at the battle of Plataea in 479 B.C., money from the sale of the booty was used to build a Persian Porch in Athens that had effigies of the Persian prisoners used as columns to carry the roof on their heads. These columns, carved as male statues in Persian costumes, were the original telamones. Similar columns, carved to look like men with arms upraised to support the roof structure, are sometimes called "atlantes," the plural of Atlas, the demigod who, in mythology, supported the sky on his shoulders. These atlantes were often used in Roman baths and public buildings as decorative columns.

Some historians claim that the statue-columns on the Roman temple of Mercury are "termini."[4] These statues are made in the form of the deity Terminus, the god who presided over boundaries and who punished the unlawful usurpation of land. He was originally represented by an upright, large rectangular rock, but later a human head was added to the top. Termini, as sculptures, became the lot-line, boundary posts used by the Romans as permanent markers. These statues were respected by the people as inviolable, and a religious festival, the Terminalia, was held for the god Terminus on the 21st day of each February.

However, several historians believe that the statue-columns on the temple of Mercury are "herms," the stone idols related to the god Hermes and found in Greek mythology.[5] Herms were rectangular monuments, with the head of Hermes on top and a phallus projecting from the middle. Sometimes feet or toes were carved at the bottom, but the dominating element of the statue was the plain, stone pillar forming the body. The herm was originally a fertility symbol placed in front of

2 *The Monuments of Ancient Rome as Coin Types,* by Philip V. Hill, Seaby, London, 1989, page 37.
3 *The Ten Books on Architecture,* by Vitruvius, Book I, 1.5, translated by M.H. Morgan, Dover Publications, New York, 1960, page 6.
4 See the *Dictionary of Roman Coins,* by S.W. Stevenson, B.A. Seaby Ltd., London, 1964, page 681.
5 *Architectura Numismatica,* by T.L. Donaldson, Argonaut, Chicago, 1965, page 91.

Greek houses as a good luck charm.

Later, it was also placed in front of temples or at cross-roads as boundary and signposts. This practice may indi-cate an assimilation of the fertility herms with the marker function of the termini statues. However, the herms were also considered to be the protectors of travellers and tra-ders, and therefore became associated with itinerant mer-chants and the god Mercury. Because of this multifunc-tional religious purpose, the herms were treated as im-portant, sacred objects. The Greek leader Alcibiades was politically persecuted and banished from Athens in 415 B.C. because, one evening, he and his drunken companions mutilated most of the herms in the city. By the time of Marcus Aurelius, the herms had been transformed into fertility and good luck charms associated with the Roman god Mercury. They were commonly used by the Romans as garden statues, to decorate the landscape and to stimulate plant growth. Such statues have been found in the gardens of houses excavated in Pompeii and in Rome.

A Roman herm of the first century B.C. These were used in Roman gardens as decorations and as good luck charms. The head probably represents some form of the ancient god of fertility, Hermes/Mercury.

The statue-columns used on the Temple of Mercury may have been any of the above pillar-type sculptures, but herms are the most logical choice given that their Roman function was directly connected to Mercury. Positive con-firmation of this can be found in the historical reasons for this peculiar temple appearing on the coinage of Marcus Aurelius. Some historians believe that Marcus Aurelius restored the original temple of Mercury in Rome, and recorded the event by portraying this design on his coinage.[6] Others suggest that the coin has a more complicated and dramatic history. They say that it commemorates a miracle that took place during a battle between the Romans and the Quadi in A.D. 172. The legend on the coin, RELIG AVG, the Religion of the Emperor, announces that his religious piety and devo-tion caused this miracle to happen.[7]

The event occurred one hot day when the Romans were fighting with the Quadi, a Germanic tribe living in the area near the Danube river. Suffering from the heat, exhaustion, and thirst, the outnumbered legionaries were losing the battle when a freak thunderstorm struck. The heavy downpour cooled off the Romans and slaked their thirst, while the thunder, lightning, and hail accompanying the storm terrified the barbarians, and caused them to break off their attack and retreat into the woods. Dio Cassius, the Roman historian, A.D. 163-235, records this event in great detail.[8] Credit for the rain miracle was given to the prayers of Marcus Aurelius and to the god Mercury, whose help had been invoked by an Egyptian seer named Arnuphis. This magi-cian was present at the battle as part of the emperor's entourage, and he pleaded for help from "Hermes, the ancient god of the air."

This miracle scene is illustrated on the famous Column of Marcus Aurelius, which was erected

6 *A Topographical Dictionary of Ancient Rome,* by S. Platner and T. Ashbey, Oxford University Press, Oxford, 1929, page 339.
7 *Coins of the Roman Empire in the British Museum,* (BMC) Vol. IV, by H. Mattingly, British Museum, London, page cxxxix.
8 *Roman History,* by Dio Cassius, translated by E.W. Cary, Loeb Classical Library, Harvard University Press, 1924, Book LXXI.8.

A sketch of the sculptural panel on the Column of Marcus Aurelius showing the "Rain Miracle" during the battle against the Quadi.

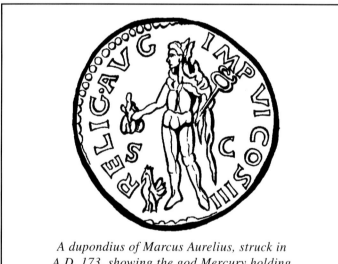

A dupondius of Marcus Aurelius, struck in A.D. 173, showing the god Mercury holding a caduceus and a purse. The god's personal symbol, a cock, can be seen at his feet. RIC, 1071.

in Rome in A.D. 176 to commemorate the emperor's victories over the Germans and Sarmatians. One panel of the frieze shows the battle against the Quadi. In this sculptured relief, the Roman soldiers are embraced and protected by the enormous wings of a grotesque, bearded rain-god whose long hair pours down like water.[9] The Quadi and their horses are shown at the right, defeated and fallen. The god shown in this sculpture is not the usual representation of Hermes, nor of Jupiter Tonans (the Thunderer), the Roman deity of thunder and lightning who would normally receive the credit for such a rain miracle. As the sculpture obviously represents the legend of the rain miracle, the god-figure on the column is perhaps an artistic assimilation or combination of the god Hermes/Mercury with Jupiter Tonans.

This miracle must have been a remarkable and memorable event because many other coins were struck by Marcus Aurelius as thanksgiving to Mercury. These coins are inscribed with the same RELIGIO AVGVSTI legend, but show a standing figure of Mercury holding the caduceus and a purse or a patera. Sometimes a cock, Mercury's personal symbol, is seen at his feet. These coins are cataloged as denarii, RIC Marcus Aurelius 285, 308, 309, and dupondii, RIC 1070-1073. Later, when the Roman empire became Christianized, the rain miracle was transferred and accredited to the prayers of the Christian soldiers in the battle, who served in Marcus Aurelius' Legio XII Fulminata, called the "Thundering Legion" in numismatic literature. More precisely, this regiment should have been called the Thunderbolt Legion, because a fulmen in Latin was a bolt of lightning. Marcus Aurelius had persecuted the Christians during his reign and, possibly, this Christianizing of the legend was a petty revenge taken by early Christian writers who wished to denegrate the emperor's pagan beliefs.

Some numismatists state that the temple shown on the coins of Marcus Aurelius has a decidedly Egyptian form and shape, in order to honor the timely prayers of the Egyptian soothsayer Arnuphis.

---

[9] *A Pictorial History of Ancient Rome, Vol I*, by E. Nash, A. Zwemmer Ltd., London, 1961, plate 330, page 279.

This may be a sound conjecture because a temple to the Egyptian goddess Isis, constructed in Rome during the reign of Caligula, did have a semicircular pediment similar to the one shown on the Temple of Mercury. This temple to Isis can be seen on a coin struck by Vespasian, RIC Vespasian, 453, but the original ancient temple of Mercury predated the temple of Isis in Rome by about four centuries. Other historians suggest that this temple of Mercury was designed as a tribute to the Roman god, but employed an architectural shape that recalled the Egyptian origins of Hermes. This theory may give the most reasonable explanation for the unusual form of the structure.

If attributing the rain miracle to the emperor's piety and prayers to Mercury seems strange, the appearance of the temple itself is even more so. The size and proportions are very small, and not really grand enough for a temple structure. Also, the use of the statue-like columns would be contrary to the contemporary style for temples constructed in Rome during the fifth to first centuries B.C. In those days, most temples used only the Ionic or Corinthian orders of columns. Therefore, a good argument can be made that the facade displayed on the coins actually represents a shrine or tabernacle for the cult statue, called a *sacellum* in Latin, which was located inside the temple. The semicircular top would be the fabric or thin metal canopy or "baldachin" traditionally used over such interior shrines. This is a fair assumption, and it fully accounts for the use of the herms as columns, because they were normally seen only on small scale monuments such as shrines. If this hypothesis is valid, the coin of Marcus Aurelius does not show the ancient temple itself, but a magnificent, new tabernacle for the cult statue placed in the middle of the cella and facing the main door. This peculiar shrine may have been built by Marcus Aurelius inside the old temple as full payment for the rain miracle.

According to Roman mythology, Mercury was a minor deity, popular only among the lowly merchant classes who were generally despised by the Romans. After all, the merchants were the offspring of slaves. But on this single occasion, and in the reign of only one emperor, a fortuitous thunderstorm gave Mercury his great, one day of glory, and momentarily raised him up to the highest level of Mount Olympus.

A reconstruction of the shrine of Mercury, shown located inside a traditional Ionic style temple of the fifth century B.C. The architectural details of the shrine are taken directly from the coin of Marcus Aurelius.

PART V

ROMAN STRUCTURES
AND MONUMENTS
ON COINS

Chapter 27

The Round Temples of Rome

Circular or round temples (tholos in Greek) were common in the ancient world and many of them are illustrated on coins. The Roman poet Virgil, 70-19 B.C., in his epic poem *The Aeneid*, IX, 408, remarked that circular temples were dedicated chiefly to the deities Vesta, Diana, Hercules, and Mercury. The most famous Roman circular temple was the small temple of Vesta located near the temple of Castor and Pollux at the foot of the Palatine Hill in the Forum Romanum. The construction for such circular temples was described by Vitruvius in his work, Book IV, Chap. VIII, 3. He explained that there were two types of circular temples, the "monopteral" and the "peripteral". The monopteral consisted of columns arranged in a circle as a colonnade on a stylobate. The columns carried curved beams that supported the vaulted cupola or dome (rotundum tectum) made of wood or concrete and faced with stone. The cult statue of the deity stood in the open center of this plan. The peripteral plan also used columns as a freestanding colonnade, but this encircled a round cella, an enclosed chamber in the center of the temple.

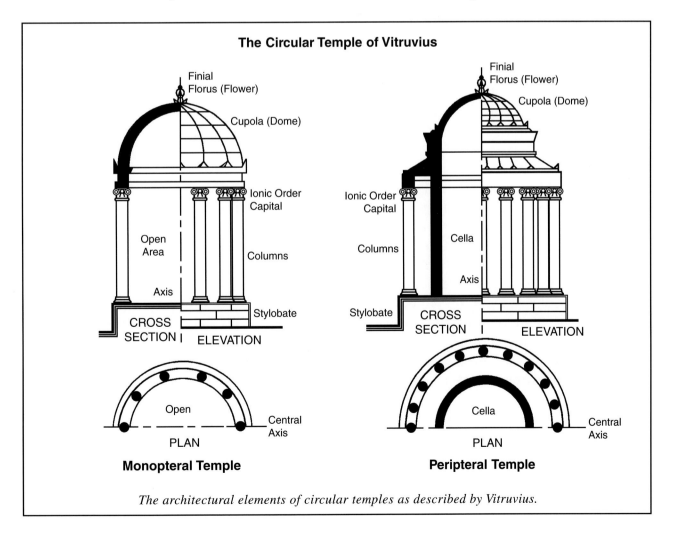

The architectural elements of circular temples as described by Vitruvius.

The round temple is usually identified with the worship of Vesta. This goddess, while only a minor deity, played an important part in the daily lives of the Romans. This can be proven by her many temples and the appearance of her image on a multitude of coins. Vesta can be seen on Roman Republican denarii, and on the coins of 34 different emperors beginning with Julius Caesar and ending with Gallienus in A.D. 268. Her legend on these coins was usually only her name, VESTA, but this may also have been supplemented with the titles *Augusta* (Revered), *Aeterna* (Eternal), *Felix* (Fortunate), and *Mater* (Mother). Vesta was closely identified with and adapted from the Greek deity of fire, Hestia. According to the Greek poet Hesiod, who lived in the 8th century B.C., Hestia was the virgin sister of Zeus and the goddess of the hearth.[1] The names Vesta and Hestia are supposedly both derived from the same Sanskrit root, *Vas,* which expresses the concept of "shining."

In ancient days, fire was essential to life because it was the only source of heat and light. In those prehistoric times, when fire was difficult to make, it was necessary to keep a constantly burning, communal fire in a central hut of the village. The task of maintaining this fire was left to the young girls of the community who were not needed to work in the fields. In time, this guardianship of the fire became a sacred institution, and these young women were personified by the goddess Hestia, the virgin sister of Zeus. Vesta, the Roman adaption of Hestia, became the deity symbolizing fire and the hearth, and then the family. In the earliest Roman legends, the goddess Vesta was supposedly introduced into Italy by Aeneas, the Trojan hero who escaped from Troy and whose son, Iulus, founded Alba Longa, the mother city of Rome.

Numa Pompilius, the second Etruscan king of Rome, is reputed to have built the first temple dedicated to Vesta. The Palladium of Troy, carried to Italy by Aeneas, was placed in the sanctuary, and a fire was kept constantly burning by the young guardians who were called the Vestal Virgins. If this fire went out, it was considered to be an evil omen and the Roman people would suffer from some disaster. If the fire was accidentally extinguished, it could be relit only by the pure rays of the sun using a concave mirror, a procedure described by Plutarch in the chapter on Numa Pompilius.[2] The Vestals were closely connected with the early college of Pontifices in Rome. At first there were only two Vestal Virgins to represent the ancient Roman tribes, Ramnes and Tatienses. Afterwards, two others were added for the Luceres tribe, and later, two more were added to make a maximum of six. Vestals were chosen from patrician families and they had to be between six and ten years old, without any physical blemishes. They devoted thirty years to the service of Vesta; ten years as a novice, ten as an active priestess, and ten as the teacher of novices. After thirty years, a Vestal could return to her family and get married or remain in the service of the temple. The goddess Vesta or the Vestals are usually portrayed on coins with their symbol of purity, a white veil called a *suffibulum,* tied under their chins.

The Vestal Virgins were carefully protected against insult or temptation, and any offense to a Vestal was punishable by death. In public places everyone, even the consuls, made way for these priestesses. The Vestals' prime responsibility was tending the eternal flame, and if it went out through negligence they suffered corporal punishment at the hands of the Pontifex Maximus. Once established as a cult, the Vestals became a powerful political influence in Roman society, and a large house, the "Atrium Vestae," with a magnificent atrium garden was built for them adjacent to their temple. The Vestals took a vow of absolute chastity and breaches of this vow were punishable by death. Guilty priestesses were beaten with rods and then walled-up, still alive, in a tomb. However, Vestals accused of impurity could prove their innocence by carrying water to the temple from

1 *Theogony,* by Hesiod, translated by H.G. Evelyn-White, The Loeb Classical Library, Cambridge, 1936.
2 *Plutarch's Lives*, The Translation called Dryden's, revised by A.H. Clough, Vol. I, Little, Brown and Co., Boston, 1888, page 140.

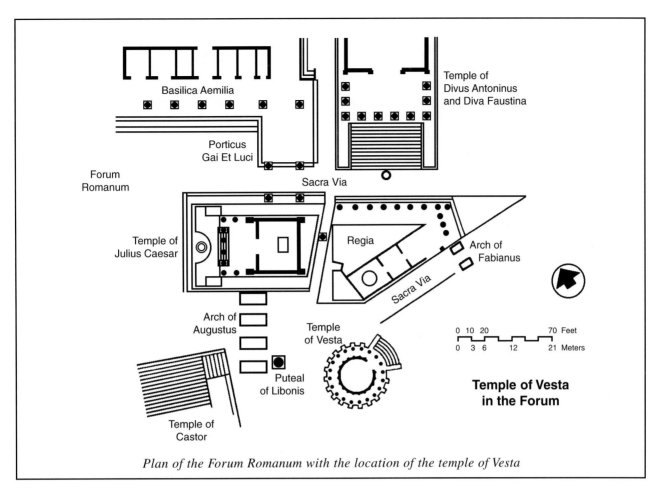

Plan of the Forum Romanum with the location of the temple of Vesta

the Tiber in a sieve. It is recorded that one, named Tuccia, actually did this (Pliny, Book XXVIII, 2), presumably when cold weather turned the water of the Tiber into ice. We know of only twenty Vestals being put to death for breaking their vows during the eleven centuries of their history.[3]

According to Plutarch, Numa Pompilius, who built the first temple to Vesta, chose the circular building plan to represent the universe. It is more likely, as suggested by some art historians, that the round form of the temple is derived from the conical, rough huts of the early Latin people. These circular, primitive abodes were made by sticking limbs of trees in the ground in a circular plan, and then tying the tops together to form a dome structure. This was covered by branches and clay or thatch to keep out the weather. Usually, a fire would be kept burning on the central stone hearth in this round shelter. An example of such an old-fashioned round hut was kept on the Palatine Hill as a shrine to Romulus, the founder of Rome, and this hut was maintained as a national monument up to the middle of the fourth century A.D.[4] The form of these

[3] *New Larousse Encyclopedia of Mythology*, page 205.

[4] *The Ruins and Excavations of Ancient Rome*, by Rodolfo Lanciani, reprint of the 1897 edition, Bell Publishing Co., New York, 1967, page 130.

The early funeral "Hut-Urns," made of clay, found in Alba Longa, probably dating to the eighth century B.C.

A denarius of Q. Cassius, 57 B.C., with the head of Vesta, Syd. 917, or, with the head of Libertas, Syd. 918. The reverses show the fourth temple of Vesta surmounted by a statue. A curule chair is shown within the hexastyle temple. Also illustrated are a voting urn on the left and a tablet on the right inscribed with "AC" for Absolvo, Condemno.

See plates, coin 39.

A dupondius of Tiberius, A.D. 14-37, struck to commemorate the deified Augustus. The reverse shows a round, hexastyle temple using an eye level one-point perspective. It is flanked by two tall altars, with an animal facing inwards on each. RIC Tiberius 74.

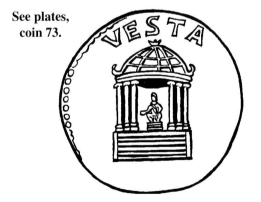

See plates, coin 73.

An aureus of Nero, A.D. 54-68, showing the fifth temple of Vesta in Rome. RIC Nero 61. The same temple appears on a denarius, RIC 67.

houses can be clearly seen in the terracotta funeral urns of the early Latin people, which were made circular with domed roofs to resemble the primitive huts in which they lived.

The original temple to Vesta in Rome, probably built as a round thatched hut, was eventually replaced by a masonry structure, and this second temple was destroyed by the Gauls in 390 B.C. The third temple dedicated to Vesta was destroyed by a fire in 241 B.C. A fourth temple was immediately built for the cult of Vesta, and this structure can be seen on a Roman Republican denarius struck in 57 B.C.

In the time of Augustus, a flood seriously damaged this fourth temple, and it was restored or totally rebuilt in marble on the same site. This fifth temple is believed to appear on coins struck by Tiberius, A.D. 14-37, but the identification is uncertain. However, noting its circular shape, most authorities describe it as the fifth temple of Vesta built by Augustus and located in the Forum (Aedes Vestae in Foro). Other writers identify it as the shrine to Vesta which Augustus built near his palace on the Palatine Hill (Aedes Vestae in Palatio) when he became Pontifex Maximus in 12 B.C.[5]

As Vesta came to represent the sanctity and unity of the family, and as Augustus was considered to be the head of the Roman national family, a close connection developed between the worship of Vesta and the cult devoted to Augustus. Therefore, the temple on the coin above may be related to the cult of Divus Augustus instead of to Vesta. This may be verified by the animals on the flanking altars. They are often described as a ram on the right and a calf on the left, and this recalls the fact that a ram and calf were the usual animals sacrificed to Divus Augustus.[6]

---

[5] The explanation for this is given in "Divus Augustus Pater," by C.H.V. Sutherland, in the *Numismatic Chronicle*, 1941, footnote 25 on pages 115-116.

[6] Mentioned by the early Christian poet Aurelius Prudentius Clemens, writing about paganism in his work *Contra Symmachum*, translated by H.J. Thompson, The Loeb Classical Library, Cambridge, 1949, page 245.

However, the succeeding fifth temple, which probably resembled the round temple of Divus Augustus, lasted for many years, and it is shown on early coins of Nero. It appears as a compact, domed monopteral structure with a statue, perhaps of Vesta, inside. The temple is approached by a monumental stairway, a feature that reappears on later coins showing this structure.

The fifth temple to Vesta was destroyed by fire in the conflagration of A.D. 64, and was entirely rebuilt as the sixth temple by Nero. Vespasian and his sons probably embellished Nero's temple to Vesta and displayed it on several of their coins. The principal coins in this Vesta series were struck about A.D. 73, and may have publicized the devotion of the emperor to family life and to the Roman people rather than the rebuilding of the temple. According to Michael Grant, the coins may also commemorate the centenary of the "republica restituta," the restitution of the Republic.[7]

In later times, Faustina Jr., the daughter of Antoninus Pius, A.D. 138-161, sponsored a medallion-like sestertius, RIC Antoninus Pius 1384, showing three priests and three Vestals sacrificing over an altar before a hexastyle,

See plates, coin 74.

An aureus and an As of Vespasian, A.D. 69-79, showing Nero's sixth temple of Vesta. Aurei RIC Vespasian 59, 304, the As, RIC 548. Similar coins depicting the temple of Vesta were struck by Vespasian for his sons. For Titus as Caesar, aurei RIC Vespasian 157, 162, 171, 180, and also an As, RIC 659. For Domitian as Caesar, aurei RIC Vespasian 230, 249, and also Asses, RIC 690, 705.

circular temple. This is believed to be the same sixth temple of Vesta, and the coin may record Faustina's supposed piety and devotion to family life, or perhaps her vows taken for the safe return of her father from the frontier. This coin became the model for many later coins illustrating the ceremonial rituals in front of the temple to Vesta. In A.D. 191, during the reign of Commodus, another terrible fire destroyed the temple of Vesta and much of the Forum. The last recorded restoration, which resulted in a seventh or perhaps eighth temple, was undertaken by Septimius Severus and Julia Domna, and this structure is celebrated on their coins from about A.D. 204 onwards. This family struck a

See plates, coin 75.

An As of Julia Domna struck under her son Caracalla in A.D. 211-217, showing four Vestals sacrificing in front of the round temple. RIC Caracalla 607.

large quantity of coins, in all denominations including medallions, to commemorate their temple of Vesta. Julia Domna seemed to have been totally involved in the cult of Vesta, and she struck many coins under her husband or her son Caracalla to illustrate her ceremonial religious connection to the temple.

---

[7] *Roman Anniversary Issues,* by Michael Grant, reprint by Attic Books, New York, 1977, page 163.

Many coins showing the architecture of this temple were struck in the name of Julia Domna by her husband, Septimius Severus. These are denarii, RIC Septimius Severus 584, 585, 586. Also, a sestertius, RIC 868, and a dupondius or an As, RIC 892, 893. Several more similar coins were struck under her son Caracalla. These are aurei, RIC Caracalla 392, sestertii, RIC 594, and also an As, RIC 607. All these coins closely resemble the coins struck by Faustina Jr., and show two, four, or six Vestals and sometimes also two children sacrificing over an altar before a circular temple. Some authorities claim this scene portrays the ceremonies of public worship by Julia and vows for the safe return of Caracalla from the wars on the frontier. There are also coins struck for Caracalla with the same architectural composition. These are aurei dated to A.D. 214, RIC Caracalla 249, 250, and 271. They show the emperor sacrificing at an altar with Vestals, priests, and a child before the round temple. The coin, RIC 250, also shows Julia Domna standing beside the emperor. These coins probably document the vows taken by the emperor before leaving for the wars. The date of these coins, however, corresponds exactly with the bicentenary of the death of Augustus, and they may actually be commemorating this anniversary.

There are several very rare medallions which duplicate the scene shown on these temple coins. These are bronze medallions of Faustina Sr., the wife of Antoninus Pius, A.D. 138-141, Cohen 318; a bronze medallion of Lucilla, wife of Lucius Verus, 161-169, Cohen 105; one of Crispina, wife of Commodus, 177-192, Cohen 45; and a rare silver medallion of Julia Domna, Cohen 240.

Generally, all these coins illustrate the round temple with Vestals sacrificing over an altar in the foreground. This architectural scene probably proclaimed the faithfulness of the emperors and empresses to their religious vows and to family life by showing their devotion to the goddess of the Roman hearth and home. After the defeat of Eugenius in A.D. 394, Theodosius II suppressed the cult of Vesta, banished the Vestal Virgins, closed the doors of the temple, and extinguished the flame that had burned continuously and brightly for over 1,000 years.

The temples of Vesta were by no means the only round temples in Rome. The deities Minerva, Hercules, Mercury, and even some princes and princesses of the imperial family were honored with circular shrines. Not as famous as the temple to Vesta, another splendid tholos structure was built in Rome for Minerva Chalcidica. This shrine was erected on the Campus Martius by Domitian, A.D. 81-96. Little is known about this temple, but it was sited near the temple to Isis and Serapis, and it appears on the Severan marble plan of Rome, the "Forma Urbis Romae." Chalcis was the chief city of Euboea and home of a

A silver medallion of Julia Domna, struck before A.D. 217, showing the round Temple of Vesta in Rome and six vestals sacrificing over an altar. Cohen 204 and Gnecchi I, plate 22, no. 4.

See plates, coin 76.

A denarius of Domitian struck in A.D. 88-96 showing the temple of Minerva Chalcidica. RIC Domitian 206.

large and influential cult to Minerva which was later transplanted to Rome. A coin of Domitian shows this round temple or shrine with Corinthian columns, and an armed and helmeted statue of the goddess in the center.

A very historical coin with pathetic undertones shows a fine round temple dedicated to an imperial princess named Claudia. This daughter of Nero and Poppaea died in A.D. 63 when she was only four months old. Poppaea, who is mentioned and perhaps shown in the tem-

See plates, coin 77.

An AE19, struck at some unknown colonial mint after A.D. 65, showing Claudia as a young woman, standing in a round, Corinthian style temple or shrine. The obverse shows the deified Poppaea seated in an Ionic style temple, probably tetrastyle even though only two columns are shown. Sear GIC 673.

ple on the obverse of the coin as DIVA—deified—was kicked to death by an insane and furious Nero in A.D. 65.

The round or circular temple was not merely a passing architectural fad; it had a venerable tradition going back into the early history of Rome. Also, the circle was a powerful sign to many ancient cults and religions because it represented the universe, perfection, faithfulness, and eternity. Laden with this symbolism, the circular plan was considered appropriate for use in the shrines of deities and as the monuments of individuals who displayed these pure virtues.

Chapter 28

The Temple of Divus Romulus

Of the many round or circular temples in Rome, the most unusual was the temple of Divus Romulus, built sometime after A.D. 309. Round temples normally consist of a circular colonnade around an open space or a closed in cella, but the temple dedicated to Romulus has a rectangular porch, a circular cella, and enclosed wings at each side. This temple was located on the Via Sacra near the Temple of Antoninus and Faustina. The emperor Maxentius built this edifice for his son, M. Valerius Romulus, who died in A.D. 309, and this structure gives us a perfect example of how coins can often clarify historical information about ancient buildings.

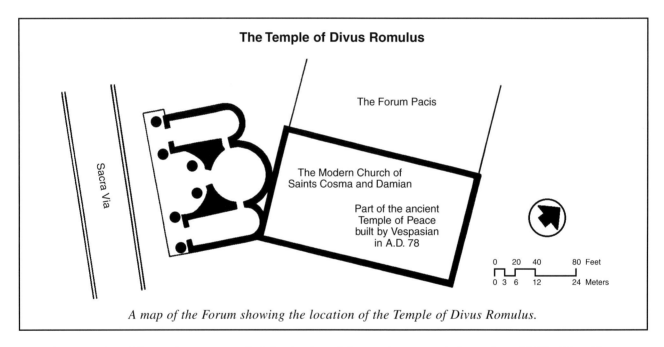

The Temple of Divus Romulus

The Forum Pacis

Sacra Via

The Modern Church of
Saints Cosma and Damian

Part of the ancient
Temple of Peace
built by Vespasian
in A.D. 78

0 20 40   80 Feet
0 3 6   12   24 Meters

A map of the Forum showing the location of the Temple of Divus Romulus.

The temple of Romulus was unfinished when Maxentius was defeated and killed by Constantine the Great at the Milvian bridge in A.D. 312. Constantine then completed this temple, and also the basilica of Maxentius which stood nearby, and dedicated them to his own family. But the name "Templum Romuli" appears in medieval documents describing this building and there is some confusion about this identification. The temple appears on coins, but two different versions of the building are illustrated. Most numismatists account for the two building designs shown on the coins by explaining that, as well as a temple in Rome, a tomb for Romulus was built along the Appian Way, and the solid masonry building without columns displayed on some of the coins is this tomb. The tomb structure, as seen on the coins, appears to be more solidly constructed, and the heavy masonry is easily recognized by the joints in the walls and the absence of columns on the facade. Remains of this round tomb have actually been found by archaeologists near the Circus of Maxentius, about three miles (5 km) outside of Rome on the Via Appia. It was a two-story structure with a lower tomb chamber and a round temple above. The temple had a hexastyle porch facing south to the road.

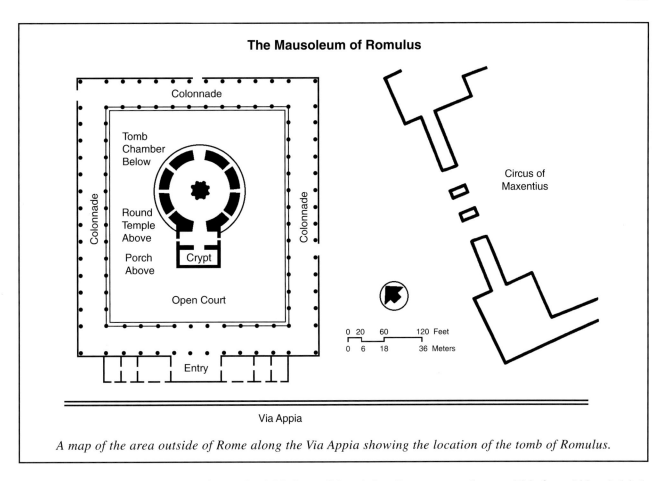

The Mausoleum of Romulus

Colonnade

Tomb Chamber Below

Round Temple Above

Porch Above

Crypt

Colonnade

Colonnade

Open Court

Entry

Circus of Maxentius

0 20 60 120 Feet
0 6 18 36 Meters

Via Appia

A map of the area outside of Rome along the Via Appia showing the location of the tomb of Romulus.

The building was approximately 109 feet (33 m) in diameter and was 132 feet (40 m) high overall. It had a rectangular burial crypt attached to its rear under the porch of the temple. The coins showing the tomb are RIC 207, and they were struck posthumously at mints in either Rome, with a letter "R" mint mark, or in Ostia, which used the "OST" abbreviation for a mint symbol.

The two types of coins of Divus Romulus appear to have been struck in two periods of time. First, coins struck in 310 immediately after Romulus' death illustrated the tomb building and carried the inscription AETERNAE MEMORIAE. This coin shows the solidly constructed masonry tomb near the Circus of Maxentius, with an eagle on the dome to symbolize the soul of the dead prince ascending. The open door is an artistic convention to indicate that the tomb was always open for visitors to pay their respects. The second coin, probably struck in 311, shows the proposed temple for Divus Romulus in Rome, dedicated but not yet completed. It also displays a dome structure, but with a frontal porch consisting of six Corinthian columns. Sometimes this coin appears with only four columns, but the legend is always the same, AETERNA

See plates, coin 78.

An AE follis of Romulus, struck posthumously by his father Maxentius after A.D. 309, showing the round tomb with an eagle on top. RIC 207.

See plates, coin 79.

An AE follis of Romulus, struck by his father around A.D. 311, showing the Temple of Divus Romulus in Rome. RIC 256.

MEMORIA. Again, the eagle and open door are used symbolically on the coin. From the part of the building still visible in Rome today, the temple was small, about 124 feet (38 m) wide and 90 feet (27 m) deep.

We do not know how Constantine I used this building when he converted it to his own purposes, but probably it became a monument dedicated to one of his victories. In early Christian times, the church of S. Cosma and S. Damiano was built into a part of Vespasian's temple of Peace, which lay just behind the Temple of Romulus. Pope Felix IV, 526-530, cut an opening between the two buildings and made the Temple of Romulus the entrance or vestibule to the church. Because of this secondary use, almost the entire temple was preserved and can be seen in Rome today. The bronze doors have been relocated to their original position and the two smaller columns, which may have flanked the doors, are in place.

These two coins explain that a round temple to Divus Romulus existed in Rome, and that a round tomb, more massive than the temple, was also located outside Rome among the other funeral monuments on the Via Appia. The actual appearances of these two buildings, while similar, are clearly illustrated on the coins so that no mistake in recognizing the structures is possible. These examples are confirmation that coins can be indispensable for the identification of ancient buildings when literary evidence is inconclusive or does not exist.

A reconstruction of the Temple of Divus Romulus.

Chapter 29

Triumphal Arches

The ancient architectural monuments we call triumphal arches were an entirely Roman invention; no precedent for them existed in Greek or eastern societies. The only possible ancestor for these arches may have been the Etruscan custom of erecting three spears tied together in a rectangular arch, and under which vanquished soldiers were forced to march in the stooped posture of subjugation. In fact, the English word subjugate comes from the Latin phrase *sub jugum,* meaning "under the spear," and this procession of defeated warriors was the origin of the triumphal march later adopted by the Romans. However, many historians attribute these structures to the Romans' great love of the arch form used as a structural element in large buildings. Others state that the triumphal arch was created specifically as a distinctive monument and symbol to represent the might and power of the Roman nation. The arch was called a *fornix* in Latin (*fornices,* plural), and although originally invented by the Etruscans or Greeks, it became an important structural device only when it was adopted by the Romans, who used concrete and formwork in their construction.

The earliest triumphal arches in Rome may have been the structural arches of the aqueducts, which were converted into commemorative monuments by simply adding statues and an inscription to the top. This was done to celebrate the victory of the Romans over their enemies perhaps as early as the third century B.C. The first recorded free-standing triumphal arches built in Rome were two erected in the Forum Boarium and one on the spina, the central platform, in the Circus Maximus. These arches were constructed beginning in 196 B.C. They were paid for by the proconsul of Spain, L. Stertinius, from the profits of his activities and land holdings in that province.[1] Three more arches are known to have been raised in Rome in the second century B.C. One, for Scipio Africanus, was erected in 190 B.C. to commemorate his defeat of Carthage. Another was built for the triumph celebrating the conquest of the city state of Corinth. We also know from historical records that one arch, called the Fornix Fabius, erected in 121 B.C., was rebuilt in 57 B.C.[2] Despite all this early arch-building activity, it was not until the reign of Augustus and his successors that the triumphal arch became a popular monument. Pliny the Elder, A.D. 27-79, in his work *Natural History*, Book XXXIV, 27, stated that the triumphal arch was a very new architectural fashion in Rome.

The most famous of these monumental structures is the Arch of Titus, which still stands in Rome today. It was built by the emperor Domitian in A.D. 81 to honor Titus' deification and the defeat of Judaea in A.D. 70. This renowned arch contains sculptural panels on the inside which illustrate the triumphal parade of Titus and the spoils taken from Jerusalem by the victorious Romans.

Most triumphal arches were constructed with a single opening, but sometimes three arches, a large one in the center and two smaller at the sides, were used to make a more impressive monument. Several plan forms of the arches were used over the centuries. These included single openings, double, triple, and *quadrifrons* types. A quadrifrons arch used four openings facing in

1 *History of Rome,* by Livy, translated by P.G. Walsh, Book XXXIII, 27, Loeb Classical Library, Cambridge, 1959.
2 *Roman Architecture,* by Frank Sear, Cornell University Press, Ithaca, New York, page 43.

A reconstruction of the Arch of Titus in Rome.
The quadriga on the top disappeared centuries ago.

The renowned sculptural panels inside the Arch of Titus.
These are the finest examples of first century A.D. Roman
sculptural reliefs and are important historical documents.

four directions, and this type was often used in the middle of the intersection of two main streets. The arch structures varied in size, but were usually from 50 to 80 feet (15-24 m) high, adorned with columns and statues, and with a triumphal quadriga grouping on the top. The attic panel at the top was often carved with a lengthy dedicatory inscription.

Triumphal arches were erected by most of the emperors, starting in the first century A.D., to commemorate their military victories and triumphal parades. These arches were usually placed in important intersections of main roads, or at prominent entrances to a public space such as a temple precinct or a forum. Triumphal arches were placed at the entrance to the forums of Julius Caesar, Augustus, and Trajan. Also, the senate erected several arches for Octavian, before he was called Augustus, in the Forum of Rome and in the principal cities of the provinces.

The most prominent arch for Augustus was located on the Sacra Via at the entrance to the Forum Romanum. This triple arch is believed to have been built in 20 B.C. to celebrate the diplomatic treaty made with the Parthians and the return of the Roman standards captured by them from Crassus in 63 B.C., Decidius Saxa in 40 B.C., and from Mark Antony in 36 B.C. The loss of these military ensigns to the enemy was a great disgrace to the Roman people, and recovering them was the cause of national rejoicing. The Parthian Arch is believed to have been built near or on top of the foundations of an earlier, single span arch, built in 29 B.C. and dedicated to Octavian for his victory over Mark Antony and Cleopatra at the battle of Actium in 31 B.C.

Archaeologists excavating the Forum area in Rome discovered the remains of the earlier Actian Arch lying directly in front of the Parthian Arch, perhaps indicating that the new arch was constructed

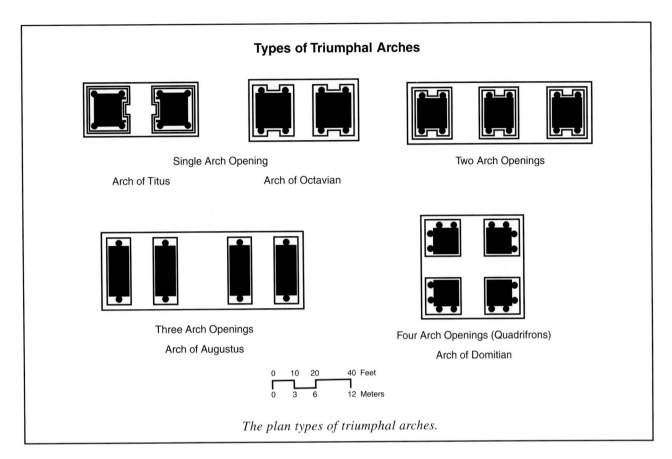

Types of Triumphal Arches

Single Arch Opening

Arch of Titus

Arch of Octavian

Two Arch Openings

Three Arch Openings

Arch of Augustus

Four Arch Openings (Quadrifrons)

Arch of Domitian

| 0 | 10 | 20 | 40 | Feet |
| 0 | 3 | 6 | 12 | Meters |

The plan types of triumphal arches.

before the old arch was removed. In comparing the coins showing the two arches, it appears that perhaps the bronze quadriga statue on the Actian Arch was reused on the later Parthian Arch. Also, the coin illustrates the Parthian Arch with three equally sized arch openings, but the archaeological excavations indicate that the monument had a larger central opening.

The return of these lost standards was not the result of a war with the enemy but of diplomatic negotiations. Nevertheless, it was such a momen-

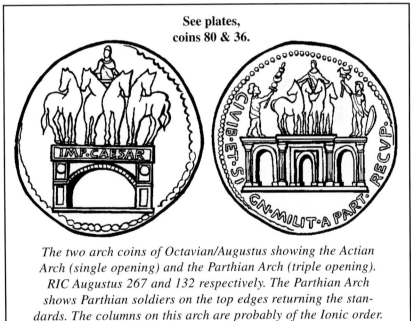

See plates,
coins 80 & 36.

The two arch coins of Octavian/Augustus showing the Actian Arch (single opening) and the Parthian Arch (triple opening). RIC Augustus 267 and 132 respectively. The Parthian Arch shows Parthian soldiers on the top edges returning the standards. The columns on this arch are probably of the Ionic order.

tous occasion that several triumphal arches were erected to commemorate the event. Augustus struck many coins, in different parts of the empire, showing some form of this Parthian Arch with the legend SIGNIS RECEPTIS, meaning the "Standards Retaken or Returned." An outstanding silver coin, a "cistophorus" equal to three Roman denarii, was struck in Pergamum, a Roman dependency in Asia Minor, showing the Parthian Arch and the legend SPQR SIGNIS RECEPTIS. The inscription on the attic panel, IMP IX TR PO V, records the date of the coin by giving Augustus' titles, Imperator for the ninth time and recipient of the Tribunicia Potestas,

190

See plates, coin 81.

A cistophorus, struck in Pergamum for Augustus in 19-18 B.C., showing a form of the Parthian Arch to commemorate the return of the lost standards. RIC Augustus 509.

the tribunican power, for the fifth time. These correspond to the years 19-18 B.C.

Some triumphal arches commemorated the civil deeds and acts instead of the military victories of Augustus, and were erected in cities all over the empire. The road building and highway restoration program initiated by Augustus was celebrated by a special series of coins, and many of these displayed a triumphal arch built over a viaduct. These coins are called the "Munitae" coins because their legends usually incorporate the abbreviation for the Latin word *munitare*, literally to open up, but meaning in this case to rebuild. Some of these arches are unusual in design and incorporate statues of a biga of elephants, the supreme form of the triumphal chariot used by the emperors. Pompey the Great, 106-48 B.C., was the first Roman to use elephants to draw his victory chariot in a triumphal procession. The inscription on the coin, QVOD VIA MVNT SVNT, the abbreviation of "for having caused the highways to be rebuilt," also indicates that this arch commemorated the emperor's restoration of the roadway system.

An aureus of Augustus showing a triumphal arch, surmounted by a biga of elephants, to commemorate his road rebuilding activities. RIC Augustus 141.

Nero Claudius Drusus, the stepson of Augustus, was a popular and successful general who subjugated the German tribes. He died prematurely in 9 B.C., while on campaign, and was mourned by the whole nation. His son, Claudius, when he became the emperor in A.D. 41, belatedly commemorated his father's great victories by erecting several triumphal arches in Rome. One was built on the main road of Rome, the Via Appia, and this arch appears on an aureus struck by Claudius in A.D. 51-52. It shows an equestrian statue of Nero Drusus holding a horizontal spear, with bound captives in front of trophies of arms at each side. The arch has

See plates, coin 82.

An aureus of Claudius, struck in the name of his father, Nero Tiberius Drusus, in A.D. 41-45, showing the triumphal arch on the Via Appia. The bust of Nero Tiberius Drusus and his inscription appear on the obverse. RIC Claudius 69.

Ionic style columns flanking the opening. The abbreviated legend, DE GERM, for DE GERMANIS, appearing on the attic panel identifies the arch with the victories in Germany.

The emperor Claudius displayed other arches, or perhaps another form of the one erected for his father, on his bronze coinage. There are several sestertii of Claudius which show a similar triumphal arch, but with four Ionic columns and a distinct temple-like pediment structure, RIC 98. The arch is surmounted by an equestrian statue holding a spear downwards, and two trophies of arms but no bound captives. These coins carry the bust of the emperor Claudius and his inscription on the obverses.

Claudius himself celebrated several triumphs over Germany and Britain, and had many arches dedicated to his military victories even though the actual battles were won by his generals. Some of these arches are recognized as converted arches of aqueducts, and the remains of several of these double-pur-

A sestertius of Claudius, struck in A.D. 41-50, showing the arch dedicated to his father's victories in Germany. RIC Claudius 98.

pose structures have been found in Rome. A good example of this type of arch is the ancient Porta Praenestina, now called the Maggiore gate, in Rome. This triumphal arch and gateway in the later Aurelian wall, built around Rome, supports three of the aqueducts bringing water into Rome. Also, to celebrate the triumph over Germany, Claudius converted an arch of the Aqua Virgo into an elaborate monument which bore the inscription DE GERMANIS, RIC 3. The remains of this arch can be seen near the modern day Trevi fountain in Rome. This arch appears on the coins of Claudius, and a close examination of the shape of the structure suggests that it is part of the aqueduct arcade. The coin, dated to A.D. 64, shows two Ionic columns each side of the opening and an equestrian statue on top. Two trophies of arms are located at each side, but the architectural composition seems incomplete at the edges.

A second similar coin also commemorates the Claudian triumph over Britain. Remains of this arch were found as part of the arcade of the Aqua Virgo located on the Via Flaminia, the main north road of Rome. The coin was struck in A.D. 46, 49, and 51-52, and shows a converted aqueduct arch. The panel with the inscription DE BRITANN extends well out from the ends of the arched opening, indicating that more of the structure existed on each side. Also, the inscribed panel appears as if it was "tacked on" to a

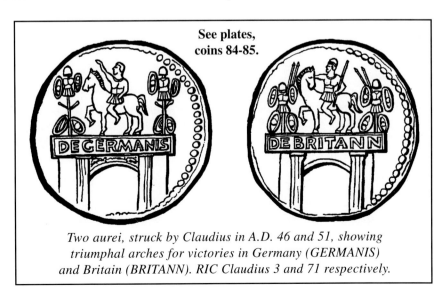

Two aurei, struck by Claudius in A.D. 46 and 51, showing triumphal arches for victories in Germany (GERMANIS) and Britain (BRITANN). RIC Claudius 3 and 71 respectively.

water channel rather than built as an integral part of the entablature. On top of the monument is an equestrian statue with trophies of arms on each side. See RIC 71.

After Claudius' reign, the emperor Nero raised several triumphal arches in Rome and in the provinces. One of them was so historically remarkable that it will be discussed separately in the next chapter.

The emperor Galba, embroiled in the terrible civil war following Nero's death, ruled for only nine months but still found time to strike a substantial coinage which featured several triumphal arches. These coins celebrated his victories in the battles of the civil wars and were essentially propaganda pieces. Three outstanding arch designs appeared on Galba's coinage, and they recorded the special types of triumphal arches built in the chaotic years of A.D. 68-69. Perhaps the earliest coin is a denarius struck sometime in June to December A.D. 68. This coin shows an elaborate structure with Corinthian columns and a substantial entablature. It is surmounted by a quadriga and other sculpture. The composition is rendered with an oblique graphics technique so that the two sides of the monument and the corner can be seen. This coin was struck at a mint in Spain, the province and home base of Galba.

A denarius of Galba struck in A.D. 68 showing an elaborate triumphal arch. The obverse bust of Galba shows the blob at the end of the neck, which is usually an identifying mark for coins struck at the mint of Lugdunum, modern Lyons, in Gaul. RIC Galba 33.

See plates, coin 86.

A sestertius of Galba, struck at the end of A.D. 68 or the beginning of 69, showing the triumphal arch and the remission of taxes legend. RIC Galba 134.

A spectacular As was struck by Galba during September to December 68, also at a Spanish mint, to celebrate some victory by showing an arch with three bound captives and an officer marching through the opening. This scene is reminiscent of the defeated soldiers marching *sub jugum* in the Etruscan tradition. The arch is topped by two equally important equestrian statues, and historians cannot explain this unusual feature. It usually means the arch was dedicated to two people as co-emperors. The legend QVADRAGENS REMISSAE translates into "The Fortieth is Remitted," and this refers to the remission of a tax perhaps named the "fortieth" or of one-fortieth of some recently imposed taxes. No historian has yet offered a theory as to what the remission of taxes has to do with a triumphal arch, but it may be that the victory celebrated by the arch made this tax redundant. The structure is adorned with Corinthian columns and is delineated by an oblique projection to show both sides and the corner of the monument.

The final coin of Galba that illustrated a triumphal arch is also connected to the remission of taxes. It is a sestertius struck at a mint in Gaul, perhaps Narbo or Lugdunum. It was made in the final months of the emperor's life, December 68 to January 69, and it shows a finely rendered Corinthian style arch surmounted by a quadriga. The emperor is shown as if he was in a triumphal procession, driving the chariot, holding an eagle tipped

An As of Galba struck in September-December, A.D. 68, showing a triumphal arch and the legend concerning the remission of taxes. RIC Galba 77.

scepter and with Victory holding a wreath over his head. The Legend of XXXX REMISSA again refers to the relief from the mysterious fortieth tax.

Following the civil wars, Vespasian and Titus erected many fine triumphal arches, especially for their victory over Judaea, but surprisingly, none of these appear on their coinage. This is most unfortunate because, judging from the appearance of the Arch of Titus, built by his brother Domitian, the monuments for Vespasian and Titus may have set new standards for architectural design in Rome. The newly developed, elegant Composite Order of columns made its first appearance on the Arch of Titus, and it may have been invented and used by Vespasian much earlier than this date. However, Suetonius said that Domitian, the second son of Vespasian, erected several triumphal arches in Rome, and one appears on his coinage.[3] From these coins, we could observe that Domitian, an emperor who reportedly indulged in most of the excesses of life, decided to exceed the well established norms of triumphal arch design. His monument is a quadrifrons type, opening in four directions, with pairs of Corinthian columns at the sides of each opening. The attic panel has a sculpted frieze, and two bigas of elephants, back-to-back, surmount the cornice. This remarkable arch is shown on a sestertius struck in A.D. 92-96, and it probably commemorates the emperor's wars with the German tribes, where he personally commanded the

armies in the field. This heavily embellished arch may have set the pattern for the much more ornate arches built by later emperors. The actual location of Domitian's arch in Rome is unknown, but we are told by historians that an arch for Domitian was built at the intersection of the Via Flaminia and the Vicus Pallacinae in A.D. 85, and another was erected on the Capitoline in front of the temple to Jupiter. As the arch on this coin is "quadrifrons," it was designed for the intersection of two roads, and the Via Flaminia site meets this requirement.

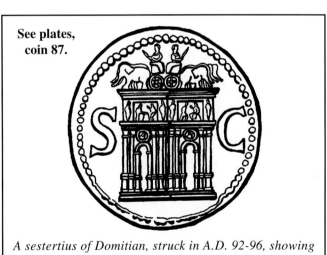

See plates, coin 87.

A sestertius of Domitian, struck in A.D. 92-96, showing the ornate triumphal arch built on the Via Flaminia, celebrating his victory over Germany and possibly his fifteenth anniversary as emperor. RIC Domitian 416.

---

3 *The Twelve Caesars*, Domitian, xiii.2, by Suetonius, translated by Robert Graves, Penguin Classics, London, 1967, page 304.

194

A sestertius of Trajan, struck in A.D. 103-111, showing the ostentatious triumphal arch celebrating the emperor's victory over Germany and perhaps his fifth anniversary of rule. RIC Trajan 572-574.

Following the ostentatious pattern set by the arch of Domitian, the emperor Trajan crassly surpassed all the boundaries of good taste and erected an overly decorated, pretentious arch to honor his victories over the German tribes. A coin issued for the fifth anniversary of Trajan's rule in A.D. 100 shows this elaborate structure. It is adorned with large Corinthian columns and a full pediment structure so that it looks like a temple. Every inch of its surface is covered with sculptured scenes, including a wolf in its cave, soldiers, mythological heroes, bigas, and bound captives in front of trophies of arms. Two imperial eagles sit at the rooftop edges. The structure is surmounted by a six-horse chariot led by two Victories. The pediment also contains sculptures of Jupiter Maximus and other deities. The abbreviated legend IOM for IOVE OPTIMVS MAXIMVS, that is "Jove the Best and Greatest," appears on the attic panel above the pediment. Trajan, who ruled over the Roman empire at the apex of its military power, apparently "pulled out all the stops" in the design of this monument. The sculptures on this triumphal arch are virtually a complete catalog of all the architectural and artistic devices that could ever be used on such monuments, but despite all this gaudiness, it is still very impressive.

Today, at the northern end of the Forum Romanum, the almost intact arch of Septimius Severus sits as a reminder of the military might of Rome. This triple arched monument exalts the emperor's victory over the Parthians, and the large friezes above the side arches show panoramic views of the campaigns. The lengthy inscription on the attic panel originally contained the names of Caracalla and Geta, the two sons of the emperor, but Geta's name was removed after he was murdered by Caracalla in A.D. 212. This historic monument appears on very rare Asses of Septimius Severus and Caracalla struck in A.D. 204 (RIC Septimius Severus 764, RIC Caracalla 419). These coins show much detail of the arch, but they are usually found in very worn condition and the artwork cannot be appreciated.

A denarius of Septimius Severus, struck in A.D. 202-210, showing the triumphal arch that still exists in the Forum Romanum. RIC Septimius Severus 259 and also RIC Caracalla 87.

The arch also appears on denarii struck in A.D. 206 to celebrate the fifteenth and tenth anniversaries of Sever-us and Caracalla respectively (RIC 259 and RIC 87). The structure shown on the coins is in close agreement with the architectural form of the existing monument. This arch is 76 feet (23 m) wide and 68 feet (20.5 m) high. The sculptures on the top of the arch have disappeared without a trace, but from the evidence of the coins they appear to have been the emperor in a six-horse chariot, flanked on each side by a soldier and an equestrian statue at each edge of the roof.

A reconstruction of the arch of Septimius Severus with details taken from the coins and the existing monument in the Forum. The legend on the attic panel reads as follows:

IMP.CAES.LVCIO SEPTIMI OM FIL SEVERO PIO PERTINACLAVG PATRI PATRIAE.PARTHICO.ARABICO.ET
PARTHICO ADIABENICO PONTIFIC MAXIMO TRIBVNIC POTEST. XL IMP. XI COS III PROCOS. ET
IMP. CAES. M. AVRELIO. FIL ANTONINO AVG. PIO. FELICI. TRIBVNIC. POTEST. VI. COS PROCOS. P.P
OPTIMVS. FORTISSIMIS. OVE. PRINCIPIBVS
OB. REM PVBLICAM. RESTITVTAM. IMPERIVM. QVE. POPVLI. ROMANI. PROPAGATVM
INSIGNIBVS. VERTVTIBVS. EORVM. DOMI. FORISQVE. S. P. Q. R.

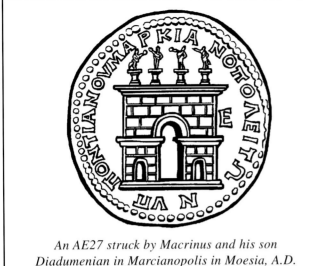

An AE27 struck by Macrinus and his son Diadumenian in Marcianopolis in Moesia, A.D. 217-218, showing the triumphal arch of that city. The obverse portrays the busts of the emperor and his son facing each other. Price and Trell, fig. 85, page 59.

The larger cities in the provinces were never overlooked when it came to the building and dedication of triumphal arches. Splendid arches were erected all over the empire, and several examples still exist because they were incorporated into the walls and fortifications of the later medieval cities. Provincial arches frequently resembled the types made in Rome, but more often they took on an appearance suitable to the local architectural styles. A good example of this vernacular approach to design can be seen in the arch built in Marcianopolis in Moesia by Macrinus and his son Diadumenian, A.D. 217-218. The heavy central arch springing from a cornice structure is an eastern architectural feature found on many local buildings. This arch actually looks like a city gate and it may have also performed that function. The statues on top may represent the emperors and the city's patron deities.

There are many other triumphal arches illustrated on coins, but these cannot be positively identified as to the builder, location, or purpose. As this chapter is not intended to be a definitive study of the triumphal arches shown on coinage, these uncertain coins are not described. The Romans built at least 36 arches in Rome; four of these still exist and can be examined today. These are the arches of Titus, Septimius Severus, the arch of the Argentarii (bankers), and the arch of Constantine built in A.D. 316. In modern times, the potent concept of the triumphal arch was copied for the famous Arc de Triomphe in Paris, built in 1808, and the Marble Arch in London, 1828. Regardless of the period of time in which the triumphal arches were erected, these commemorative structures were always regarded as advertisements of a nation's pride and its imperialistic ideals. In the descriptive terminology of historical architecture, the triumphal arch became the unique emblem of the Roman empire, and these monuments have never been surpassed as a symbol of majestic power and military glory.

Chapter 30

The Lost Arch of Nero

During the reign of Nero, A.D. 54-68, Rome was involved in a bitter war with their traditional eastern enemy, the Parthians. Despite some victories by the famous Roman general Corbulo, the hostilities continued and eventually spilled over into the kingdom of Armenia, where the Romans had installed a puppet king named Tigranes V. To end the protracted war, a face-saving diplomatic peace was arranged in which Tiridates, half brother of the Parthian king, was to be appointed as ruler of Armenia by both Parthia and Rome.[1] Under this treaty, Rome would retreat from Mesopotamia, and Parthia would withdraw from Armenia. Tiridates would then be proclaimed king by the Parthians and be crowned by Nero. This arrangement was considered to be a pragmatic Roman political victory that would guarantee peace with Parthia. To celebrate this event, Nero struck many coins in gold, silver, and bronze or brass denominations showing the Temple of Janus with its portals closed. The doors of this famous temple were shut only when there was peace in the Roman empire. These coins carried the inscription PACE P. R. TERRA MARIQ PARTA IANVM CLVSIT, meaning "Having Procured Peace for the Roman People by Land and by Sea, the Doors of the Temple of Janus were Closed". The coins are cataloged as RIC Nero 50, 58, 283, 306, and 353. Sometimes the inscription PACE P. R. VBIQ. PARTA IANVM CLVSIT, meaning "Having

Procured Peace for the Roman People Everywhere, the Doors of the Temple of Janus were Closed," was used on the smaller sized coins.

The Roman historian Tacitus, A.D. 55-120, said in his *Annals of Imperial Rome,* XV. 18, that the senate erected trophies and arches of victory over Parthia for Nero in the center of the Capitoline Hill. Over the years, the Romans had erected numerous altars, trophies, shrines, and even small temples, as well

See plates, coin 88.

A sestertius of Nero showing the Temple of Janus with the doors closed and the famous "Peace" inscription. RIC Nero 438.

as several triumphal arches, including one dedicated to Scipio Africanus, the conqueror of Carthage, in the temple courtyard on the Capitol. This area was the most prestigious location in Rome for commemorative monuments, and such a large number were placed in the temple zone that they cluttered up the ceremonial approach to the temple of Jupiter Capitolinus. Augustus had them all removed and re-erected in the Campus Martius during his civic improvement program of 9 B.C.

It is presumed that the arch for Nero was erected in front of the entrance to the Capitoline Temple, perhaps in A.D. 58, when a premature victory over Parthia was celebrated. Some his-

---

[1] *Nero, Emperor in Revolt,* by Michael Grant, American Heritage Press, New York, 1970, page 127.

198

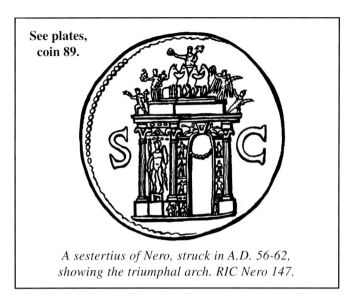

See plates, coin 89.

A sestertius of Nero, struck in A.D. 56-62, showing the triumphal arch. RIC Nero 147.

torians believe it was raised in 63 when the diplomatic accord with Parthia regarding the appointment of the ruler of Armenia was signed, or in 66 when the new Armenian king, Tiridates, visited Rome to receive his crown from Nero. However, no remains of the arch or its foundation have ever been discovered by archaeologists.

Fortunately, we do have a marvellous and accurate illustration of it preserved on the sestertii of Nero struck in A.D. 64-68, RIC 143-150. These are considered to be some of the finest architectural coin reverses ever struck by the mint in Rome. There are several variations of the design of this single span arch, but most depict it covered with numerous statues and topped by a quadriga driven by Nero, who holds an eagle tipped scepter and a victory wreath. The quadriga is escorted by Victory on the right, holding a wreath and palm branch, and by the goddess of Peace, Pax, on the left holding a cornucopia and a caduceus. On the lower roof edge and on the extreme left and right are soldiers. Judging from his headgear, the warrior on the left is a Parthian or Armenian. An enormous figure of Mars, holding a shield and spear, appears on the side panel of the arch.

An imaginary reconstruction showing the Arch of Nero, in its presumed location directly in front of the Temple of Jupiter Capitolinus, around A.D. 66.

Other figures are located on the plinths that flank the archway and on the base of the monument. A wreath, probably made up of bronze laurel leaves, hangs in the arch opening. The pilasters or columns used on the monument are of the popular Corinthian order. The composition on the coin was engraved using a zero angle, oblique projection so that the front, corner, and left side are visible. No inscription can be seen on the attic panel at the top, but a lengthy one must have been carved there to satisfy Nero's enormous ego and notorious desire for publicity.

The triumphal arch of Nero did not survive for long. It is possible that it was completely renovated and modified by later emperors who tried to obliterate the memory of the hated Nero, but more likely it was torn down immediately by Nero's successor in A.D. 68 and the sculptures re-used on other monuments. It is believed that when Rome declined and lost its status as the capital city of the empire, probably in A.D. 330, many of the great sculptures and statues were removed from the public buildings in Rome and taken to decorate the imperial palaces and theaters in Constantinople. The splendid quadriga, taken from the top of Nero's Arch, is thought to have been placed in the hippodrome, in the center of the racecourse, of Constantine's new capital city. In later years, this chariot was broken up and the bronze horses were taken to Venice, sometime after the city was captured by Crusaders in 1204 or before Constantinople fell to the Turks in 1453.[2] Some historians suggest that the four horses of Nero's quadriga can be seen today over the main door of Saint Mark's (San Marco) cathedral in Venice, built in 1042. Other art experts say that the shapes and artistic details of these horses place their manufacture sometime in the second century A.D., long after Nero's reign. However, the coins provide us with an everlasting, clear, and elegant illustration of this famous sculptural group.

---

[2] *The Architecture of Europe,* by Doreen Yarwood, Chancellor Press, London, 1974, pages 90 and 103.

Chapter 31

The Market Place of Nero

Art historians credit the Romans with developing many types of secular buildings in the ancient world. The Greeks, in their architectural endeavours, had concentrated on religious buildings, turning the design of temples into an art form. The basilica or courthouse, the market buildings, the amphitheater, and the circus were mainly Roman inventions. As a powerful nation, the Romans needed a variety of different buildings in order to administer their complex empire. Not the most important among these building types, but one of the more interesting, was the market building called the "macellum." Modern day shopping centers or malls are not a new, twentieth century idea; they were actually invented by the ancients. There were at least three large market centers in early Rome. The first was built just north of the Forum to replace the old fish, vegetable, and confectionary markets that were located there. This market place burned down in 210 B.C. and was rebuilt as a "tholos," a round type of building, in 179 B.C. by M. Fulvius Nobilior (*Livy*, xxvii.II). In 40 B.C., this market building was removed to make way for the new imperial fora. A second market center, the Macellum Liviae, was built on the Esquiline Hill by Augustus and named after his wife Livia. It was dedicated by Tiberius in 7 B.C. Later, both Nero and Trajan constructed elaborate market buildings in Rome to cater to the shopping habits of the growing upper and middle classes. Dio Cassius reported that in A.D. 59 Nero dedicated the "Provision Market" building in Rome (*Roman History*, lxi,18). This market building was called the Macellum Augusti, the Macellum Magnum, or the Macellum Caelian. This later name makes reference to its location on the Caelian Hill in Rome. The Macellum of Nero was designed by his court architects, Severus and Celer, two professionals who are mentioned by Tacitus as "having the genius and audacity to attempt by art even what nature had refused" (*Annals*, xv, 42). In this statement Tacitus was probably referring to the magnificent dome that supposedly capped the rotunda of Nero's new market building. Judging from the existing dome in the present-day church, which supposedly occupies or was constructed inside Nero's market building, the original dome may have been 120 feet (36 m) in diameter, only 22 feet (6.5 m) smaller than Hadrian's amazing dome over the Pantheon, built more than 60 years later. Several authorities believe that the present-day church of S. Stefano Rotondo stands on the foundations of the Macellum and duplicates the great ancient dome in its rotunda. Other historians dispute this theory because the building was transformed into a church by Pope Simplicius in A.D. 468-482, and was renovated several times over the years by later popes, who probably tore down the original dome structure.

Nero's Macellum is depicted on several coins struck in A.D. 62-68. These coins show a market building that must have been an outstanding structure in its day. It has flanking wings of slightly different construction, and a large, central dome dominating the architectural composition. See RIC 402.

These coins of Nero show the market building as a substantial structure, and historians believe that it was part of an extensive shopping area containing open stalls, a covered portico, and animal pens. The two-story building contained shops for luxurious goods such as gems, perfume, jewelery, silks, and gourmet foods. The second floor probably housed the stalls of silversmiths, bankers, loan brokers, and other businesses associated with commerce. Some where on the ground floor a shrine to Ceres, probably a tholos type structure, would be located. Ceres was the goddess of crops, produce, and cereals, and her shrine was always placed in or close to the market place. A large fish tank would also be somewhere in the market building to hold the fresh fish so loved by the Romans. Nero's Macellum must have been the largest in Rome at that time because it is given the subtitle *Magnum*, for "Great," in ancient literature.

This market building is last heard of in the records of Rome for the fourth century A.D.,

See plates, coin 90.

A dupondius of Nero struck in around A.D. 63 showing the Macellum Magnum in Rome, with the legend MAC AVG, for MACELLVM AVGVSTI, placed above the dome. RIC Nero 109. Other dupondii display the same elaborate building with the legend placed at the sides, RIC 402.

and archaeologists have not decided whether the church of S. Stefano Rotondo was actually built over its remains. Later Christian rulers of Rome established a policy of using existing Roman secular edifices, such as the basilicas, porticoed villas, and markets for their civic buildings, and

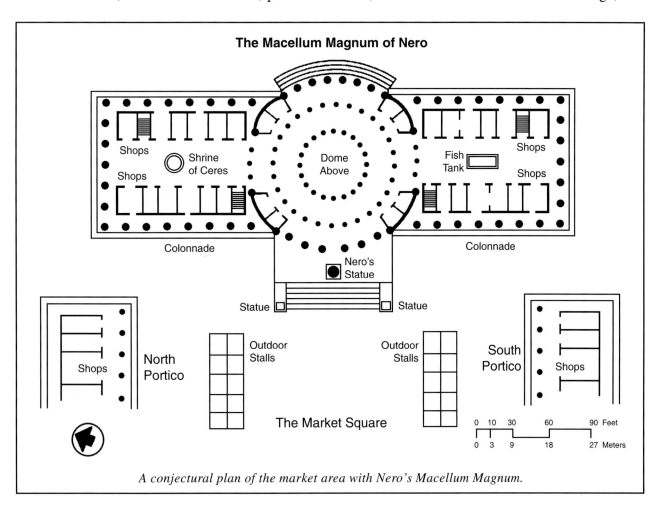

A conjectural plan of the market area with Nero's Macellum Magnum.

of converting the pagan temples into churches. As this was the common practice for many years, perhaps we may see Nero's Macellum building as the prototype for several government buildings in medieval Europe. This same domed structure appears to have been the model for all the modern state and national capitol buildings constructed in the Americas. Using the rotunda of a secular Roman building rather than the porch and colonnade of a Roman temple was perhaps more appropriate for a government building in democratic countries where the separation of church and state was a basic precept.

An imaginative reconstruction of Nero's Macellum Magnum.

Chapter 32

Pontoon Bridges

In 1995 most of the nations of the world celebrated the 50th anniversary of "VE Day," the end of World War II in Europe. To commemorate this event, many of the television stations in North America featured the dramatic war movies made during those trying and desperate years. In several of those films, the allied forces can be seen using "pontoon bridges" to cross over the rivers in war-torn Europe. Pontoon bridges are temporary military roadways supported on boats or rafts, and they have been used by armies for at least the past 2,600 years. The fundamental design of these bridges has remained virtually unchanged over these 26 centuries.

Boat-bridges were probably first used by the Assyrians sometime in the eighth century B.C. Assyria was the first society to develop an organized, professional standing army, and Assyrian engineers are credited with inventing the earliest city siege tactics and war machines such as battering rams and assault towers.[1] The armies of Assyria were formidable, technically advanced, and the first military force to make extensive use of iron weaponry. They had learned how to smelt and forge iron from the conquered Hittites. The Assyrians were an imperialistic, expansionist nation noted for military prowess and terrible cruelty in warfare. Historians have charged them with the crimes of devising systematic torture and the routine execution of prisoners of war. To expand their empire the Assyrians conquered all the neighbouring countries and then crossed the wide rivers that isolated them from more distant realms such as Egypt and Mesopotamia. A ninth century B.C. wall sculpture from the Assyrian palace at Kalhu, now in the British Museum, shows fully armed Assyrian soldiers attacking a foreign city by swimming across a river on inflated animal skins.[2] It would have taken only a minor leap in technology for the Assyrians to advance from inflated skins to boat-bridges. Xenophon, the Athenian soldier and author, later described a proposed bridge built on inflated skins in his work, *The Anabasis of Cyrus,* 401-399 B.C. (*Anabasis* III, V, 8-11).

The first written account of a pontoon bridge is given by Herodotus, the "Father of History," 484-420 B.C. In his *History*, Book I, Chapter 205, he said that Cyrus I, 559-529 B.C., the founder of the Persian empire and the conqueror of the Assyrians, built a bridge of boats over the Araxes river in 503 B.C. to attack Queen Tomyris of the Massagentae. Herodotus casually recorded this event as if the building of a boat-bridge was a well-known, standard tactic in ancient warfare. Also in his writings Herodotus documented the great wars between the Greeks and Persians. He told how the Persian king Darius I, 521-486, planned to attack mainland Greece, but first needed to subdue the troublesome Scythians who were harassing the northern flanks of his empire. Darius had a great boat-bridge built across the Bosphorus in 512 B.C. so that he could advance into Thrace and Macedonia, then move north and attack the Scythian empire from the rear.[3] Herodotus gives the name of the architect who designed the Bosphorus bridge as Mandrocles the Samian. This boat-bridge was such a great feat of engineering that the architect had a painting made of it showing

---

[1] *History of Ancient Civilization*, Vol. 1, by A.A. Trever, Harcourt Brace and Co., New York, 1936, page 99.
[2] *The Ancient World,* edited by Esmond Wright, Chartwell Books Inc., 1979, page 37.
[3] *History of Herodotus,* translated by G. Rawlinson, Book IV, Chpt. 88-97, Vol. I, Everyman's Library, J.M. Dent and Sons, New York, 1909, pages 322-325.

204

An imaginary reconstruction of the painting commissioned by the architect Mandrocles of Samos, described by Herodotus and illustrating an enthroned Darius watching his army crossing the Bosphorus.

Darius, seated on a throne, watching his army crossing over the strait. Later, Darius had another boat-bridge built over the Ister river, the modern Danube, to enable his army to move from Thrace into the heartland of Scythia, north of the Black Sea. This bridge was made up with a fleet of ships provided by the Greek tyrants of the Ionian city states who were allied with Darius during this invasion.

The most famous pontoon bridge in history was also described by Herodotus. This was the great double boat-bridge constructed for Xerxes I, 486-465 B.C., for his attempt to conquer mainland Greece. In 481 B.C. he had two boat-bridges constructed, side by side, over the Hellespont. This famous strait in Turkey, now called the Dardanelles, separating Asia from Europe, is about one mile (1.6 km) wide at its narrowest point. One bridge was for soldiers, the other for supply wagons and animals. Xerxes, a true megalomaniac, supposedly had his soldiers lash the water of the Hellespont with whips when a sudden storm broke the bridges. He also had enormous chains thrown into the strait to subdue and restrain the sea-god Poseidon. This is probably a folklore reference to the heavy chains later used to securely anchor the ships against any future storms. Herodotus has left us a description of Xerxes' pontoon double bridge that is so detailed modern engineers use it as a classical example of clarity and precision in technical writing. He said that one of the bridges was built on 360 ships. These were of two types, the older penteconters, single-banked ships with 50 oars, and the newer triremes, three-decked warships with as many as 120 rowers. Using first class warships to make a bridge was an extravagance that revealed the enormous size of the fleet available to Xerxes for his invasion. The second, parallel bridge, built on the Euxine Sea side of the narrows, was laid on top of 314 warships. The ships were moored by unusually large anchors and tied together with six thick cables fastened to the shores. Two of the cables were made of white flax and four of papyrus. Planks were laid down over the ships for a roadbed and covered with brushwood and clay, which was trodden down to make a solid mass. Bulwarks or sidewalls were placed on the edges of the bridges to prevent horses from seeing the water and becoming frightened.[4] The construction of these parallel boat-bridges was an engineering miracle that has never been repeated in history, and the design of Xerxes' bridges became the prototype for all later pontoon bridges.

The Romans were excellent military engineers, and they frequently used pontoon bridges in campaigns against their enemies. In Latin, these bridges were called "pons navalis," naval bridges. The emperor Trajan, A.D. 98-117, the most successful of all the Roman soldier-emperors, had to cross many wide rivers in his wars against the surrounding barbarian tribes, and his engineers

---

[4] *History of Herodotus*, as above, Book VII, Chpt. 36, Vol. II, page 135.

raised the science of bridge building to its highest level. The Column of Trajan, one of the most remarkable existing sculptural documents of Roman military warfare, shows several large bridges, including two boat-bridges used to cross the Danube in the battles against the Dacians. These are very similar to the descriptions of Xerxes' boat-bridges as reported by Herodotus. Also, some of Trajan's coins display a single arched bridge, which is perhaps a symbol to represent the many military and civil bridges built over the Danube river. See RIC 569.

The Roman historian Dio Cassius, A.D. 155-230, perhaps quoting from Arrian's *Campaigns of Alexander,* Book V.7, gave a good description of the pontoon bridges used by the Roman legions of his days.[5] Dio said that the Romans were very knowledgeable about boat-bridge construction, and they built many of them over the Rhine, Danube, and Euphrates rivers. He reported that flat-bottomed boats were floated down the river with the current and placed into position one by one. Large wicker baskets full of stones were used as anchors. Sections of roadway were already on each boat and, when in place, were projected out and fastened together over the river. The boat nearest the enemy shore had towers, gates, catapults, and archers to defend the bridge-head from attack.

Perhaps the most famous pontoon bridge in Roman and Christian history is the one constructed north of Rome over the Tiber River to replace the destroyed Milvian Bridge (Pons Milvius). According to the legends, the Roman emperor Constantine I, A.D. 307-337, had a famous vision of a "Cross of Light" in the sky accompanied by the words "by this sign shall you conquer." He converted to Christianity and painted the Greek letters "X P," the Chi-Rho monogram for Christ, over the pagan symbols on his legionaries' shields. Then Constantine, armed with a new faith

A sketch of one of the pontoon bridges shown on the Column of Trajan. Drawn from the photographs of panel 12 and 13 of plate VII in Trajan's Column, *by Frank Lepper and S. Frere. The other boat-bridges can be seen on plate XXXV.*

See plates, coin 91.

A sestertius of Trajan, A.D. 98-117, showing the symbolic Danube Bridge. The coin was struck in A.D. 104-111. RIC Trajan 569. Also on a dupondius, RIC 570, and on an As, RIC 569.

---

5 *Roman History,* by Dio Cassius, Book LXXI, III. I, translated by E.W. Carey, The Loeb Classical Library, Vol. VII, Harvard University Press, 1924.

and renewed strength, defeated his opponent Maxentius at the battle of the Milvian Bridge in A.D. 312. Constantine's troops pursued the defeated army onto the boat-bridge and it collapsed, drowning many of the enemy soldiers, including Maxentius. This event marked a great turning point in history when Christianity supplanted the pagan religions of the Roman empire.

The emperor Marcus Aurelius erected a sculptural column similar to Trajan's in A.D. 176. This monument celebrates and documents the Roman wars against the German and Sarmatian tribes. It also shows two boat-bridges that Marcus Aurelius had built across the Danube river.[6] These bridges are similar in detail and construction to those shown on the earlier Column of Trajan, and Marcus Aurelius also memorialized these boat-bridges on his coinage. These coins, struck in A.D. 172, RIC 1047, illustrate the emperor at the head of his legions crossing over a bridge laid on three boats in a river. He is followed by five, or sometimes six soldiers bearing standards, a vexillum,

A sestertius of Marcus Aurelius, struck in A.D. 172, showing the pontoon bridge over the Danube. RIC 1047. The scene is very similar to the one illustrated in the sculptures on his column.

A very rare aureus of Marcus Aurelius showing the pontoon bridge over the Danube. Struck in A.D. 172. RIC 270.

and spears. This coin type may actually commemorate some victory over the Marcomanni or Quadi tribes living across the Danube, or it may represent the emperor taking complete control of the Danube river and making it a Roman frontier. The legend VIRTVS AVG, meaning the Virtue or Valor of the emperor, appears below the bridge.

The details of the pontoon bridges shown on these coins perhaps describe the design and technology used to fabricate them. The bridges are shown with sidewalls made up of elaborate diagonal cross-bracing, and this has led modern engineers to conclude that the Romans had devised a prefabricated, truss type of structure that functioned as a bulwark, a strong connecting cable, and as a roadbed all at the same time. These sections could be quickly transported and assembled, even when the river was under attack. There is also a very rare aureus of Marcus Aurelius depicting almost the same scene as appears on the bronze coinage, except that the emperor is shown crossing the bridge followed by only three legion-aries. One soldier carries a military stan-dard, one rides on horseback holding a vexillium, and a third soldier, carrying a spear, brings up the rear. This coin is RIC 270, with the legend in exergue again, VIRTVS AVG, the Valor of the emperor.

6 The coinage of Marcus Aurelius is co-related to the scenes shown on his column in an excellent article (in French), "Le Monnayage de l'Empereur Marc-Aurele et les Bas-Reliefs Historiques Contemporains," by Professor J. Dobias, in *Revue Numismatique*, 1932, pages 127-172 and plates V, VI.

In A.D. 209, Caracalla as Augustus with his father, Septimius Severus, issued a medallion-like coin, RIC 441, showing the two emperors crossing a boat-bridge that looks like a direct copy of the one shown on the coins struck by Marcus Aurelius. The legend in exergue on this coin is TRAIECTVS, meaning "the crossing or passage" of the emperors. As the letters SC, the abbreviation for "Senatus Consulto," do not appear on the coin, numismatists assume that it was not official currency sanctioned by the senate, but was struck as a medal to be given to officers who participated in the event. Because the coin was made in A.D. 209 and it shows two emperors leading the soldiers, it may celebrate Caracalla's victories in northern Britain when he was co-emperor with his father, or it may simply be a propaganda piece meant to project the image of Caracalla as a victorious general and colleague of Severus. Some numismatists identify this coin directly with Severus' military campaigns in Caledonia (Scotland) in A.D. 209, when

he presumably crossed over the Firth of Forth on a pontoon bridge to attack the Picts.[7] The bridge on this coin would then represent the actual boat-bridge thrown over the Forth inlet by the Romans.

An As or medallion of Caracalla struck in A.D. 209 showing Septimius Severus and Caracalla crossing a boat-bridge. RIC 441. It is very similar to the pontoon bridge coins of Marcus Aurelius, RIC Marcus Aurelius 1047, shown above.

The pontoon bridge coin of Caracalla is extremely rare, and the few existing examples in museums are very worn or have blurred details. It is usually described as showing two emperors, one holding a baton, leading six soldiers, crossing over a boat-bridge supported by three ships. The legionaries consist of four standard bearers followed by two spearmen. Some numismatists claim that one soldier in the middle is on horseback, but the coins available for examination do not support this observation. The legend is PONTIF TR POT XII COS III, with TRAIECTVS in the exergue. See RIC 441.

Septimius Severus must have built many large bridges in his campaigns against the hostile tribes surrounding the empire because a symbolic bridge, almost exactly the same as Trajan's so-called Danube Bridge, was placed on his Asses struck in A.D. 193-211 (RIC 786c). Also, the same bridge symbol was used on aurei, Cohen 521, and on a splendid medallion probably given to the officers in the campaigns, Cohen 522.

The art and technology of warfare changed radically after the Second World

An As of Septimius Severus, A.D. 193-211, showing the symbolic bridge indicating the emperor's bridge building activities. RIC Septimius Severus 786c. The same bridge appears on his aurei, Cohen 521, and on medallions, Cohen 522.

---

[7] "The First Forth Bridge A.D. 209", by Sir Charles Oman, in the *Numismatic Chronicle*, 1931, published by the Royal Numismatic Society, London, page 137.

War. Massive air-power tactics, nuclear or chemical weapons, and laser guided missiles have transformed offensive military action into a completely new science. However, even in modern times, the use of infantry and the common foot-soldier is still the only practical method of seizing and holding the fields of battle. As long as the occupation of enemy land remains one of the main objectives of warfare, pontoon bridges will be essential pieces of military equipment, and they will undoubtedly be used for many centuries into the future.

Chapter 33

The Baetyl,
Fantastic Architecture

Ancient architecture is much admired by people today because they see in it an integrity and a beauty of proportions that is often missing in modern, mass produced buildings. There is also an element of the unusual and fantastic in some ancient monuments. Early people were very fond of incredible architecture and, when they could afford it, they built wonderful religious structures. Perhaps one of the most unusual monuments built for the deities was the "Baetyl," a sculptural pillar often described in numismatic literature as a "likeness" of the deity, or a *simulacrum* in Latin. The word Baetyl was adapted from the Semitic phrase "Bet El," meaning literally the "house of god." Sometimes this term is applied to statues, but more often to sacred stones

or monuments which symbolically represent a god or goddess. One of the best known of ancient Baetyls seen on coinage was the sacred conical stone of Aphrodite, the Roman Venus, contained in the sanctuary courtyard of her temple located in the city of Byblos, Phoenicia. This simulacrum can be seen on coins struck in this city by the emperor Macrinus, A.D. 217-218.

A more spectacular and mysterious simulacrum dedicated to an important goddess was the monument or Baetyl of the Pergaean Artemis, the Latin Diana, erected in Perge (Perga in Latin), or sometimes called Murtana, in Pamphylia. This large sculp-ture was contained inside the temple, but was visible from the front porch. It is the most fantastic piece of architecture ever used as a likeness of a deity. Fortunately, it was

A bronze coin, 30 mm in diameter, struck at Byblos, Phoenicia by Macrinus, A.D. 217-218, showing the temple to Artemis with the conical stone Baetyl located in the open courtyard. Sear GIC 2963.

depicted on many Roman Provincial coins, complete with many of the details of its form and decoration. How it was actually used in the temple rituals is still being debated by historians.

In mythology, Artemis was the daughter of Zeus, a twin sister of Apollo and, like him, one of the most widely revered deities in the Greek world. She was the city goddess of many of the Greek colonial cities in Asia Minor, including Magnesia, Myndus, Ephesus, Patraem, and Perge. Her cult was very powerful and influential in Perge, and she appears on the coinage of this city from the third century B.C. to late Roman times. See Sear Greek 5413.

Perge was an important trade center located near the south coast of Pamphylia, now southern Turkey, between two rivers, the Cestus and the Catarrhactes, which led from the fertile interior to the Mediterranean Sea. The original Greek city of Perge was an independent city-republic

210

A tetradrachm of Perge in Pamphylia, struck in around 190 B.C., showing the bust of Artemis on the obverse, and also the figure of Artemis standing, on the reverse. She is accompanied by her usual companion, a hart, and her guardian, a sphinx, appears before her. The importance of Artemis to the city may be indicated by the fact that she appears on both sides of the coin. Sear Greek 5413.

A bronze coin, 19 mm in diameter, struck in Perge in the 2nd to 1st century B.C. It shows a distyle temple containing the primitive Baetyl of Artemis. Sear Greek 5422.

under the political control of Lydia until the arrival of Alexander the Great. It then became a flourishing Hellenistic center. Perge expanded under Roman rule, and its many buildings were embellished by the emperors of the first and second centuries A.D. They improved or renovated the temples, baths, triumphal arches, a stadium for 25,000 spectators, a theater for 12,000 people, and a large basilica.

Perge is noted in the Bible as the city where Artemis was worshipped, and where the apostles Paul and John stopped on their way from Paphos to Antioch (Acts, XIII. 13). The Temple of Artemis in Perge was renovated several times, but the Baetyl must have been of ancient manufacture, perhaps dating to the fifth century B.C. or even earlier, to a time when the deities had not assumed human form and were represented by natural objects. The earliest representation of the Baetyl of the Pergaean Artemis appears on a bronze coin struck in Perge during the second to first century B.C.

Details of the other coins showing this simulacrum of Artemis indicate that it was between 30 to 40 feet high, conical in shape, with sculptured panels, a wreath at the top, and with niches inset into the lower half. Barclay Head, in his work *Historia Numorum* (page 702), says that the sculptured figures on the monument are bands of dancing deities. The Baetyl was probably made out of large blocks of expensive marble. Coins showing the temple to Artemis in Perge with the Baetyl revealed in the porch usually depict the temple as distyle, that is, with two frontal columns. It probably was at least hexastyle, with six columns, but the central columns were omitted by the coin engraver to better show the very important Baetyl monument.

Such temple coins showing the Baetyl were struck by several emperors during the first three centuries A.D. These include the quasi-autonomous bronze coins of Flavian times (Sear GIC 5134), and imperial silver cistophori and bronzes of Nerva (RIC 116), Trajan (Sear GIC 1050), Hadrian (BMC 19.26), and Antoninus Pius (Sear 1463), as well as those struck by all the succeeding emperors up to Tacitus, A.D. 275-276 (*Sylloge Nummorum Graecorum, Sammlung*

211

A silver cistophoric tetradrachm, valued at three denarii, of Nerva, A.D. 96-98, struck at Perge and showing the temple for DIANA PERG and the Baetyl of the goddess. The central columns of the temple are omitted to reveal the simulacrum. RIC Nerva 116.

A bronze coin, 30 mm in diameter, struck in Perge by Hadrian, A.D. 117-138. It shows clearly the details of the Baetyl of Artemis. BMC Pamphylia 26.

von Aulock, no. 4759). This coin of Tacitus was perhaps the last Roman coin struck to represent the famous temple and Baetyl of Artemis.

The details of the Baetyl of Artemis are clearly shown on the large imperial bronzes struck in Perge. A coin struck by Hadrian, A.D. 117-138, perhaps gives the most detailed picture of the monument, including the associated cult symbols such as the dancing figures and guardian sphinxes.

The question about the function of the Baetyl has not been satisfactorily resolved. Some historians claim that it was simply a stone abstract representation of the deity, but others believe it was a large altar structure even though its shape is unsuitable for this purpose. Most numismatic reference books avoid the issue and refer to the Baetyl as a "simulacrum," or likeness

of the deity (Sear), and other coin catalogs call the monument a "cultic statue" of the deity (RIC). This is fair enough for purposes of identifying and labelling the object, but the monument apparently had much more significance in history and mythology.

The origin of this Baetyl may be found in the religious customs surrounding Artemis' twin brother, the powerful god Apollo. Artemis was actually born a minute before Apollo, and she is usually directly connected to him in the myths. Among their many manifestations, they were linked together in that he was god of the sun and she was goddess of the moon. The ancients always united these two great lights in the sky. In the extensive mythology of Apollo, he is sometimes represented by a conical stone or column, often incorrectly called an obelisk in numismatic literature. In fact, this sacred conical stone appears to be a type of Baetyl. The mythology is confusing, but this conical stone is called an "Aguieus," and it is a symbol of the god as "Apollo Aguieus." Aguieus means "He of the Ways," and refers to Apollo's function as protector of highways and travellers or wayfarers. It also makes reference to Apollo as the deity, the sun god, who lights the way for travellers. Artemis the moon deity, by association with Apollo, would then be the goddess who lights the way for travellers at night. The Greek author Valerius Harpocration of Alexandria, writing in the second century A.D., describes the Baetyl of Apollo as "a pillar tapering to the end, which they set up before doors. And some say

See plates, coin 92.

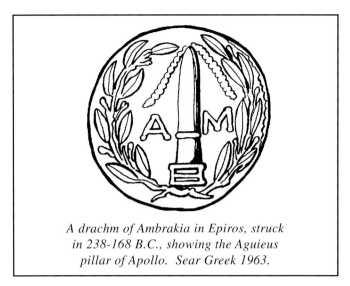

A drachm of Ambrakia in Epiros, struck in 238-168 B.C., showing the Aguieus pillar of Apollo. Sear Greek 1963.

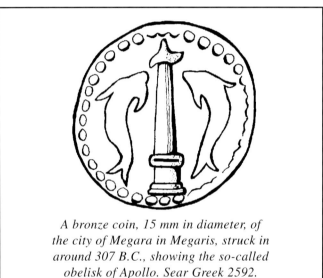

A bronze coin, 15 mm in diameter, of the city of Megara in Megaris, struck in around 307 B.C., showing the so-called obelisk of Apollo. Sear Greek 2592.

A drawing of a part of the vase in the Villa Albani showing the Aguieus pillar to Apollo as a votive stele. It clearly resembles the Baetyl of the Pergaean Artemis as shown on the coins.

that they are proper to Apollo."[1] These Aguieus pillars are of ancient origin, and are often shown on coins struck in cities where Apollo was worshipped. For example, coins struck during the fourth to second centuries B.C. at Byzantium in Thrace, Megara in Megaris, Apollonia in Illyria, and Ambarakia in Epiros use such tapering pillars as the main feature in their designs. The Aguieus form has a distinct resemblance to the Baetyl of Artemis, especially in the form of the base and the wreath at the top.

To supplement and reinforce the information given on these coins, a fourth century B.C. Greek painted vase, now in the Villa Albani museum (Villa Torlonia) in Rome, clearly illustrates a tapering Aguieus pillar. Around the base can be seen dancing figures representing Apollo playing his lyre, Pan playing on his pipes (the syrinx), and three Horae, the goddesses of order in nature who cause the seasons to change. Wreaths are placed on pegs projecting from the face of the pillar. Also, Clement of Alexander (Titus Flavius Clemens), born about A.D. 150, an early Christian writer, said that in the temple to Apollo in Delphi there was a high pillar on which were hung tithes and spoils votive to Apollo (Clement, *Stromata* or *Miscellanies*, Book I. 348).

From this ancient evidence, and by comparing the Aguieus obelisk of Apollo to the Baetyl of his twin sister Artemis, it can be concluded that the simulacrum of Artemis at Perge was also a votive pillar or stele erected to display the donations to the goddess. The niches in the lower half of the Baetyl shown on the coins probably were the receptacles for offerings of food, oil, incense, and money in containers such as jugs or caskets. Also, on the coins, a wreath

---

[1] *Epilegomena to the Study of Greek Religion and Themis, a Study of the Social Origins of Greek Religion,* by Jane Ellen Harrison, University Books, New York, 1962, page 407.

is prominently shown suspended on the upper half of the monument, similar to the wreath shown on the Aguieus pillar. If this theory is correct, it is possible to reconstruct the Baetyl from the coins to indicate its function as a votive holding monument.

Assuming this reconstruction is accurate, it proves again that ancient coins are capable of linking together evidence from other art forms and from ancient literature to confirm the function and appearance of the architectural monuments used in the religious ceremonies of classical days.

The author's reconstruction of the Baetyl of the Pergaean Artemis from the details of the coins, and showing its function as an Aguieus pillar or a votive holding monument located in the porch of the temple.

A bronze coin, 28 mm in diameter, struck by Lucius Verus in A.D. 161-168, showing the Baetyl with niches and wreaths. Description de Medailles Antiques, Greques et Romaines, *by T.E. Mionnet, Vol. 3, no. 93, page 463.*

A bronze coin, 28 mm in diameter, struck, as the last coin showing the temple, by Tacitus, A.D. 275-276. The Baetyl is surrounded by a barrier fence. Sylloge Nummorum Graecorum Sammlung von Aulock, *no. 4759.*

Chapter 36

Altars

There is an architectural monument found on the reverses of many Roman coins and it is always described in numismatic literature as a "large altar." This identification is logical and understandable because the structure looks exactly like the ornate, waist-high altars (*arae* in Latin, singular *ara*) used for sacrificial offerings in religious ceremonies. These altars were usually located in front of Roman temples. However, this description was not formulated by architecturally trained historians, but by antiquarians who were only familiar with the low Roman altars found all over Europe. These waist-high altars fall into two categories. The first is a round, short, column-like altar sometimes called a *cippus,* although the name cippus means a stake or shaft and is usually associated with a stele or a milestone marker. The cippus group includes a type of altar called the "puteal," which may have been an altar, a sacred wellhead cover, or a tomb for the thunderbolts of Jupiter. The puteal was sometimes erected as a sacred altar to Jupiter on the spot where lightning had struck the earth.

A Republican denarius of Lucius Scribonius Libo, struck in 62 B.C., showing the puteal (cippus) located in the Forum. Syd. 927.

A round marble altar resembling the Puteal of Scribonius Libo. Found at Veii, now in the Vatican Museum, Rome.

The second group of low altars used by the Romans consisted of rectangular stone tables with "horns" at the corners. This variety of altar was an imitation of the altars used by older eastern religions, and was adopted by the Romans early in their history. These altars had horn-like elements projecting from the four corners of the top, and they can be seen on many coins struck in the eastern provinces. The origin of the horns is unknown.

A sculptural form of these horns, usually transformed into an ornate scroll ornament, also appeared on the so-called large altars seen on Roman coins, and this was the graphic evidence that misled the early historians into identifying the structures as the waist-high types of altars. It is interesting that the scholars totally disregarded the obvious doors, always shown on these large altars, and concentrated only on the rectangular shape and the horn-like corners. Doors are incongruous and foreign elements to the architecture of ancient altars, but they are functional and make sense if the structure is a building or walled enclosure. However, early numismatists needed some immediate, definitive term for these monuments in order to prepare their catalogs, and "large altar" seemed to be the most practical choice.

As these early catalogs became the basic reference sources upon which the study of numismatics was founded, the term "large altar" was perpetuated and still appears frequently in modern day catalogs. In light of recent archaeological research, this traditional identification of the object as a "large altar" should be challenged. Serving the interests of scientific accuracy, it is perhaps important to re-examine the altars seen on coins and to propose a more suitable term for this monument. From an architectural point of view, it appears that the large altars were actually buildings used as an "altar enclosure" or a "shrine."

A Roman shrine was usually a building that contained an altar, provided an appropriate setting for the ceremonies, and housed the sacred implements and effigies of the deity. It may have also served as a chapel where small groups of people or priests assembled to perform some religious rit-uals. It was the size of a small house, and

An AE27 struck at Caesarea in Samaria by Severus Alexander, A.D. 225-235. It displays a typical horned altar with two sacred trees behind. The tree on the left is the palm, and on the right, the fig. Guide to Biblical Coins, by David Hendin, no. 245.

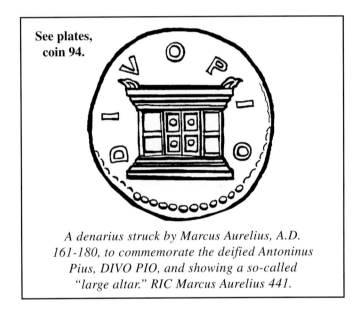

See plates, coin 94.

A denarius struck by Marcus Aurelius, A.D. 161-180, to commemorate the deified Antoninus Pius, DIVO PIO, and showing a so-called "large altar." RIC Marcus Aurelius 441.

was usually open to the sky to directly relate the altar to the heavenly deity and to allow the smoke from the altar fires to escape. Such enclosures may have also been necessary to keep the uninitiated from observing the sacred or magic rites performed by the priests. The ancients called such rituals "mysteries," and for good reason; in many cults these ceremonies were kept as deep, dark secrets. If the enclosure was such a shrine, it needed doors in order to function as a physical separation of the sacred from the profane.

Perhaps the correct word in Latin for such an enclosed shrine would have been an "aedicula," a little temple, but other terms, "sacellum" and "sacrarium," have similar meanings. Some other Latin words meaning a sanctuary, such as "fanum," "asylum," and "delubrum" may have also been used. The word aedicula appears most frequently in ancient literature, and it was derived from the word "aedes." This Latin word originally meant a building (edifice), and later was applied to a building used for religious purposes. The word "templum" for temple usually referred to an important, more magnificent building, perhaps something like a cathedral as compared to a church today. A "lararium" was a private shrine or chapel located in a house and dedicated to the Lares and

Penates, the private household gods, or to the patron deity of the family. The lararium usually took the form of a large cabinet with doors, and it looked somewhat like the so-called large altars. The fact that there were so many Latin terms for religious structures confirms that religious worship was an important, everyday activity for the ancient Romans. The word "sacellum" is frequently used to designate a shrine in numismatic documents, but unfortunately, in many reference texts and illustrations, all the descriptive labels for religious buildings are loosely applied or interchanged so that there is some confusion as to whether a building was a templum, an aedes, a fanum, an ara (altar), or a sacellum.[1]

Hundreds of the waist-high, table types of sacrificial altars were erected in cities all over the empire. These were usually made of stone, in a rectangular form but with the usual horns projecting at the corners. These low altars are often displayed on coins, and are easily recognized because the decorations and inscriptions clearly indicate their function. Also, sometimes they are shown in conjunction with priests or ritual objects which indicate their correct size, scale, and purpose. One spectacular example of a low altar seen on coinage will be sufficient to illustrate this point. An ara used for sacrifices to the emperor Augustus is shown on a coin struck under Tiberius at the city of Tarraco in Spain. This low altar is famous in history because a small palm tree grew, all by itself, out of a crack in the top. The city council of Tarraco excitedly wrote to Augustus to tell him of this miracle, because the palm was a symbol for victory and this was a good omen for the emperor. According to the Roman historian Quintillian, Augustus, who was well-known for his sense of humor and his dry wit, replied tongue-in-cheek that the growing palm seedling showed how infrequently the citizens lit the sacrificial fire on his altar.[2]

An AE33 of Tarraco, Spain, struck under Tiberius, A.D. 14-37, showing the low ara and the miracle of the palm tree growing from the top. Sear GIC 234.

The so-called large altars are usually shown as isolated monuments, without other objects whose size and scale would be known. However, the architectural details, such as doors, door handles, decorations, columns or pilasters, cornices, and bases give distinctive clues as to the altar's height and real function. The most famous large altar shown on Roman coins was the Altar of Lugdunum

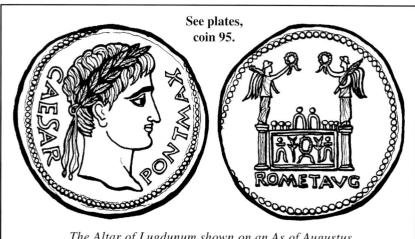

See plates,
coin 95.

The Altar of Lugdunum shown on an As of Augustus struck at Lugdunum around 10 B.C. RIC Augustus 230.

[1] *The Monuments of Ancient Rome as Coin Types,* by Philip V. Hill, Seabys, London, 1989, pages 9-39. In the chapter on temples and shrines, Mr. Hill clearly differentiates between the building types shown on coins, but as his descriptions are based on the terminology used in existing catalogs, he does not create clear categories that differentiate between shrines, temples, and altars.

[2] *The Power of Images in the Age of Augustus,* by Paul Zanker, University of Michigan Press, Ann Arbor, 1988, page 305.

in Gaul, built in 10 B.C. and dedicated to Roma and Augustus. These altar coins were struck at the mint of Lugdunum for Augustus and, later, for Tiberius (RIC Augustus 229-248 and RIC Tiberius 31-32). Augustus refused the dedication of this altar to himself alone and insisted that it be for Roma and Augustus, hence the legend ROM ET AVG which appears on the reverse.

Some historians suggested that this Altar of Lugdunum may have been copied from the "Ara Pacis Augustae," the famous altar of peace built for Augustus in Rome around 9 B.C. The Ara Pacis was erected by the senate to honor the triumphal return of the emperor from his campaigns in Gaul. For propaganda purposes, Augustus decided that it should be erected to commemorate Pax, or peace in the empire. It was built on the Campus Martius, and many large fragments of the structure were discovered by archaeologists in 1568 and later in 1859. It has been fully reconstructed, and can be seen today in Rome on the banks of the Tiber River next to the remains of Augustus' mausoleum.[3] Because of the marvellous sculptures and ornaments on the walls, the Ara Pacis is considered to be the greatest existing artistic monument of the Augustan Age.

The Ara Pacis is believed to have been inspired by the famous Greek Altar of Pity in the market place (agora) of ancient Athens. The name Ara Pacis actually refers to the altar inside the building, but appears to have been later applied to the whole structure. From its reconstruction, it is clearly a shrine building, open to the sky, and it should properly be called a sacellum or an aedicula. If the Ara Pacis is indeed the prototype for the Altar of Lugdunum, the two buildings would have been identical in architectural form. However, the Altar of

A cut-away perspective view of the Ara Pacis Augustus showing how the altar functioned. A low relief sculpture of the procession of Augustus, his family, and court appears on the upper wall panels. The traditional horns projecting from the roof had been transformed into scroll-like ornaments. There probably were doors on the front opening to the shrine, as shown on the coins of later emperors.

Lugdunum is illustrated on Roman coins as if it was a low, waist-high altar with ritual vessels placed on top. This may be an artistic misinterpretation of its size and scale because the die engraver lacked the skill to render the altar in true graphic perspective. Also, the vessels on top of the altar may in fact represent statues in the court behind the altar, but are shown above it, as is done with the artistic conventions used by Roman engravers to suggest depth in space.

Proof that the Altar of Lugdunum was actually a shrine building with doors may be found in some medieval coinage struck in France. A coin issued by Charlemagne in about A.D. 808 probably shows the Roman Altar of Lugdunum. The coin is a silver denier struck at Lugdunum (Lyons in France). The city's ancient Roman name, LVGDVNVM, is engraved around the

3 *The Mute Stones Speak,* by Paul MacKendrick, St. Martin's Press, New York, 1st edition, 1960, pages 160-171.

218

A silver denier of Charlemagne, A.D. 768-814, struck at Lugdunum (Lyons) in France and showing the original Roman Altar of Lugdunum built in Gaul in 10 B.C. Carolingian Coinage, *by Karl F. Morrison, The American Numismatic Society, 1967, coin 167, plate VI.*

A very rare As or perhaps a dupondius of Domitian, A.D. 81-96, clearly showing the Ara Pacis erected in 9 B.C. RIC Domitian 336.

monument.4 In the reference books and catalogs of these coins, this structure is described as a gate of the city, but it is obviously an accurate depiction of the famous Gaulish altar that is shown on Roman coins, complete with the flanking statues on columns. On Charlemagne's medieval coin, the view of the building is taken from behind, and the doorway to the shrine building is clearly seen. This can be taken as confirmation that the Altar of Lugdunum survived in its original form until at least the ninth century A.D. By that time, it had probably been converted into a Christian church, despite the fact that the columns and pagan statues of Victory were still evident.

For some unknown reason, Augustus never commemorated the Ara Pacis on his coinage, but two unidentified, low type of altars are found on his quadrantes (RIC Augustus 422, 425, 443-464). Some numismatists claim that these altars are really anvils, but the most current scholarship confirms that they are indeed altars. However, we can see an accurate representation of the Ara Pacis Augustae on a coin of Domitian struck in A.D. 86. This coin is a fine example of the great skill used by Roman engravers when they illustrated an existing building. The reverse of the coin is described in numismatic texts as showing a "large altar." The coin is rare and always found in worn condition, but the details are clear enough to identify the altar as the Augustan shrine to Peace. The sculptured figures on the wall panels, the stairs leading to the entrance, the pilasters, and the horn or scroll ornaments projecting from the roof corners duplicate exactly the elements found on the reconstructed Ara Pacis. The priests or statues shown flanking the shrine, although their heights are somewhat exaggerated, give a visual clue to the size and scale of the structure, and clearly show that it was not a waist high altar but a shrine building. Also, the inscription, PACIS SC, helps to identify the shrine as the original building erected for Augustus in 9 B.C.

The emperor Tiberius, A.D. 14-37, began a long tradition of striking coins showing a large altar or shrine building. He produced a multitude of Asses which honored the deified Augustus and displayed a shrine dedicated to Providentia, the personification of the providence or foresight of the emperor (RIC Tiberius 80-81). This monument is always described as a "large altar" in catalogs,

4 *Traite de Numismatique du Moyen Age, Vol. I,* by Arthur Engel and Raymond Serrure, reprint by Scorpion Publishers, Amherst, New York, undated, figure 399, page 220.

but it is most likely a sacellum. It appears as a large rectangular shape with two doors, a decorated cornice, and a base of steps typically used on religious buildings. This altar for Providentia must have been an important and significant shrine for the Roman people because several succeeding emperors copied this coin type, and the structure that appeared on the later coins was an exact imitation of the monument found on the coins struck by Tiberius. It was used on Asses of Galba, RIC 499; Vitellius, RIC 129, 163; Vespasian, RIC 494, 544, 712, 746, 763, 785; Titus as Caesar, RIC 621, 655; Domitian as Caesar, RIC 687, 698; Titus as emperor, RIC 140a; and on a restoration coin for Divus Augustus by Titus, RIC 191.

Nero, A.D. 54-68, was the first emperor to actually use the legend "ARA PACIS", the Altar of Peace, on his coins. A large shrine appears on some of his Asses, struck in about A.D. 60-64, and this structure is clearly labelled as the Ara Pacis in the legend. It could represent the altar built for Augustus in 9 B.C., or more probably, Nero's own altar shrine, a copy of Augustus' altar, commemorating peace with Parthia in A.D. 64. The coin was struck at Lugdunum, a mint city that also produced the famous coins of Nero showing the temple of Janus with the doors closed (RIC Nero 263). Because of its early artistic style, some numismatists relate this altar shrine to the peaceful settlement of the Armenian problem in A.D. 59.[5] The reverse is engraved in the finest artistic style, typical of all the architecture shown on coins struck by Nero, and the monument is easily recognized as being a building by its doors and steps.

A later coin struck by Titus, A.D. 79-81, shows an altar shrine to Salus, the goddess of health (RIC Titus 105). The most authoritative reference text, *The Roman Imperial Coinage*, remarks on the elaborate detail of this altar and describes it as an "altar in the form of a temple."[6] This expression is an excellent euphemism for a

5 *The Coinage of Nero*, by E.A. Sydenham, reprint by Sanford J. Durst, New York, 1982, page 63.

6 *Roman Imperial Coinage, Vol. II*, by H. Mattingly and E.A. Sydenham, Spink and Son Ltd., London, 1926, page 128, coin 105.

See plates, coin 96.

The large altar, probably a sacellum, to Providentia on a bronze coin of Divus Augustus struck by Tiberius in honor of the deified Augustus in A.D. 22-23. RIC Tiberius 80. The reverse design was copied by several later emperors.

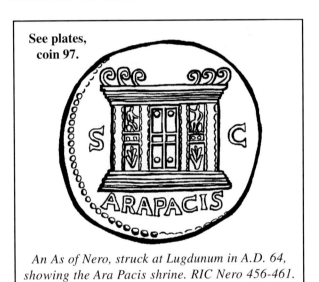

See plates, coin 97.

An As of Nero, struck at Lugdunum in A.D. 64, showing the Ara Pacis shrine. RIC Nero 456-461.

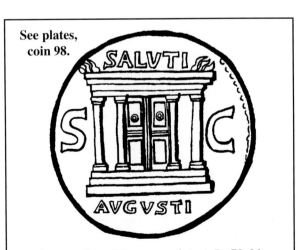

See plates, coin 98.

A sestertius of Titus, struck in A.D. 79-81, showing the Shrine to Salus. RIC Titus 105.

220

sacellum or shrine, and it betrays some reservation by the author of the RIC in identifying it as the traditional "large altar." The legend SALVTI AVGVSTI refers to the health of the emperor. Titus was ill at this time, and the shrine was built as a plea to Salus to restore good health to the beloved emperor. This coin reverse was copied many times by Domitian, A.D. 81-96, the brother of Titus and his successor. It appears on his coins, RIC Domitian 242, 250, 271, 272, 304, 338, and 396. Domitian was greatly concerned with his own health, and the numerous coins he struck commemorating the shrine of Salus indicated his deeply seated hypochondria.

One of the most elegant depictions of the large altar or shrine appears on a cistophorus of Domitian as Caesar, struck under Titus, to commemorate the deceased Vespasian. The architectural details are clearly shown on this coin, and a close observation of the monument's doors, door handles, cornice, columns, and stepped base leaves no doubt that this is a shrine building and not a large altar. The rectangular object on the roof may represent the altar inside the shrine rising above the roofline of the open structure, or it may be a common artistic distortion of the composition, enabling the engraver to show the altar inside in the same view as the exterior of the shrine.

A rare silver cistophoric tetradrachm struck at a mint in Ephesus, Asia Minor, for Domitian as Caesar, under the emperor Titus in A.D. 80-81. It commemorates the deified Vespasian by showing an altar shrine. RIC Titus 75.

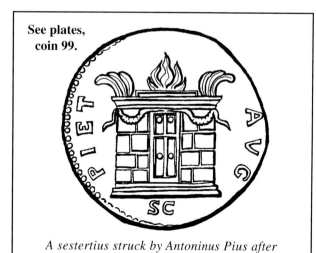

See plates, coin 99.

A sestertius struck by Antoninus Pius after A.D. 141 to commemorate his deceased wife, Faustina Senior. The flame-like ornament appears over the doors. RIC Antoninus Pius 1191.

Later, the large altar/shrine was used by the emperors to honor a deceased and deified relative or predecessor. This reverse type can be seen in the coinage of Hadrian, Marcus Aurelius, and Commodus. These coins are usually referred to in reference works as "Consecratio" coins because the Latin word CONSECRATIO, meaning consecrated, often appears in the inscription. A denarius struck under Hadrian in A.D. 138, RIC 422, showing such a shrine with the legend PIETATI AVG, the piety of the empress, honored his deceased wife Sabina. Also, Antoninus Pius struck a beautiful sestertius sometime after A.D. 141, RIC 1191, to commemorate his late wife Faustina Senior. The design of this coin and the legend PIET AVG is almost a direct copy of the coin struck by Hadrian to honor Sabina. This coin sometimes shows the shrine with a flame-like decoration on top. In fact, the altar was usually raised above the roofline of the shrine, as shown in the reconstruction of the Ara Pacis, so this fire decoration may represent a sacrificial fire burning on top of the altar.

The shrine building eventually became a standard consecration symbol on many coins and, over the years, it was used by the emperors to commemorate the deification of the preceding emperor. The consecration shrine was used on coinage up until the reigns of Claudius II Gothicus and Quintillus, A.D. 270. A posthumous antoninianus of Claudius II, 268-270, RIC 259, illustrates the longevity of this reverse type. This coin, probably struck by Quintillus, shows a shrine which is an imitation of the type struck by earlier emperors. It is always described in references as a lighted altar, but once again, the doors, door pulls, cornice, and stair-like base clearly indicate its function as a shrine building despite the flame on top.

The architectural details on the coins give the most conclusive evidence that the large altars were probably buildings. Roman coin artists were known for their attempts to accurately illustrate their subject matter. They often rendered the early emperors' portraits in the most truthful and realistic manner, warts

See plates, coin 100.

A posthumous antoninianus of Claudius II, A.D. 268-270, showing a so-called "lighted large altar," but probably a shrine containing an altar dedicated to Claudius' consecration. RIC 259-264.

and all, no matter how unpleasant the image. Although less talented artists were reputed to have engraved the reverses of the coins, judging from other architectural coins, their penchant for preciseness of detail cannot be denied. If the engravers showed doors on an altar, we must believe that they were not indulging in a whim or fantasy, but were meticulously recording what they saw. In light of this tradition of accuracy among the Roman engravers, it should be judged that if a monument had doors, it was probably a building and not an altar.

Perhaps the time has come to recognize the phrase "large altar" as a misnomer, and that it tends to trivialize the purpose of the monument. By continuing to use this clumsy label, we conceal the relevance and diminish the importance of these coins to history. As the study of numismatics moves towards becoming a modern science, closely related to archaeology and history, it is necessary to devise a more accurate terminology for the architecture depicted on ancient coins. Perhaps we can begin this procedure by replacing the ambiguous label of a "large altar" with the more correct architectural term, a sacellum or shrine.

PART VI

APPENDICES

Afterword

The architectural coins illustrated in this book are only a special few selected from the thousands issued by the ancients. It would take several books and a lifetime of work to describe every ancient coin that displayed some work of architecture or engineering. Unfortunately, many of the greatest ancient monuments were never commemorated on coins. For example, the magnificent theaters of Marcellus, Pompey, and Balbus in Rome, as well as the enormous and impressive bath buildings of the emperors Nero, Titus, Trajan, Caracalla, Diocletian, and Constantine were never exhibited on coinage. Even the exceptional Mausoleum of Hadrian, now the Castel Sant' Angelo in modern Rome, and the mausoleum of the emperor Augustus were never illustrated on coins although they must have been the most outstanding buildings constructed in their times. It seems that the Roman minters followed a well-defined political and religious propaganda agenda when they designed the coins, and many outstanding buildings did not fit into this rigid program.

Several other famous examples of ancient architecture were never considered to be appropriate for use on coins. The great pyramids of Egypt were totally neglected as an architectural subject for coinage simply because they were already ancient and obscure when coins were invented. The Greeks and Romans admired and appreciated the pyramids as antiquities, but never fully understood their purpose or grandeur. However, the geometric form of the pyramid was copied by some patrons of the arts and used for private tombs or mausoleums in Rome. Two such Roman pyramid tombs are known to archaeologists. One, erroneously called the Tomb of Romulus or the "Meta Romuli," stood near the Mausoleum of Hadrian. It was also called the "Sepulcrum Scipionis Africani," the sepulchre of Scipio Africanus, in the Middle Ages because local antiquarians believed that such a magnificent structure could only have been built for some mighty Roman hero. Its true origins are unknown, and it disappeared completely at the end of the fifteenth century.

The other pyramid in Rome still stands. It is the tomb of C. Cestius, a prominent Roman who served as a praetor and tribune plebis. He may have become familiar with the pyramid when he served as an administrator in Egypt. Cestius, who died around 12 B.C., was a relative of Marcus Agrippa, the associate and son-in-law of Augustus. His steeply sloping pyramid tomb, made of brick-faced concrete and covered with a veneer of marble, was constructed by his relatives after his death. It is located next to the gate of the Via Ostiensis, and was incorporated into the city defensive walls constructed by the emperor Aurelian, A.D. 270-275. Today it marks the location of the so-called Protestant cemetery in Rome, where the English poets Keats and Shelly are buried.

The pyramid of Cestius is a remarkable monument for its period of time. It is 89 feet (27 m) high and has a base size of 72.5 feet (22 m) square. These dimensions make it about one-fifth the height and one-fiftieth the volume of the great pyramid of Cheops in Egypt, but it is still an impressive mass for an ancient structure. The interior burial chamber is 19.5 feet (5.95 m) long by 13.5 feet (4.1m) wide and 15.8 feet (4.8m) high. Inscriptions on the face of the pyramid and on statue bases found nearby record that the heirs of Cestius built the tomb. In the Middle Ages this monument was known as the "Sepulcrum Remi," to complement the other pyramid in Rome, which had been named the Sepulcrum Romuli. Romulus and Remus were the mythical twins who, by legend, were instrumental in founding the city of Rome in 753 B.C. The pyramid of C. Cestius survived the fanatical destruction of pagan monuments that took place in the Middle Ages only because it was given as a gift to the church by the last Roman emperors. It remains today in excellent condition, and is the landmark monument of the nearby necropolis.

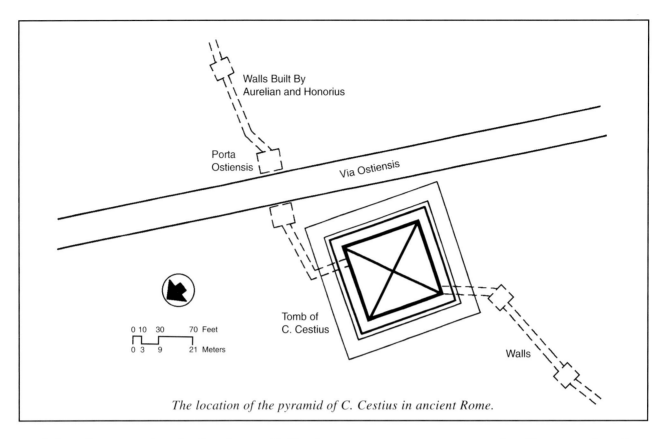

The location of the pyramid of C. Cestius in ancient Rome.

It is unfortunate that the Sepulcrum C. Cestius was never commemorated on Roman coins. Cestius was a prominent contemporary of Augustus, perhaps his friend and ally, and a direct relative of the faithful companion of the emperor, Agrippa. His tomb was an exceptional monument which must have added much to the architectural environment of the newly refurbished Rome of 12 B.C. Marcus Agrippa also died sometime in 12 B.C., so the pyramid of his relative could have been appropriated as a cenotaph for this admirable Roman warrior and administrator. The coin artists of ancient Rome must have often looked out of the windows of their workshops and seen this pyramid rising up to the sky. Politicians and bureaucrats, doing their rounds in the nearby commercial and dock areas of Rome, may have passed by it daily, yet no coin we know of illustrates this unusual tomb. To correct this historical oversight, I have produced an imaginary Roman coin showing this tomb of C. Cestius. Perhaps such a fantasy coin is a suitable invention with which to end this book, because it exemplifies the major objective of using ancient coins as propaganda to describe and publicize the architecture that made Rome the *Caput Mundi,* the capital city of the world. It may be that some day an archaeologist will discover such a coin buried in the ruins of Rome, and this will encourage a whole new generation of authors to begin a fresh study and investigation of the architecture and engineering illustrated on ancient coins.

A fantasy coin showing the Sepulcrum C. Cestius as it would have appeared on a coin after 12 B.C.

Glossary of Numismatic Terms

Aedes	A temple structure.
Aedicule	A small shrine structure usually attached to a temple or triumphal arch.
Aegis	The cloak or shield of Zeus worn by his daughter Athena.
Amphora	A two-handled, large jug used to store liquids or cereals.
Antoninianus	A double denarius coin introduced by Caracalla in A.D. 215 (plural - Antoniniani)
Aquila	An Eagle, the standard of the legion, surmounted by a golden eagle.
Ara	A rectangular altar made of stone (plural - Arae)
Argentius	A silver coin equal in fineness to the denarius of Nero, introduced by Diocletian, A.D. 284-305 (plural - Argentii)
As	A bronze coin equal to one-sixteenth of a denarius (plural - Asses)
Augustus	Literally "revered." A title conferred on Octavian in 27 B.C. by the Senate and assumed by all the succeeding emperors.
Aureus	A gold coin of the late Republic and the Empire equal to 25 denarii (plural - Aurei)
Biga	A two-horse or animal-drawn chariot.
Bisellium	A ceremonial seat for two people, usually placed on a speakers' dais.
Blank	The round coin metal piece. See also Flan and Planchet.
Caduceus	A herald's staff associated with the gods Mercury or Hermes.
Caesar	The last name of the Julian family but used as part of the emperors' titles, and after A.D. 138 used to designate heirs to the throne.
Caryatids	Columns sculpted in the form of Greek women.
Cippus	A short, round stone pillar used as a monument or highway marker.
Cistophorus	A silver coin (tetradrachm) struck in Roman Imperial Asia Minor, showing a mystic basket (Cista Mystica) in its design, usually equal to three denarii.
Congiarium	The distribution of grain or money to the populace by the emperor.
Contorniates	Bronze medallions with raised rims and edges.
Cornucopia	The Horn of Plenty carried by deities.
COS	Abbreviation for CONSVL, the title of the two chief magistrates of Rome.
Countermark	A mark of letters or symbols stamped on a coin to re-validate and re-tariff it, or to identify it with a new authority.
Curule Chair	A folding stool used as a chair of state for officials.
Denarius	The silver coin of the Republic and Empire, equal to 16 Asses.
Diademed	Wearing a headband with a fillet.
Die	The metal tool engraved with the coin's design, used to strike the blank.
Didrachm	A silver Greek coin equal to two drachms.
Divus, Diva	"Divine," titles given to deified emperors or empresses respectively.
Donitiva	Presents of money given by the emperor to his soldiers.
Dupondius	A bronze or brass coin equal to two Asses (plural - Dupondii)
Draped	Wearing a toga or cloak draped around the shoulders.
Electrum	An alloy of silver and gold found in nature.
Exergue	The area on a coin's reverse below the design.
Field	The background area around the design on a coin.
Flan	The round metal coin piece. Same as a Blank and a Planchet.
Follis	A large bronze coin with a thin silver wash introduced by Diocletian, A.D. 284-305.

Fulmen	A thunderbolt, usually associated with Jupiter (Jove or Zeus).
Genius	The guardian spirit of a place or person.
IMP	The abbreviation in inscriptions for IMPERATOR, a general with the Imperium, the right to command. The title assumed by the emperors.
I O MAX	Abbreviation on coins for IOVE OPTIMVS MAXIMVS, Jove the Best and Greatest. Sometimes shown as I O M.
Laureate	Wearing a wreath of laurel, oak, or olive leaves.
Legend	The inscription on a coin.
Medallion	A large size medallic coin usually not bearing the SC legend.
Metae	The goal or turning posts in the circus.
Millennium	The one-thousand-year anniversary.
Mint mark	Letters or symbols on a coin indicating the city where it was made.
Modius	A vessel to measure grain or cereals.
Obverse	The "Heads" side of a coin.
Palladium	A sacred statue of Athena usually associated with Troy and Rome.
Patera	A flat bowl used for ceremonial religious libations.
Pellet	The dots used on coins to represent elements too small to engrave.
Pileus	The conical cap of Liberty.
Planchet	The same as the Flan or Blank of a coin.
PON MAX	Or PM or PONT MAX. The abbreviation in inscriptions for PONTIFEX MAXIMVS, the chief priest of the Roman religion, usually the emperor.
PP	The abbreviation in inscriptions for PATER PATRIAE, Father of the Fatherland, a title granted to the emperors.
Princeps	First citizen (Prince).
Quadrans	A small bronze coin equal to one-quarter of an As (plural - Quadrantes)
Quadriga	A four-horse or animal-drawn chariot.
Radiate	Wearing a crown of rays (the radiate crown of Apollo or Helios).
Reverse	The "Tails" side of a coin.
Rostra	The bronze beaks or rams of warships. The term was given to the speakers' dais in the Forum, which had trophies of rostra attached to its facade.
Sacellum	Also Sacrum, a small shrine structure.
S C	Abbreviation on coins for SENATVS CONSVLTO, meaning "by the authority of the Senate."
Semis	A small bronze coin equal to one-half of an As (plural - Semisses)
Sestertius	A large bronze coin equal to four Asses (plural - Sestertii)
Similacrum	A "likeness." An abstract monument representing a deity.
Sphinx	A winged creature with the head of a woman and the body of a lion.
SPQR	Abbreviation on coins for SENATVS POPVLVSQVE ROMANVS, meaning (for) "the Senate and Roman People".
Stater	An early Greek silver coin equal to two drachms, a didrachm.
Tetradrachm	A large Greek silver coin equal to four drachms, usually tariffed at three denarii in Roman provincial areas.
Tholos	A round temple structure.
Togate	A figure on a coin wearing a toga.
Triga	A three-horse or animal-drawn chariot.
TR POT	Also T P or TR P. An abbreviation in inscriptions for TRIBVNICIA POTESTAS, the Tribunican Power. The Tribunican number is the usual method of dating an emperor's coins.
Vexillum	A military flag used as a standard or ensign for a maniple, a company-sized section in a legion. Also used by cavalry detachments.

Index

List of Plate Coins

(All enlargements shown in the plates are 1.5x)

1 Silver drachm of Knossos, Crete. Reverse: Labyrinth. Svoronos 70. *Classical Numismatic Group, Auction 34, lot 114.*

2 Bronze 27 mm of Heliopolis, Coele Syria, minted under Septimius Severus. Reverse: Temple of Jupiter. Cf. BMC 2 (variant obverse legend). *Numismatic Fine Arts, Auction XX, lot 253.*

3 Gold aureus of Cn. Domitius L.f. Ahenobarbus. Reverse: Temple of Neptune. Crawford 519/1, Sydenham 1176, Cohen 1. *Numismatic Fine Arts, Auction XXII, lot 26.*

4 Bronze sestertius of Nero. Reverse: Temple of Janus. RIC 173, Cohen 146. *Numismatic Fine Arts, Auction XII, lot 194.*

5 Bronze 29 mm of Zeugma, Commagene, minted under Philip II. Reverse: aerial view of temple. Sear GIC 3954, BMC 35. *Superior Galleries, Antiquities and Ancient Coinage Mail Bid Sale, September 21, 1990, lot 130.*

6 Bronze sestertius of Trajan. Reverse: Temple of Jupiter Victor. RIC 577, Cohen 549. *Classical Numismatic Group, Auction 40, lot 1480.*

7 Bronze sestertius of Titus. Reverse: Colosseum (Flavian Amphitheater). RIC 110, Cohen 400. *Numismatic Fine Arts, Auction I, lot 325.*

8 Bronze sestertius of Trajan. Reverse: Port of Trajan at Ostia. RIC 471, Cohen 305. *Classical Numismatic Group, Auction 42, lot 894.*

9 Bronze 45 mm of Pergamum, Mysia, minted under Caracalla. Reverse: Temple of Aesclepius. SNG von Aulock 1411-1412. *Numismatic Fine Arts, Auction XVI, lot 495.*

10 Bronze 30 mm of Ephesos, Ionia, minted under Trajan. Reverse: cult statue of Artemis. Cf. Mionnet Supp. VI, 375. *Classical Numismatic Group, Auction 39, lot 934.*

11 Silver cistophoric tetradrachm of Pergamum, Mysia, minted under Claudius. Reverse: Temple of Artemis/Diana. RIC 120. *Classical Numismatic Group, Auction 37, lot 1448.*

12 Bronze 34 mm of Amaseia, Pontos. Reverse: city plan. SNG von Aulock 44. *Classical Numismatic Group, Auction 31, lot 1233.*

13 Silver denarius of C. Considius Nonianus. Reverse: Temple of Venus, Eryx, Sicily. Crawford 424/1, Sydenham 887. *Numismatic Fine Arts, Auction X, lot 282.*

14 Silver tetradrachm struck during Year 2 of the Bar Kokhba War. Obverse: Temple of Jerusalem. Mildenberg 14. *Superior Galleries, The Bromberg Collection of Jewish Coins, Part II, lot 397.*

15 Silver tetradrachm struck during Year 3 of the Bar Kokhba War. Obverse: Temple of Jerusalem. Mildenberg 95. *Superior Galleries, The Bromberg Collection of Jewish Coins, Part II, lot 437.*

16 Bronze sestertius of Antoninus Pius. Reverse: Temple of Venus and Roma. RIC 622, Cohen 699. *Numismatic Fine Arts, Auction XVI, lot 443.*

17 Potin tetradrachm of Alexandria, Egypt, minted under Commodus. Reverse: ship and Pharos lighthouse. Sear GIC 2067, Milne 2683. *Classical Numismatic Group, Auction 43, lot 1181.*

18 Bronze drachm of Alexandria, Egypt, minted under Antoninus Pius. Reverse: Isis Pharia sailing toward Pharos lighthouse. BMC 1120. *Classical Numismatic Group, Auction 13, lot 111.*

19 Bronze hemidrachm of Alexandria, Egypt, minted under Hadrian. Reverse: Pharos lighthouse. Milne 1381. *Classical Numismatic Group, Auction 18, lot 391.*

20 Bronze drachm of Alexandria, Egypt, minted under Hadrian. Reverse: Isis Pharia sailing toward Pharos lighthouse. Milne 1417 var. *Classical Numismatic Group, Auction 41, lot 1153.*

21 Bronze sestertius of Divus Antoninus Pius struck under Marcus Aurelius. Reverse: Ustrinum of Antoninus Pius. RIC (Marcus Aurelius) 1266, Cohen 165. *Leu Numismatics, Auction 71, lot 394.*

22 Bronze sestertius of Divus Antoninus Pius struck under Marcus Aurelius. Reverse: Column of Antoninus Pius. RIC 1269, Cohen 354. *Classical Numismatic Group, Auction 35, lot 818.*

23 Bronze sestertius of Divus Marcus Aurelius struck under Commodus. Reverse: Ustrinum of Marcus Aurelius. RIC (Commodus) 662, Cohen 98. *Numismatic Fine Arts, Auction XXXIII, lot 1592.*

24 Bronze sestertius of Divus Septimius Severus struck under Caracalla. Reverse: Ustrinum of Septimius Severus. RIC 490b, Cohen 90. *Superior Galleries, An Official New York International Auction, December 10-11, 1993, lot 1935.*

25 Silver denarius of Augustus. Reverse: arch and quadriga. RIC 144, Cohen 233. *Numismatic Fine Arts, Fall Mail Bid Sale, 10/18/90, lot 1981.*

26 Silver denarius of Augustus. Reverse: cippus inscribed in six lines. RIC 362, Cohen 543. *Numismatic Fine Arts, Auction XXV, lot 331.*

27 Silver denarius of Trajan. Reverse: Via Traiana. RIC 266. *Classical Numismatic Group, Auction 37, lot 1532.*

28 Bronze sestertius of Nero. Reverse: aerial view of the Port of Ostia. RIC 178, Cohen 38. *Classical Numismatic Group, Auction 40, lot 1392.*

29 Silver denarius of L. Marcius Philippus. Reverse: equestrian statue above the Aqua Marcia. Crawford 425/1, Sydenham 919. *Classical Numismatic Group, Auction 42, lot 740.*

30 Bronze As of C. Censorinus. Reverse: aqueduct arches. Crawford 346/3, Sydenham 716. *Classical Numismatic Group, Auction 42, lot 734.*

31 Bronze sestertius of Trajan. Reverse: reclining river god commemorating the Aqua Traiana. RIC 463. *Superior Galleries, The August 22, 1994 Mail Bid Sale, lot 2376.*

32 Bronze sestertius of Tiberius. Obverse: Temple of Concordia. RIC 67, Cohen 70. *Classical Numismatic Group, Auction 38, lot 875.*

33 Silver denarius of Lollius Palicanus. Reverse: Rostra. Crawford 473/1, Sydenham 960. *Classical Numismatic Group, Auction 40, lot 1291.*

34 Silver denarius of Augustus. Reverse: statue of Gaius and Lucius Caesars. RIC 207. *Classical Numismatic Group, Auction 42, lot 800.*

35 Bronze sestertius of Hadrian. Reverse: Hadrian addressing citizens from the Rostra Julia in front of the Temple of Divus Julius. RIC 639, Cohen 416. *Numismatic Fine Arts, Auction XII, lot 261.*

36 Silver denarius of Augustus. Reverse: Parthian Arch. RIC 131. *Classical Numismatic Group, Auction 37, lot 1400.*

37 Silver denarius of L. Scribonius Libo. Reverse: Puteal of Scribonius. Crawford 416/1c, Sydenham 928. *Numismatic Fine Arts, Auction XXVII, lot 496.*

38 Silver denarius of Octavian. Reverse: Temple of Divus Julius. Crawford 540/2, Sydenham 1338, Cohen 90. *Numismatic Fine Arts, Fall Mail Bid Sale, 10/18/90, lot 1392.*

39 Silver denarius of Q. Cassius Longinus. Reverse: Temple of Vesta. Crawford 428/2, Sydenham 918. *Classical Numismatic Group, Auction 42, lot 743.*

40 Silver denarius of M. Aemilius Lepidus. Reverse: Basilica Aemilia. Crawford 419/3b, Sydenham 834. *Numismatic Fine Arts, Auction XXVII, lot 504.*

41 Silver denarius of L. Mussidius T.F. Longus. Reverse: Shrine of Venus Cloacina. Crawford 494/42a, Sydenham 1093. *Numismatic Fine Arts, Auction XX, lot 50.*

42 Bronze As of Nero. Reverse: Temple of Janus. RIC 198, Cohen 171. *Numismatic Fine Arts, Auction XII, lot 196.*

43 Silver denarius of Augustus. Reverse: Curia Julia. RIC 266. *Classical Numismatic Group, Auction 41, lot 1712.*

44 Silver denarius of P. Licinius Nerva. Reverse: citizens voting in the Comitium. Crawford 292/1, Sydenham 548. *Numismatic Fine Arts, Auction XXVII, lot 382.*

45 Silver denarius of Octavian. Reverse: rostral column. RIC 271. *Classical Numismatic Group, Auction 40, lot 1328.*

46 Silver denarius of Trajan. Reverse: equestrian statue. RIC 291, Cohen 497. *Numismatic Fine Arts, Auction XII, lot 253.*

47 Gold aureus of Trajan. Reverse: arch gateway to the Forum of Trajan. RIC 257, Cf. Cohen 168. *Numismatic Fine Arts, Auction XXV, lot 378.*

48 Gold aureus of Trajan. Reverse: Basilica Ulpia. RIC 246-247, Cohen 42. *Numismatic Fine Arts, Auction XXXIII, lot 475.*

49 Bronze dupondius of Trajan. Reverse: Corinthian temple. RIC 576, Cohen 554. *Classical Numismatic Group, Auction 43, lot 1946.*

50 Gold aureus of Trajan. Reverse: Corinthian temple. RIC 145. *Classical Numismatic Group, Auction 38, lot 961.*

51 Bronze As of Trajan. Reverse: Column of Trajan. RIC 600 var. *Classical Numismatic Group, Auction 37, lot 1542.*

52 Silver denarius of Trajan. Reverse: Column of Trajan. RIC 356, Cohen 284. *Numismatic Fine Arts, Auction XVIII, Part II, lot 470.*

53 Bronze sestertius of Trajan. Reverse: Circus Maximus. RIC 571, Cohen 545. *Numismatic Fine Arts, Auction XII, lot 249.*

54 Gold aureus of Hadrian. Reverse: Genius of the Circus, commemorating the Natalis Urbis festival. RIC 144, Cohen 162. *Numismatic Fine Arts, Auction XVI, lot 431.*

55 Gold aureus of Septimius Severus. Reverse: Stadium of Domitian. RIC 260, Cohen 571. *Leu Numismatics, Auction 71, lot 447.*

56 Bronze sestertius of Caracalla. Reverse: Circus Maximus. RIC 500(b), Cohen 236. *Numismatic Fine Arts, Auction XXV, lot 423.*

57 Bronze contorniate, A.D. 364-375. Reverse: Circus Maximus. Alfoldi 520. *Antiqua Inc., Catalogue I, lot 25.*

58 Bronze contorniate, A.D. 364-375. Reverse: Circus Maximus. Alfoldi 26.2. *Classical Numismatic Group, Auction 36, lot 2508.*

59 Silver legionary denarius of Mark Antony. Reverse: standards honoring Praetorian cohorts. Crawford 544/8, Sydenham 1213, Cohen 7. *Numismatic Fine Arts, Fall Mail Bid Sale, 10/18/90, lot 1394.*

60 Silver legionary denarius of Mark Antony. Reverse: standards honoring Speculatores cohorts. Crawford 544/12, Sydenham 1214, Cohen 6. *Numismatic Fine Arts, Fall Mail Bid Sale, 10/18/90, lot 1393.*

61 Silver denarius of Claudius. Reverse: Castra Praetoria. RIC 24, Cohen 44. *Numismatic Fine Arts, Auction XII, lot 185.*

62 Silver argenteus of Diocletian. Reverse: Castra Praetoria. RIC 27a. *Numismatic Fine Arts, Auction XXXIII, lot 662.*

63 Silver denarius of M. Volteius M.F. Reverse: Temple of Jupiter Capitolinus. Crawford 385/1, Sydenham 774. *Classical Numismatic Group, Auction 35, lot 547.*

64 Silver denarius of Petillius Capitolinus. Reverse: Temple of Jupiter Capitolinus. Crawford 487/1, Sydenham 1149. *Numismatic Fine Arts, Auction XXVII, lot 582.*

65 Silver denarius of Petillius Capitolinus. Reverse: Temple of Jupiter Capitolinus. Crawford 487/2c,

Sydenham 1152. *Numismatic Fine Arts, Auction XXVII, lot 583.*

66 Silver denarius of Vitellius. Reverse: Jupiter seated in the Capitolium. RIC 56, Cohen 39. *Numismatic Fine Arts, Fall Mail Bid Sale, 10/18/90, lot 1509.*

67 Silver cistophoric tetradrachm of Domitian. Reverse: Capitolium. RIC 222. *Classical Numismatic Group, Auction 37, lot 1511.*

68 Silver denarius of Augustus. Reverse: Temple of Jupiter Tonan. RIC 276. *Superior Stamp & Coin Co., Fixed Price List, Winter 1988/89, lot C91.*

69 Bronze sestertius of Caligula. Reverse: Caligula sacrificing before the Temple of Divus Augustus. RIC 44, Cohen 10. *Numismatic Fine Arts, Auction XXVII, lot 99.*

70 Silver denarius of Antoninus Pius. Reverse: Temple of Divus Augustus. RIC 290a. *Classical Numismatic Group, Auction 43, lot 2001.*

71 Base silver antoninianus of Probus. Reverse: hexastyle temple, possibly the Temple of Venus and Roma. RIC 186. *Numismatic Fine Arts, Auction XX, lot 434.*

72 Silver denarius of P. Fonteius P.F. Capito. Reverse: Villa Publica. Crawford 429/2a, Sydenham 901. *Numismatic Fine Arts, Auction XXVII, lot 519.*

73 Silver denarius of Nero. Reverse: Temple of Vesta. RIC 62, Cohen 335. *Numismatic Fine Arts, Auction XX, lot 122.*

74 Gold aureus of Vespasian. Reverse: Temple of Vesta. RIC 69c. *Classical Numismatic Group, Auction 40, lot 1422.*

75 Bronze As of Julia Domna struck under Caracalla. Reverse: Vestal Virgins and the Temple of Vesta. RIC 607, Cohen 234. *Numismatic Fine Arts, Fall Mail Bid Sale, 10/18/90, lot 1644.*

76 Silver denarius of Domitian. Reverse: Temple of Minerva Chalcidica. RIC 206, Cohen 171. *Leu Numismatics, Auction 71, lot 353.*

77 Bronze 20 mm of Panias, Judaea, minted under Nero. Obverse: Diva Poppaea in temple. Reverse: Claudia in temple. Sear GIC 673. *Superior Galleries, The May 30, 1990 Sale, lot 7161.*

78 Bronze follis of Romulus. Reverse: Temple of Divus Romulus. RIC 207. *Superior Stamp & Coin Co., Fixed Price List, Winter 1988/89, lot C132.*

79 Bronze follis of Romulus. Reverse: Temple of Divus Romulus. RIC 256, Cohen 10. *Numismatic Fine Arts, Winter Mail Bid Sale, 12/14/89, lot 1214.*

80 Silver denarius of Augustus. Reverse: Actian Arch. RIC 267, Cohen 123. *Numismatic Fine Arts, Auction XVIII, Part II, lot 414.*

81 Silver cistophoric tetradrachm of Augustus. Reverse: Parthian Arch. RIC 510. *Classical Numismatic Group, Auction 37, lot 1415.*

82 Silver denarius of Nero Claudius Drusus struck under Claudius. Reverse: triumphal arch. RIC (Claudius) 70. *Classical Numismatic Group, Auction 40, lot 1379.*

83 Bronze sestertius of Claudius. Reverse: triumphal arch. RIC 114, Cohen 48. *Bank Leu, Auction 38, lot 235.*

84 Silver denarius of Nero Claudius Drusus struck under Claudius. Reverse: triumphal arch. RIC (Claudius) 72, Cohen 4. *Numismatic Fine Arts, Winter Mail Bid Sale, 12/14/89, lot 1097.*

85 Gold aureus of Claudius. Reverse: triumphal arch. RIC 33. *Classical Numismatic Group, Auction 41, lot 1768.*

86 Bronze As of Galba. Reverse: triumphal arch. RIC 81. *Classical Numismatic Group, Auction 35, lot 749.*

87 Bronze sestertius of Domitian. Reverse: triumphal arch. RIC 416, Cohen 531. *Classical Numismatic Group, Auction 39, lot 1418.*

88 Bronze sestertius of Nero. Reverse: Temple of Janus. RIC 438. *Classical Numismatic Group, Auction 35, lot 741.*

89 Bronze sestertius of Nero. Reverse: triumphal arch. RIC 147. *Numismatic Fine Arts, Auction XXXII, lot 297.*

90 Bronze dupondius of Nero. Reverse: Macellum Magnum. RIC 109, Cohen 130. *Classical Numismatic Group, Auction 38, lot 905.*

91 Bronze sestertius of Trajan. Reverse: Danube bridge. RIC 569. *Superior Stamp & Coin Co., Fixed Price List, Winter 1988/89, lot C98.*

92 Silver cistophoric tetradrachm of Perge, Asia Minor, minted under Nerva. Reverse: Baetyl inside Temple of Diana Pergamum. RIC 116, Cohen 42. *Superior Galleries, 1980 Chicago International Coin Fair Auction Sale, lot 2370.*

93 Silver denarius of L. Aemilius Lepidus Paullus and L. Scribonius Libo. Reverse: Puteal of Scribonius. Crawford 417/1a, Sydenham 927. *Numismatic Fine Arts, Auction XXVII, lot 497.*

94 Silver denarius of Divus Antoninus Pius struck under Marcus Aurelius. Reverse: "large altar" of Divus Antoninus. RIC (Marcus Aurelius) 441. *Classical Numismatic Group, Auction 42, lot 937.*

95 Bronze sestertius of Augustus. Reverse: Altar of Lugdunum. RIC 361, Cohen 236. *Numismatic Fine Arts, Auction XII, lot 160.*

96 Bronze As of Divus Augustus struck under Tiberius. Reverse: altar to Providentia. RIC 81, Cohen 228. *Classical Numismatic Group, Auction 43, lot 1779.*

97 Bronze As of Nero. Reverse: Ara Pacis shrine. RIC 460. *Classical Numismatic Group, Auction 41, lot 1790.*

98 Bronze As of Domitian. Reverse: Shrine to Salus. RIC 272, Cohen 417. *Numismatic Fine Arts, Fall Mail Bid Sale, 10/18/90, lot 1534.*

99 Bronze As of Diva Faustina struck under Antoninus Pius. Reverse: "large altar." RIC 1191A, Cohen 257. *Classical Numismatic Group, Auction 37, lot 1590.*

100 Silver antoninianus of Divus Claudius II. Reverse: "large altar." RIC 261 var. *Classical Numismatic Group, Auction 39, lot 1652.*

Plate I

Plate II

Plate III

Plate IV

38

39

40

44

43

46

42

45

47

48

50

49

Plate V

Plate VI

Plate VII

242

Plate VIII